THE PUB JOKE BOOK Ever!

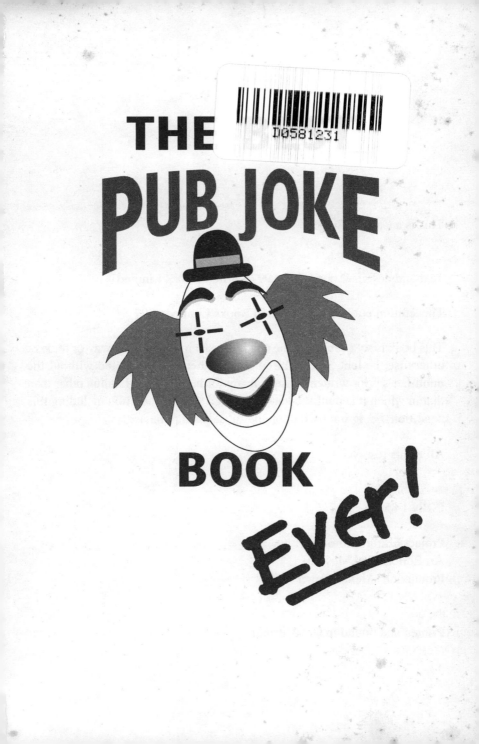

ISBN 1 85868 335 1

Project Editor: Simon Kirrane
Art Editor: Paul Messam
Production: Alexia Turner

Printed and bound in Great Britain

THE BEST
PUB JOKE

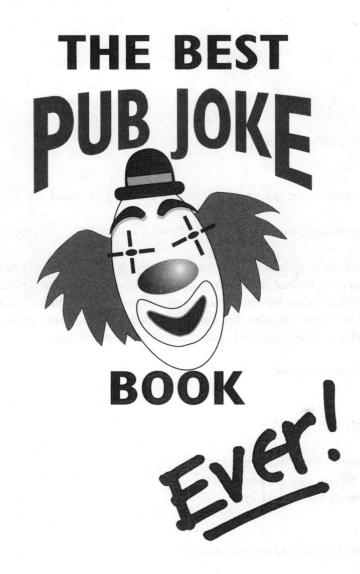

BOOK
Ever!

CARLTON

CONTENTS

Introduction

A drink and a laugh. The two things are bleeding synonymous. They were made for each other. I mean, when God invented the left tit, it was just right and proper that he invent the right tit to go with. The one without the other would look stupid. Batman and Robin. Morecambe and Wise. Huntley and Palmer. Mike and Berni Winters. Fish and chips. They all fit together like the finished jigsaws they are.

Of course, it's not just any drink that goes with a drink and a laugh, oh no. It's got to be a drink down the boozer with your mates. I mean, sitting at home on your own having a stiff one or cracking a few tinnies; where's the laughs in that? 'Oh ha ha, here I am alone and I'm getting pissed, ha ha ha.' What's that all about? If you do that you're just going to get more and more miserable thinking about how much of a real laugh you'd be having if you were down the pub with your mates. So, you see; a drink down the pub and a laugh – now *that's* what it's all about.

Much as the great atmosphere of the pub – with its noisy hubbub, smoky air, constant music pumping out of the jukebox, shouts at the bar and vomit – is highly conducive to a great laugh, sometimes, just sometimes, you're sitting there thinking, 'Shit, that was a great gag Barry just told and the way Barbara's looking at him now I reckon he's in there, the lucky bastard.'

Now, on the surface no one would be more pleased than your good self to see Barry get his end away with Barbara, especially as he hasn't had much luck in that department since he was discovered six months ago in a compromising position with a vacuum cleaner – come to think of it, *that* was on a night when he'd stayed in on his own with a few cans – but deep down, you know that you want to shag Barbara. In fact, Barbara knows that you want to shag her and she'd be up for it, too. It's just you can't find the right word, the right anecdote, the right line... the right gag to open the gates of heaven.

If only there was some way you could sneak off to the bogs and rub something vigorously, but lovingly. Something that would produce a genie. A genie who could turn you into the wittiest man in the boozer with a joke for every occasion. Then things would be different.

Oh, you'd also wish that Barry could get a shag with Barbara's mate Tracey, who's got a lovely personality, and that you could win the lottery every week – though occasionally every other week when it's a rollover – and that you could have five mansions in every continent of the world, and a new car, and be the greatest footballer in the world. But when it came down to it, what you'd really want is to be able to get those laughs. To see the adoring faces all around you, tears of happiness in their eyes, subconsciously saying, 'He's a great lad. So, so funny. They don't make many like him. He's one in a million, he is. Shame he's got such a small cock, mind.' 'Course by then it'd be too late and the genie would have gone, but there's always going to be one thing you forget to ask for.

Anyway, the point is that in some small way this book is like that genie. No, it won't give you a bigger dick, or bigger breasts if you're a woman, unless you use the correct lubricant, but it will equip you to go out there on to the social battlefield and hit 'em with a few punches. And then a few jabs. And then a few uppercuts. Maybe one or two below the belt, and then back for the big knockout finish. And it won't just be for the one night, either. There are so many laughs contained herein, that you'll be the funniest guy in the pub for years to come. Even after that you'll still be funny because the alcohol will have destroyed you and all your mate's memories, so you can just tell all the jokes again. There, you see? This is just like your own personal little genie. And you didn't even have to rub anything.

Chapter 1
Jokes Not To Tell The Hard Bloke

You know what it's like when you've had a few. You get a bit of Dutch courage up. So you sidle over to the big, psychopathic-looking guy whose been sitting in the corner looking like it's just a matter of time before he beats someone up and, in an attempt to become his mate so that it won't be you, you tell him the one about the guy whose wife's vagina was so big there was an echo when he went down on her.

'Course the psycho's two brain cells get confused by this attempt at friendship and he thinks it's his wife you're talking about. The resulting six months you spend in hospital give you ample time to think about where you went wrong that night and what a terrible state the NHS is in.

Here are some more jokes it's best to tell only to very good friends who are not particularly strong…

****

This bloke wakes up one morning to find a gorilla in a tree in his garden. He looks in the phone book for a gorilla removal service until he finds one.

'Is it a boy gorilla or a girl gorilla?' the service bloke asks.

'Boy gorilla', replies the man.

'Righto,' says the service bloke. 'I'll be round in a jiffy.'

An hour later the service bloke shows up with a stick, a Pit Bull Terrier, a shotgun and a pair of handcuffs.

'Right,' he says to the man. 'I'm going to climb the tree and poke the gorilla with the stick until he falls. When he does, this highly trained Pit Bull will tear the gorilla's balls off. When the gorilla crosses his hands over his crotch to protect himself, you slip the handcuffs on.'

'OK,' says the man, 'but what's the shotgun for?'

'I'm glad you asked that,' says the service bloke. 'If I fall out of the tree before the gorilla does, then blow the dog's brains out.'

****

This bloke Sam's been working on the stock exchange for 15 years and the stress has finally got to him. So he quits his job and buys a cottage in the middle of nowhere, right up in the highlands of Scotland.

For six months he doesn't see a soul, until one evening, just as he's finishing his dinner, there's a knock on his front door. He opens it and there, on his door step, is a gigantic, ginger-bearded Scotsman in a kilt.

'Name's Hamish. I'm your your neighbour from the other side of the glen. I'm having a party on Saturday and I thought you might like to come along.'

'That's very kind of you,' says Sam. 'After six months of this I'm ready to meet some of the locals. Thank you very much.'

'Good,' says Hamish with a smile. 'I better warn you, though, there's gonna be some serious drinking done.'

'No problem,' replies Sam. 'After 15 years in the stock markets I can drink with the best of them.'

'More than likely be a bit of punch-up at some point as well,' says Hamish.

'Oh, I'm sure I'll be OK,' says Sam. 'I can look after myself, and besides I tend to get along with most people.'

'One last thing,' says Hamish as he turns to leave, 'I've seen some pretty wild sex at these parties, as well.'

'Well, now you're talking,' says Sam, 'what time should I come over?'

'Oh, whatever time suits you,' says Hamish. 'After all, it's only going to be the two of us.'

****

A sergeant-major in the Paras was giving a lecture to some raw recruits.

'If you want to be a part of this regiment,' he shouted at them, 'then you need to have COMMITMENT! What do you need?'

'COMMITMENT, sergeant-major!' the recruits all shouted back.

'Right, I shall now demonstrate my COMMITMENT to this regiment.' The sergeant-major then ordered one of the men to open a nearby door.

Almost as soon as the squaddie turned the handle, the door was pushed open and in slithered a 10-foot-long alligator, snarling and snapping.

The sergeant-major then undid his belt and dropped his trousers. Almost as soon as he did so, the alligator ran up and sank his teeth right into the sergeant-major's love-truncheon. The sergeant-major barely winced. 'This,' he shouted. 'is what we in the Parachute Regiment call COMMITMENT!' He waited several seconds more to make his point and then swiftly jabbed the alligator in both eyes with his fingers.

The alligator flipped over on his back, jumped up, and ran into the corner of the office, glaring angrily at the sergeant-major.

'That, you 'orrible bunch, is what we in the Paras call COMMITMENT. Now which one of you 'orrible little men is ready to demonstrate his COMMITMENT?'

There was much shuffling of feet and murmuring until finally one young lad stepped forward. 'I will, sergeant-major,' he said, 'but you've got to promise not to poke me in the eyes.'

✳✳✳✳

Some tourists were touring an Arab bazaar when they saw a man on his knees next to a camel. The tour guide approached the man. 'Excuse me, Sir,' said the tour guide. 'You wouldn't happen to have the time, would you?'

The Arab grabbed the camel by the balls and said, 'Ten past two.'

The tour guide couldn't believe what he was seeing so he rushed off to get the rest of his party. 'You won't believe what I've just seen,' he told them. 'Follow me.'

They all trooped back to where the Arab and the camel were standing. 'Excuse me, Sir,' said the tour guide. 'Could you tell me the time again, please?'

The Arab thought this was a slightly strange request but once again, he grabbed the camel by the balls and said, 'Just gone Ten minutes past two.'

The tour party were amazed.

'Excuse me, Sir,' said the tour guide to the Arab. 'But I've worked in this part of the world for many years now, and I've never seen anything like this. If you don't mind me asking, how on earth do you tell the time by grabbing the camel's balls like that?'

'Well,' said the Arab demonstrating the manoeuvre again, 'by moving his balls over to one side I can see that clock on the wall over there.'

✱✱✱✱

It was the stockbroker's first day in prison and on meeting his psychotic-looking cell mate he became even more nervous than ever.

'Don't worry, mate,' said the prisoner when he noticed how scared the stockbroker looked. 'I'm in for a white-collar crime, too.'

'Oh, really?' said the stockbroker with a sigh of relief.

'Yeah,' said the prisoner. 'I murdered a priest.'

✱✱✱✱

A young man goes to a restaurant and orders a chicken dish. The waiter brings it to him and just as he's ready to tuck in, the *maître d'* comes running over and says, 'I'm terribly sorry, sir, but I'm afraid there has been a mistake. You see that police officer sitting at the next table? Well, he's a regular customer of ours and he usually orders the same dish. The problem is, this is the last chicken in the house. I'm afraid I'll have to take your meal to him and arrange for you to have something else from the menu.'

The young man, however, refuses to give up his food, so the waiter walks over to the other table and explains the situation to the policeman. A few minutes later the policeman walks over to the man's table and says, 'Now you listen to me, young man, and listen good. That is MY chicken you're about to eat and I'll warn you, whatever you do to that chicken I'll do the same to you. You pull out one of its legs, I'll pull out one of yours. You break one of its wings, I'll break one of your arms!'

The young man looks calmly at the policeman, then calmly at the chicken, sticks his finger into the bird's arse, pulls it out and licks it.

✱✱✱✱

This bloke went to the Far East on business and three months later – after a successful trip – arrived home only to find he'd contracted a strange disease in the genital region. He goes to the doctor who, after a thorough examination, informs the businessman that he's got no choice but to amputate the man's penis.

'I refuse to believe that's the only option,' says the businessman. 'I shall consult another physician.'

So the businessman sees numerous doctors all over Europe and North America, but they all come to the same conclusion. His member has got to be chopped off.

Just when he's about to accept the doctors' verdict, however, the businessman has a brainwave. If it's an Oriental, Far Eastern disease, he figures, then why doesn't he consult an Oriental doctor?

An appointment is made with the finest doctor in London's Chinatown. After a full examination the Oriental doctor says to him, 'No, I don't think amputation is necessary.'

The businessman is over the moon. 'Brilliant! I saw dozens of doctors from Europe and America and they all said amputation was the only way.'

'Pah!! Western doctors!', says the Chinese doctor with disdain. 'What do they know? Any doctor worth his salt could tell you that it'll drop off by itself in four to six weeks!'

****

There was a middle-aged bloke called Steve who decided to go back to college to take a degree. Not being sure of what he wanted to take, he began to look around campus at all the different colleges. He saw the College of Physics, the College of Sociology, the College of Psychology and the College of Assuming. Having never heard of a College of Assuming, Steve was puzzled. While he stood there pondering what it was, the Dean of the college happened by and asked Steve if he needed any help.

'It's just that I've never heard of the College of Assuming,' said Steve, and I just wondered what it is.'

'Well, I'm the Dean of the college,' said the Dean, 'and here in the

College of Assuming, we raise assumption to the level of an art form.'

'I'm sorry,' said Steve, 'but I still don't understand.'

'Let's try this,' said the Dean. 'Can I assume you have a dog?'

'Why yes, I do have a dog,' replied Steve.

'And can I assume you have a garden for your dog to play in?' inquired the Dean.

'Why yes, I do have a garden for my dog,' said Steve.

'OK, and can I further assume that because you have a garden you also have a house?' said the Dean.

'Why yes, I do have a house,' said Steve beginning to be amazed.

'Now, because you have a house and a dog, and a garden, can I then assume you have a wife,' said the Dean.

'That's amazing! Yes, I do have a wife,' said Steve.

'Then because you have a wife, can I assume you are not gay?' inquired the Dean.

'Why no, I'm not gay,' replied Steve.

'There you see,' stated the Dean. 'From the simple fact of assuming you had a dog, I was able to assume you had a house with a garden, a wife, and that you are not gay.'

Clearly amazed, Steve enrolled in the class of assumptions. One day, about three weeks later while waiting for class to start, Steve saw a very puzzled man in the halls. Wanting to try his new skills and be of assistance, Steve approached the man.

'Can I help you?' asked Steve.

'Why, yes,' replied the man. 'What is the College of Assuming?'

Delighted, Steve replied, 'The College of Assuming takes assumption to the level of an art form.'

'I'm still not sure I understand,' replied the man. 'Well let me give you an example,' said Steve. 'Do you own a dog?'

'No,' replied the man.

'Aha,' said Steve, 'then you must be a poof.'

****

Three mice are at a bar, having drinks, talking about how tough they are. The first mouse slams down a shot of booze and says, 'Let me tell you how tough I am. I spot a trap and go for the cheese. When it snaps, I snatch the bar and bench-press it 20 or so times and before it can close I'm out of there!' and he tosses down another shot.

The second mouse slams down a shot and says, 'You think that's tough? When I find a pile of rodent poison, I crush it and snort it like it's cocaine.' With that he throws down another shot and slams his shotglass on the bar.

The first two stare at the third mouse, waiting to see what he has to say for himself. He fires down a shot of booze, throws down his glass and heads for the door. His buddies look at each other, then at him and say, 'Hey, where are you going?' The third mouse says, 'I haven't got time for this shit, I'm going home to fuck the cat.'

****

A general and his paratrooper son are sitting at home having a couple of beers.

'So, son, tell me about your first jump,' says the general.

'Well, by the time the plane got over the jump site,' says the son, 'I was really scared. When it was my turn to jump, I got to the door and I just couldn't do it.

'What happened, then?' asks the general.

'Well,' says his son, 'the sergeant came up behind me, pulled out his dick and said, "Jump or I'll stick this up your arse."'

'So you jumped? says the general.

'A little,' says the son, 'but only at first.'

****

Two old drunks were getting wankered in a pub. The first one says, 'You know, when I was 30 and got a hard-on, I couldn't bend it with both hands. By the time I was 40, I could bend it about 10 degrees if I tried really hard. By the time I was 50, I could bend it about 20 degrees, no problem. I'm 60 next week, and now I can almost bend it in half with just one hand.'

'So,' says the second drunk, 'What's your point?'

'Well,' says the first, 'I'm just wondering how much stronger I'm gonna get!'

****

An armless man walked into an empty pub. He ordered a drink and when he was served, asked the barman if he'd get the money out of his pocket for him, since he had no arms. Of course, the barman obliged.

He then asked if the barman would tip the glass to his lips. The barman did this until the man finished his drink. He then asked if the barman would get a hanky from his pocket and wipe the foam from his lips.

'It must be very difficult not to have any arms,' said the barman as he wiped the man's face.

'Yes, it can be a bit embarrassing at times,' said the armless man. 'By the way, mate; where's your bog?'

'About three miles away down the end of this road,' replied the barman.

****

Once there was a beautiful woman who loved to work in her vegetable garden, but no matter what she did, she couldn't get her tomatoes to ripen. One day when she was admiring her neighbour's garden, which had beautiful, bright red tomatoes, she asked him what his secret was.

'It's really quite simple,' her neighbour explained. 'Twice each day, in the morning and in the evening, I expose myself in front of the tomatoes and they turn red with embarrassment.'

Desperate for perfect tomatoes, she decided to take his advice and proceeded to expose herself to her plants, twice daily. Two weeks passed and her neighbour stopped by to check her progress.

'So,' he asked, 'any luck with your tomatoes?'

'No,' she replied excitedly. 'But you should see the size of my carrots!'

****

A urologist, a gynaecologist and a sex therapist met one afternoon to discuss their results from a similar study.

'I spent £100,000 on my study,' said the urologist and my results conclusively prove that the reason the head of a man's penis is wider than the shaft is so that the man will feel more pleasure during intercourse.

'Well, I spent £200,000 on my study,' said the gynaecologist, 'and my results conclusively prove that the reason the head of a man's penis is wider than the shaft is so that the woman will feel more pleasure during intercourse.'

'Oh yeah,' said the sex therapist. 'Well, I only had to spend £100 on my study and my results conclusively prove that the real reason the head of a man's penis is wider than the shaft is to prevent a man from accidentally hitting himself in the forehead while he's having a wank!'

✱✱✱✱

A husband and wife are cooing over their new born baby.

'Look at his todger,' says the man. 'It's massive!'

'Yes, dear,' says the woman. 'But at least he's got your eyes.'

✱✱✱✱

Four surgeons were taking a coffee break and discussing their work. The first said, 'I think accountants are the easiest to operate on. You open them up and everything inside is numbered.'

The second said, 'I think librarians are the easiest to operate on. You open them up and everything inside is in alphabetical order.'

The third said, 'I like to operate on electricians. You open them up and everything inside is colour-coded.'

The fourth one said, 'I prefer to operate on lawyers. They're heartless, spineless, gutless, and their heads and arses are interchangeable.'

✱✱✱✱

There's this woman who's a faithful churchgoer. She's been looking forward to a particular guest speaker coming to give a sermon at her local church for some months, but on the weekend he's due to speak, the woman gets ill. She's too sick to attend the service, but because she doesn't want to miss what the guest speaker has to say, she asks her husband – who never goes to church – to attend for her and give her a full report. After a big row he finally agrees and goes off to the church. On his return his wife is amazed to see he's got two black eyes.

'What in God's name happened to you?' she asks him.

'Well,' he replies, 'before the guest speaker got up to give his sermon, we were asked to stand and sing. I noticed this fat woman in front of me had her dress stuck in her crack, so I reached over the pew and pulled it out. Her husband saw me and twatted me in the eye.'

'OK,' says the wife. 'So how did you get the second black eye?'

'Well, I figured I'd upset him by taking the dress out of her crack,' said the husband, 'so I tried to make amends by slipping it back in.'

****

This little old lady calls 999. When the operator answers she yells, 'Help, send the police to my house right away. There's a damn Labour MP on my front porch and he's playing with himself.

'I beg your pardon?' said the operator.

'I said there's a damn Labour MP on my front porch playing with himself and he's weird; I don't know him and I'm afraid! Please send the police,' the little old lady repeated.

'Well, now,' said the operator. 'How do you know he's a Labour MP?'

'Because if he was a Tory,' said the old lady, 'he'd be screwing somebody!'

****

Three elderly men are talking about their aches, pains and bodily functions. The 70-year-old man says, 'I have this problem. I wake up every morning at seven and it takes me 20 minutes to tinkle.

The 80-year old man says, 'My case is worse. I get up at eight and I sit there and grunt and groan for half-an-hour before I finally have a movement.'

The 90-year old says, 'At seven I piss like a horse, at eight I shit like a cow.'

'So what's your problem?' ask the other two.

'Well, you see,' says the 90-year old, 'I don't wake up until nine.'

****

A man with a 50-inch long dick goes to his doctor to complain that he was unable to get any women to have sex with him because his knob was too long.

'Doctor,' he asks, in total frustration, 'is there any way you can shorten it?'

'Medically, I'm afraid there is nothing I can do for you,' replies the doctor, 'but, I do know this witch who may be able to help.'

So the doctor gives the man with the king-sized knob directions to the witch and the man goes off to visit her.

'Witch,' he says when he gets there. 'My dick is 50 inches long and I can't get any women to have sex with me. Can you help me shorten it?'

'Pull it out,' says the witch, 'and let me look at it.'

The man uncoils his 50-inch love wand and the witch stares in amazement, scratches her head, and then says, 'I think I may have a solution to your problem. What you have to do is go to this pond deep in the forest. In the pond you will see a frog sitting on a log who can help solve your dilemma. First you must ask the frog to marry you. Each time the frog declines your proposal, your dick will shrink by Ten inches.'

The man's face lights up and he dashes off into the forest. Sure enough he comes upon the pond in the middle of which is the frog. 'Will you marry me?' he calls out to the frog.

The frog looks at him and replies, 'No'. The man looks down and just as the witch had said, his dick is Ten inches shorter.

'WOW!' he screams out loud, 'This is great!! But it's still 40 inches too long. I'll ask the frog to marry me again 'Frog, will you marry me?'

The frog rolls its eyes back in its head and screams back, 'NO!' The man feels another twitch in his dick, looks down, and finds it is another 10 inches shorter.

'This is fantastic,' says the man, 'but 30 inches is still a monster; just a little less would be ideal. So, I'll ask the frog to marry me one more time.' Grinning, he looks across the pond and yells out, 'Frog, will you marry me?'

The frog looks back across the pond shaking its head. 'How many times do I have to tell you? NO!... NO!!... and for the last time... NO!!!'

****

A girl was a prostitute, but she didn't want her grandma to know. One day, the police raided the brothel where the girl worked and the police had all the prostitutes line up outside. Just then, the girl's grandma came by and saw her granddaughter. Not wanting her granny to know the truth, the girl said the first thing that came into her head.

'I'm queueing up for some free oranges, granny, they're handing them out here today.'

'Ooh, that's nice, dear,' said the granny. 'I'll think I'll get some, too.' And with that she joined the back of the queue.

By this time, a policeman was going down the line asking for information from the prostitutes. When he got to grandma, he was bewildered and asked, 'You're so old, how do you do it?'

'Oh, it's easy,' replied Grandma. 'I just take my dentures out and suck them dry.'

****

On his first day in prison this young bloke gets put in a cell with an old con and the first thing the old con asks him is, 'Do you like church?'

'It's OK,' replies the young bloke.

'On Sundays we get to go to church,' says the old con. 'You're gonna love Sundays.

'Yeah, right.' says the young bloke.

Next the old con asks him if he likes football.

'Yeah, I like footie,' says the young bloke.

'Well, you're gonna love Mondays then,' says the old con. 'We play football on Mondays. What about cricket?'

'Yeah, cricket's all right,' replies the young bloke. '

'Well, you're gonna love Tuesdays,' says the old con. 'We always play cricket on Tuesdays – unless, of course, it rains. Then we play cards. You like cards?'

'Yeah, I like cards,' says the young bloke.

'What about sex?' asks the old con. 'You like sex?'

'Course I do.' says the young bloke.

'Who do you like sex with best?' asks the old con. 'Men or women?'

'Women.' says the young bloke getting a little bit worried.

'You don't like sex with men?' says the old con.

'No I most certainly do not.' says the young bloke.

'Oh dear,' says the old con. 'You're gonna hate Wednesdays.'

****

Two Welshmen are out rounding up sheep when all of a sudden a ewe takes off and goes wild, runs into a fence and gets her head stuck. The two shepherds run over to the fence to get her out when one says to the other: 'Hey, boyo, this is too good an opportunity to pass up.' So he unzips his fly, yanks out his wang and fucks the this ewe for about ten minutes. When he's finally finished he looks round to his mate and says, 'That was bloody marvellous. D'you fancy a go?'

'Bloody right I do!' grins his mate, as he drops his trousers and sticks his head through the fence.

****

Two young lads are picked up by the Old Bill for smoking dope. When they appear in court, though, the magistrate says: 'You two seem like such nice young men, I'd like to give you a second chance. I want you to go out this weekend and try to show others the evils of drug use and get them to give up drugs forever. I'll see you back in court on Monday morning.'

Come Monday morning, the two lads are in court, and the magistrate says to the first one, 'So, how did you do over the weekend?'

'Well, your honour,' he replies, 'I managed to persuade 17 people altogether to give up drugs forever.'

'Seventeen people?' says the magistrate. 'That's wonderful, news. What did you tell them?'

'I used a diagram, your honour,' replied the first lad. 'I drew two circles like this:

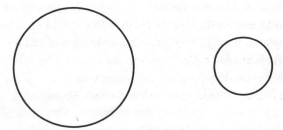

and told them this (the big circle) is your brain before drugs and this (small circle) is your brain after drugs.'

'That's admirable,' said the judge . 'And how did you do?' he asked the second lad.

'Well, your honour,' he replied. 'I persuaded 156 people to give up drugs forever.'

'One-hundred and fifty-six people!' cried the judge. 'That's amazing! How did you manage to do that?'

'Well, I used the same two circles. I pointed to the small circle and told them, 'this is your arsehole before you go to prison…'

****

This bloke John gets a new job, but on the Monday morning when he's supposed to start work he phones his new boss and tells him, 'I'm sick.' The boss excuses him and when John shows up for work on Tuesday morning the boss says he hopes he's feeling better. John works throughout the rest of the week without any problems, greatly impressing everyone with his diligence and ability. The next Monday, however, he again calls his boss to tell him, 'I'm sick'. The boss reluctantly excuses him again, but notices that this is the second Monday in a row John's claimed to be ill.

Once again, John shows up on Tuesday morning and works throughout the week, even faster and better than the previous week. The following Monday, however, he phones his boss again to tells him, 'I'm sick' and although the boss once again excuses him, he decides that this time he'll take John to task on Tuesday. Tuesday comes and as soon as John shows up, the boss calls him into his office.

'What's the story?' asks John's boss. 'I can see you're a hard worker, but you've only been here three weeks and you've called in sick every Monday.'

'Well,' says John, 'my sister's in a bad marriage and I go over to console her every Monday morning before work. One thing leads to another and we end up making love all day long.'

'With your sister!?!' says the boss. 'That's disgusting!'

'Well,' says John, 'I told you I was sick.'

****

Ten things not to say to the hard bloke in the pub:

10. Oi! Lurch! Get out of the fucking way!

9. I think of homosexuality as a perfectly acceptable extension of one's personality… my, you've got very big arms haven't you?

8. Yeah, you might be a big feller, but I reckon I'd have you.

7. Oi, you! You just spilled my pint. Tosser!

6. What'll you have, Piña Colada is it Tiny?

5. Honestly though, don't *you* think your relationship with your mum is a bit... well, unnatural?

4. Is that your bird? I heard she bangs like a barn door in a blizzard.

3. You look like Boy George. I bet you mince when you walk too.

2. What's your job then? Guard dog? Paperweight? Go on? What do you do?

1. Is this your pint… *(drinks some)* mmm, that tastes nice and that's Lager is it?

****

Q: Why did they have to draw a circle round your mouth when you were born?

A: Because you were so ugly they were afraid they might feed your arse by mistake!

****

Little Johnny thinks he's old enough to start swearing, so when he comes down for breakfast one morning and his mum wishes him a good morning and asks him what he'd like for his breakfast, Johnny replies: 'I'd like some fucking cornflakes...'

Obviously, his mum's outraged. 'Go to your room now!' she screams. Once he's gone, she turns to Johnny's brother Ivor and asks him what he'd like for breakfast.

'Well,' says Ivor. 'I'm definitely not having the fucking cornflakes...'

****

Q: What do you call a Manc lad in a filing cabinet?

A: Sorted!

****

Two friends are out taking a walk in the Australian outback when one of them goes for a piss behind a tree. In the middle of his piss a snake appears, slithers up his leg and bites him on the knob. Writhing in agony he shouts to his friend for help. Luckily his friend has a mobile phone and calls the doctor.

'Doc, doc!' shouts the friend. 'My mate just got bitten by a snake. What should I do?'

'OK, just calm down,' says the doctor. 'Firstly, take a knife and make a small incision where the bite is and then suck out all the poison; it's quite a simple operation. But if you don't do it I'm afraid your friend will die.'

By now his mate is writhing around in agony. 'What the doc say?' he asks his friend with the phone.

'Sorry, mate', he replies, 'but he says you're going to die.'

****

Q: How can you tell a Frenchman's been in your garden?
A: Your dustbin's empty and your cat is pregnant

****

Q: Why do the marines send three men out on a patrol?
A: One to read the map and two to guard the intellectual.

****

Q: What do you call a Welshman with a sheep under his arm?
A A newlywed.

****

Q: What do you call a Welshman man with two sheep under his arms?
A: A pimp.

****

During the war an officer got caught getting a blow-job by a female spy. He was later court martialed for insertion in the face of the enemy.

****

Q: What's the similarity between a lawyer and a sperm?
A: Only one in a million turns out to be a human.

****

Q. What did the elephant say to the naked man?
A. How do you breathe through that thing?

****

An Essex man goes to a fancy dress party, with blonde draped over his shoulder. 'I've come as a tortoise,' he says, and points to the girl on his back, 'and this is Michelle.'

****

Q: What's the violent, alcoholic, mental patient's catchphrase?
A: I'd rather have a bottle in front of me than a frontal lobotomy

****

Q: How many intelligent Arsenal fans does it take to screw in a light bulb?
A: Both of them.

****

Q: Why don't men have mid-life crises?
A: They stay stuck in adolescence.

****

Q: How do men buy lingerie for a woman?
A: They hrows it on the floor to see if it looks good, cuase that's where they wants to see it anyway.

****

Q: How are men and dogs alike?
A: If they can't eat it or screw it, then they just piss on it.

****

Q: What's the difference between men and cheese?
A: Cheese matures.

****

Q: What is the difference between a puppy and a man?
A: Eventually the puppy will grow up and stop whining.

****

Q: Why is sleeping with a man like a soap opera?
A: Just when it's getting interesting, they're finished until next time.

****

Q: Why do men like love at first sight?
A: It saves them a lot of time.

****

Q: What do you call a virgin in a $300 Hat?
A: The Pope.

Chapter 2
My Wife Doesn't Understand Me

Getting pissed can go three ways. Up, down or fast asleep. Up is good because you're loud, boisterous and having a laugh. Fast asleep isn't too bad until you wake up, but down is not good. When the booze starts working on you in such a way that your eyes fill with tears and you put your arm round the nearest person of the same sex (it has to be someone of the same such otherwise you're not telling them your problems, you're trying to shag them) and start telling them the most intimate details of your personal life and why it's all going wrong, you're in trouble. But don't panic; even though you're probably being more honest and open with a complete stranger than you've ever been with anyone before in your life, neither of you will remember a bleedin' word you said the next morning...

****

While on a car trip, the old couple stopped at a service station for lunch. The old woman left her glasses on the table, but didn't miss them until her and her husband were back on the motorway. By then, they had to travel quite a distance before they could find a place to turn around. The old man was fuming and moaned on at his poor wife all the way back to the service station. When they finally arrived, as the old woman got out of the car to retrieve her glasses, the old man called after her, 'And while you're in there, you might as well pick up my hat, too.'

****

You may have heard about a new bride who was a bit embarrassed to be known as a honeymooner. So when she and her husband pulled up to the hotel, she asked him if there was any way that they could make it appear as if they'd been married a long time. 'Sure,' he said. 'You carry the suitcases.'

****

A young man said to his girlfriend's dad, 'I realise this is only a formality, but could I ask you for your daughter's hand in marriage?'

'Who says it's only a formality?' replied her dad angrily.

'Her obstetrician,' replied the young man.

****

This lad was getting married and two days before he was due to tie the knot, a cricket ball hit him in the bollocks.

'Sorry son,' his doctor told him. 'But your tackle will need to go in a splint.'

On his wedding night, his virginal bride strips off and points at her breasts. 'Aren't they beautiful?' she asks him. 'Never touched by human hands.'

He pulled down his Y-fronts and points at his crotch. 'That's nothing,' he says, 'mine hasn't even been unpacked.'

****

A boy and his dad from a developing country were visiting the Gateshead Shopping Centre. They were amazed by almost everything they saw, but especially by two shiny, silver walls that could move apart and back together again. The boy asked his dad what it was.

'Son,' he replied, ' I have never seen anything like this in my life.'

While the boy and his dad watched wide-eyed, an old lady in a wheelchair rolled up to the moving walls and pressed a button. The walls opened and the lady rolled between them into a small room. The walls closed and the boy and his dad watched small circular numbers above the walls light up. They continued to watch as the circles lit up in the reverse direction. The walls opened up again and out stepped a voluptuous 24-year-old woman.

The dad and the son stared at each other in wide-eyed amazement until the dad said, 'Son, go and fetch your mother.'

****

A Frenchman and an Italian were seated next to an Englishman on a long-haul flight. After a few cocktails, the men began discussing their home lives.

'Last night I made love to my wife four times,' the Frenchman bragged, 'and this morning she made me delicious *crêpes* and she told me how much she adored me.'

'Ah, last night I made love to my wife six times,' the Italian responded, 'and this morning she made me a wonderful omelette and told me she could never love another man.'

'And what about you?' the Frenchman smugly asked the Englishman. 'How many times did you make love to your wife last night?'

'Just the once,' he replied.

'Only once?' laughed the Italian. 'And what did she say to you this morning?'

'Don't stop,' said the Englishman.

****

A bloke walks into a pub and sees a man sitting at the end of the bar with the smallest head he's ever seen. In fact, it's only about two inches high. So, he sits down next to him and says, 'Excuse me for asking, mate. But how come you've got such a small head?'

'Well, you see,' says the man with the unfeasibly small head, 'I was stranded on a deserted island and was combing the beach, when I came across an ornate bottle. When I opened it, a beautiful genie appeared and she told me I would be granted three wishes. My first wish was for a luxurious boat to take me home, and so a large yacht appeared just offshore. For my second wish, I asked to be wealthy, so I would want for nothing when I got home, and lo and behold a large pile of gold coins appeared on the deck of the yacht. For my third wish I asked the genie if I could make mad, passionate love to her, but she refused. She told me that under no circumstances could she do that for me, so I asked her, 'How about a little head?'

****

This bloke walks into a pub with a monkey on a string. He sits at the bar and announces that the monkey's for sale.

'What do I want with a monkey?' replies the publican, 'they destroy everything, and they're a nuisance!'

The bloke replies, 'But this is a special monkey. It gives a really good blow-job. Look, go in the back and try it out.

After 10 minutes, the publican returns with a broad grin.

'You weren't kidding, were you mate? That monkey's really good! How much do you want for it?'

They agree on £200 and the money is duly exchanged. That evening, the publican returns home to his wife. 'Listen, love, he says to her. 'I just bought this monkey and it cost me 200 quid so I want you to teach it to cook and wash and then I want you to get the fuck out of my house.'

****

Customer: (to publican) My wife and I just got into a knock-down, drag-out fight!

Publican: What happened?

Customer: When it was all over, she came crawling to me on her hands and knees!

Publican: Wow! What did she say?

Customer: She said, 'Come out from under that bed right now you coward, or I'll kick your flamin' head in!'

****

A fellow decides to take off early from work and go drinking. He stays until the pub closes at 11pm by which time he's well and truly wankered. When he gets home, he doesn't want to wake anyone up, so he takes off his shoes and starts tip-toeing up the stairs. Half-way up, though, he falls arse over tit and lands flat on his backside. To make matters worse, the two bottles of lager he had in his back pockets smash, carving up his arse terribly.

Because he's so pissed, though, he doesn't realise how badly he's hurt himself until gets to his room and stars undressing. Realising that he's bleeding, he checks himself out in the mirror and, sure enough, his behind is cut up something terrible. Well, he repairs the damage as best he can under the circumstances, and goes to bed. The next morning, his head aching, and his rear's throbbing, and he's lying there under the covers trying to think up a good story, when his wife comes into the bedroom.

'Well, you really tied one on last night,' she says. 'Where'd you go?'

'I was working late,' he replies, 'and I stopped off for a couple of pints.'

'A couple of beers? That's a laugh,' she shouts. 'You got plastered last night.'

'What makes you so sure I got drunk last night?' he shouts back.

'Well,' she replies, 'my first big clue was when I got up this morning and found a load of plasters stuck on the mirror.'

****

A married couple were throwing a dinner-party for all the top people in Cannes. The wife was very excited about this and wanted everything to be perfect. At the very last minute, she realised she didn't have any snails, so she asked her husband to run down to the beach and get her a bucketfull. Reluctantly, he agreed. He took the bucket, walked out the door, down the steps and out to the beach. As he was collecting the snails, he noticed a beautiful woman strolling alongside the water just a little further down the beach. 'Wouldn't it be great if she came over and just started talking to me?' he thought for a moment, before going back to gathering the snails. Moments later, he found himself staring up into the face of the beautiful woman he'd watched earlier. The two of them got talking, and she invited him back to her place. Before long they started shagging and it got so hot and heavy that when it was over he passed out from exhaustion.

At seven o'clock the next morning he woke up and, remembering his wife's dinner party, grabbed his clothes, put them on as quickly as he could, grabbed his bucket, and ran out the door. He ran down the beach all the way home. He ran up the stairs of his house, but he was in such a hurry that when he got to the top of the stairs, he dropped the bucket of snails.

Hearing the commotion his distraught wife came to the front door. On seeing her husband she became furious. 'Where the hell do you think you've been?' she screamed at him.

The man looked at the snails all down the steps, then looked at her, then back at the snails and said, 'Come on lads, we're almost there!'

****

This couple had been married for 30 years, and on their anniversary they decided to go back to the same hotel where they'd spent their wedding night. The husband was lying on the bed when his wife came out of the bathroom totally starkers, just as she had 30 years before. She stood seductively before him and said, 'Tell me, darling, what were you thinking 30 years ago when I came out of the bathroom like this?'

The husband replied, 'I took one look at you and thought I'd like to screw your brains out and suck your boobs dry.'

'And what are you thinking now, baby?' she asked huskily.

He said, 'I'm thinking I did a pretty good job of it!'

****

Eli was a just simple country boy, and though his wife longed for the sophisticated London life she read about in glossy magazines, she loved him just the same. Around the end of harvest-time she wanted to do something special for him because he'd been working so hard, so she bought a pair of crotchless knickers. The night the harvest was finally all brought in she put them on and waited for him . When he came home she lay sprawled on the couch spread-eagled. 'Hi, honey,' she purred sexily. 'You fancy some of this?'

Eli took one look at her and said, 'No thank you. Just look at what it done to your undies.'

****

A fireman came home from work one day and said to his wife, 'You know, we have a wonderful system at the fire station. Bell One rings and we all put on our jackets. Bell Two rings and we all slide down the pole and when Bell Three rings we're ready to go on the engines. From now on we're going to run this house the same way. When I say, "Bell One," I want you to strip naked. When I say, "Bell Two" I want you to jump into bed, and when I say, "Bell Three" we're going to screw all night.' So the next night he came home from work and yelled, 'Bell One,' and his wife took off her clothes. He yelled, 'Bell Two,' and his wife jumped into bed. He yelled, 'Bell Three,' and they began to screw. After a couple of minutes, though, his wife yelled, 'Bell Four!'

'What's Bell Four?' her husband asked.

'More hose,' she replied, 'you're nowhere near the fire.'

****

This geezer had a very attractive wife, but she was always wanting clothes and jewellery and all sorts of expensive stuff he couldn't really afford. One day his wife came home with a diamond necklace.

'Where'd you get that?' asked the bloke.

'I won it at bingo,' she replied.

The very next night she comes home with a Gianni Versace coat.

'Where'd you get that?' asks the geezer.

'I won it at bingo,' she replied.

The following night she comes home with a brand-new Mercedes.

'Where'd you get that?' asks the bloke exasperated.

'Look,' shouts his wife. 'Don't keep asking where I get my things from. Go upstairs and run a bath for me.'

So off he went, but when his wife comes upstairs she finds only a small amount of water in the tub.

'Why's there hardly any water in the bath?' she demands.

'Well,' replied the guy, 'I didn't want to get your bingo card wet.'

****

Malcolm and his wife are walking down the high street one evening, window-shopping. They stop by a jewellery shop.

'Malc,' says his wife, 'I'd love those diamond earrings.'

'No problem,' says Malcolm, takes a brick out of his pocket, smashes the window and grabs the earrings. They walk hastily away and soon come upon another jewellery shop. In the window, there's this gorgeous diamond ring.

'Malc, oh please, please, please, get me that ring,' begs his wife. He looks around, sees there's nobody looking, takes another brick out of his pocket and hurls it at the window. Now she's got the earrings and this great ring, and they walk away until they come to yet another jewellery shop. This time there's this fantastic diamond necklace in the window.

'Malc, Malc, just look at it. It goes so well with the ring and the earrings. I need it!'

'For God's sake, woman,' says Malcolm. 'Do you think I'm *made* of bricks?'

****

A businessman and his secretary are overcome by passion, and the exec convinces her to nip back to his house for a lunchtime shag.

'Don't worry,' he purrs, 'my wife's on a business trip. She won't bother us.'

The pair are getting it on in the man's bedroom, when the secretary gasps, 'We've got to stop now! I'm not using any birth control.'

'No problem,' replies the man, 'I know where my wife keeps her diaphragm.'

He immediately begins rooting around in the bathroom. After half an hour, he returns to the bedroom in a fury.

'The bitch took it with her,' he said angrily. 'I knew she didn't trust me.'

****

A husband and wife were lying in bed. The husband reached over and nudged his wife. 'What do you want?' she said.

'You know,' he said.

'Can't,' she replied. 'I have to see my gynaecologist tomorrow.'

Later, the husband reached over and nudged his wife again.

'Look, I told you,' she shouted. 'I have to see my doctor tomorrow.'

'I know,' he said. 'But you don't have to see your dentist, do you?'

****

A husband comes home with a tub of ice-cream and asks his wife if she wants some.

'How hard is it?' she asks.

'About as hard as my dick,' he replies.

'OK,' she says, 'then pour me some!'

****

Man: (to friend) I'm taking my wife on an African safari.

Friend: Wow! What would you do if a vicious lion attacked your wife?

Man: Nothing.

Friend: Nothing? You wouldn't do anything?

Man: Right. Let the stupid lion fend for himself!

****

A man rushes into his house and yells to his wife, 'Debbie, pack your things, girl. I just won the lottery!'

'Shall I pack for warm weather or cold?' asks Debbie.

'I don't care,' the man responds. 'Just so long as you're out of the house by noon!'

****

Two married couples who regularly played bridge together were playing one week and took a break between hands. The wives went to the kitchen to get refreshments and the following conversation took place.

'You know, Brian, you're doing much better this week as far as remembering what's trump and whose played what and everything,' said George.

'Yeah, George,' said Brian. 'I took one of them memory courses.'

'Really? which one did you take?' asked George.

'Erm, now let me think,' says Brian. 'Erm… what's it called… a red flower… got thorns…'

'A rose?' suggest George.

'That's it!' shouts Brian. 'Rose,' he shouts into the kitchen, 'what was the name of that memory course I took?'

****

A man is holding his wife's hand as she's lying on her death-bed.

'Jerry, I… I have something to tell you before I pass on,' she whispers.'

'No, no, dear,' says Jerry. 'Everything is forgiven now. All is well.'

'No, Jerry,' she mumbles. 'I've been carrying this load for years now, and I must tell you. I… I've been unfaithful to you. I slept with your best friend, Phil. I'm so terribly sorry.'

'Yes, dear, I know,' says Jerry. 'Why do you think I poisoned you?'

****

'After a few years of married life , this bloke finds he's unable to perform any more. He goes to his doctor, who tries a few things, but nothing works. Eventually the doctor says to him 'This is all in your mind', and refers him to a psychiatrist.

After a few visits to the shrink, the shrink confesses, 'I'm at a loss as to how to cure you,' and refers him to a witch-doctor.

The witch-doctor tells him, 'I can cure this, no problem,' and throws some powder on a flame. Suddenly, there's a flash followed by billowing blue smoke.

'This is powerful healing,' the witch doctor tells the bloke, 'but you can only use it once a year! All you have to do is say "One, two, three" and it shall rise for as long as you wish!'

'What happens when it's over?' asks the guy. 'All you have to say is "One, two, three, four" and it will go down again,' says the witch-doctor. 'But be warned; it will not work again for a year!'

The bloke goes home and that night he is ready to surprise his wife with the good news. As he's lying in bed with her he says "one, two, three", and suddenly he gets an erection.

His wife turns over and says, 'What did you say "One, two, three" for?'

****

A woman reported the disappearance of her husband to the police. The officer in charge looked at the photo she handed them, questioned her, and then asked if she wished to give her husband any message if they found him.

'Yes,' she replied readily. 'Tell him Mother didn't come after all.'

****

A married couple retire to their hotel room on their wedding night. The man, who's much larger than his petite bride, takes off his trousers and throws them over to his wife, saying, 'Put these on.'

'But they're way too big for me,' giggles his wife.

'I don't care,' says the man. 'Put them on anyway.'

So she puts his trousers on and, of course, they fall down. 'I told you I couldn't fit into these...'

'That's right,' he replied. 'Now just remember who wears the trousers in this family.'

The woman then takes off her panties and throws them over to her husband, saying, 'Put these on.'

He looks at them and says, 'I can't get into these...'

'Yes, that's right,' she replies, 'and you won't be able to in the future unless you change your attitude!'

****

Men who have pierced ears are better prepared for marriage. They've experienced pain and bought jewellery.

****

A little boy asked his father, 'Daddy, how much does it cost to get married?'
    'I don't know, son,' replied his father, 'I'm still paying for it.'

****

A tramp asked a man for £2.
    'Will you use it to buy booze?' asked the man.
    'No, sir,' replied the tramp.
    'Will you gamble it away?' asked the man.
    'No, sir,' said the tramp.
    'Then will you come home with me,' said the man, 'so my wife can see what happens to a man who doesn't drink or gamble?'

****

This couple visited a sex clinic to get treatment because their sex life had become a bore. Each night, the man would arrive home. His wife would prepare supper. After supper, they'd watch two hours of telly and immediately afterwards go to bed. From that point on, every move was routine.
    'No wonder,' the sex therapist said. 'You've made sex monotonous. Stop living on a schedule. Get into sex whenever you feel like it. Don't wait until bedtime each night to do it. Do it whenever you get into the mood.'
    The couple agreed to try the advice and said they would give him a progress report the following week.
    'How did things work out?' the sex therapist asked when they turned

The Best Pub Joke Book Ever!

up a week later. The man and his wife were beaming. 'It worked! It worked great!' they both said.

'Tell me about it,' said the therapist.

'Well, two nights after we saw you last,' said the husband, 'we were eating supper when I noticed that, although it was only seven o'clock, I had this huge erection. Sweetie-pie here was staring at it with longing eyes. So I didn't wait for any shower or any news broadcast. Instead, I reached out, ripped off her blouse and bra. Then I tore off her panties. I flung her right on to the table, spilling all the wine and soup in the process. Then I unzipped and we had sex like we've never had it before!'

'That's wonderful!' said the sex therapist. 'I told you it would work if you did it when the spirit moved you!'

'Only one thing,' said the man a little sadly. 'They're never going to let us go back in that restaurant.'

****

This old bloke who's a bit hard of hard of hearing has a bit of a funny turn, so his missus takes him to see the doctor.

The doctor runs a few tests but can't find anything wrong with him. Finally, the doctor says, 'Well, I'm baffled. I'm afraid I'm going to have to undertake some more thorough tests. Could you leave me a urine, faeces and sperm sample, please?'

'What does he want me to leave him?' says the old man.

'Your underwear, dear,' says his wife.

****

This woman goes to see a psychiatrist and says, 'I've got a big problem, doctor. Every time I'm in bed with my husband, he lets out this earsplitting scream when he climaxes.'

'My dear,' says the shrink, 'that's completely natural. I don't see what problem is.'

'The problem is,' says the woman, 'that he always wakes me up.'

Since her husband became infatuated with Brigitte Bardot, Doreen's found that her love life' has gone right down the tubes. So one day she goes to the a tattoo shop, thinking that if she has the letters BB tattooed on her breasts that maybe her husband will notice and start paying attention to her again. Upon telling the tattooist her desires he explains that due to the ageing process and gravity, the tattoo on her breasts might not be so attractive in several years' time and suggests she have the initials put on her buttocks instead. She thinks it over and agrees, then leans over the table while the tattooist puts a B on each cheek. When her husband arrives home from work she greets him, turns around, bends over and lifts her dress to expose the art work.

'What do you think?' she asks.

'Who the fuck is Bob?' shouts her husband.

✳✳✳✳

Mrs Jones goes to see her obstetrician, Dr. Smith. She says, 'Dr. Smith, I'm pregnant again. I need a hearing aid.'

'Mrs Jones,' says Dr. Smith, 'I thought we decided last time that your 12 children were more than you could handle, and that you should not get pregnant again. I'm going to give you a powerful contraceptive.'

'But doctor,' says Mrs Jones, 'I don't need a contraceptive. I need a hearing aid! '

'How come, Mrs Jones?' asks the doc.

'Well,' says Mrs Jones, 'I'm kinda hard of hearing. At night, when the old man and I turn off the lights and go to bed, he asks me, "Do you want to go to sleep, or what?" And I always say, "What?"'

✳✳✳✳

A man came home after a night shift and went straight up to the bedroom. He found his wife with the sheet pulled over her head, fast asleep. Not to be denied, the horny husband crawled under the sheet and proceeded to make love to her. Afterwards, as he hurried downstairs for something to eat, he was startled to find breakfast on the table and his wife pouring coffee.

'How d'you get down here so fast?' he asked. 'We were just making love!'

'Oh my God,' his wife gasped, 'that's my mother up there! She came over early and had complained of having a headache. I told her to lie down for a while.'

Rushing upstairs, the wife ran to the bedroom. 'Mother, I can't believe this happened. Why didn't you say something?' The mother-in-law huffed: 'I haven't spoken to that good-for-nothing for 15 years and I wasn't about to start now!'

****

A woman was in bed with her lover when she heard her husband opening the front door. 'Hurry!' she said, 'stand in the corner.' She quickly rubbed baby oil all over him and then she dusted him with talcum powder. 'Don't move until I tell you to,' she whispered. 'Just pretend you're a statue.'

'What's this, darling?' her husband inquired as he entered the room.

'Oh, it's just a statue,' she replied nonchalantly. 'The Smiths bought one for their bedroom. I liked it so much, I got one for us too.'

No more was said about the statue, not even later that night when they went to sleep. Around two in the morning the husband got out of bed, went to the kitchen and returned a while later with a sandwich and a glass of milk.

'Here,' he said to the statue, 'eat something. I stood like an idiot at the Smiths' for three days and nobody offered me so much as a glass of water.'

****

Two deaf people get married. During the first week of marriage, they find they're unable to communicate in the bedroom when they turn off the lights because they can't see each other using sign language.

After several nights of fumbling around and various misunderstandings, the wife decides to find a solution. 'Darling,' she signs, 'why don't we agree on some simple signals? For instance, at night, if you want to have sex with me, reach over and squeeze my left breast once. If you don't want to have sex, reach over and squeeze my right breast once.'

The husband thinks this is a great idea and signs back to his wife, 'Great idea. Now if you want to have sex with me, reach over and pull on my penis once. If you don't want to have sex, reach over and pull on my penis 50 times.'

****

A couple go out to dinner to celebrate their 50th wedding anniversary. On the way home, she notices a tear in his eye and asks if he's getting sentimental because they're celebrating 50 wonderful years together.

'No,' he replies, 'I was thinking about the time before we got married. Your father threatened me with a shotgun and said he'd have me thrown in jail for 50 years if I didn't marry you. Tomorrow I would've been a free man!'

****

A little old man and a little old lady met in a nursing home and decided to get married. Both had been widowed some years before, and, naturally, it had been a long time since either had enjoyed conjugal relations. So on their wedding night, as she started to disrobe, the little old lady turned to her new husband and said, 'Now, before we get frisky, I just want you to know that I have acute angina.'

Her new husband, who was a little deaf, replied, 'WHAT WAS THAT, HONEYBUNCH?'

'I SAID, I'VE GOT ACUTE ANGINA!' she shouted.

'WHAT?' he yelled back.

'I SAID, I'VE GOT ACUTE ANGINA!' she screamed.

'Thank God for that,' the old man muttered, 'those wrinkley old tits of yours are a right turn-off.

****

Joe still enjoyed chasing girls even when he got to be 70. When his wife was asked if she minded, she answered, 'Why should I be upset? Dogs chase cars, but they can't drive.'

****

Doris and Fred had started their retirement years and decided to raise some extra cash by advertising for a lodger in their two-up, two-down terraced house. After a few days, a young, attractive woman applied for the room and explained that she was a model working in a nearby city-centre studio for a few weeks and that she'd like the room from Mondays to Thursdays, but would pay for the whole week.

Doris showed her the house and they agree to start straight away. 'There's just one problem,' explained the model. 'Because of my job, I have to have a bath every night, and I notice you don't have a bath?'

'That's not a problem,' replied Doris. 'We have a tin bath out in the yard and we bring it in to the living room, in front of the fire, and fill it with hot water.'

'What about your husband?' asked the model.

'Oh, he plays darts most weekdays, so he'll be out in the evenings,' replied Doris.

'Good,' said the model. 'That settles it. I'll go to the studio and see you tonight.'

That evening Fred dutifully went to his darts match whilst Doris prepared the bath for the model. After stripping off the model stepped into the bath and Doris was amazed to see that she had no pubic hair. The model noticed Doris staring, smiled and explained that it was part of her job to shave her pubic hair especially when modelling swimwear or underclothes. Later when Fred returned, Doris told him about this, but Fred didn't believe her.

'It's true I tell you,' says Doris. 'Look, if you don't believe me, tomorrow night I'll leave the curtains slightly open and you can peek in and see for yourself.'

The next night Fred left as usual and Doris prepared the bath for the model. As the model stepped naked into the bath Doris, standing behind her, looked towards the curtains, and points towards the model's naked snatch. Then she lifted up her skirt and, wearing no panties, points to her own hairy mass. Later Fred returned and they retired to bed.

'Well do you believe me now?' she asks Fred.

'Yes,' he replied. 'I've never seen anything like it in my life. But why did you lift up your skirt and show your hairy bits?'

'Just to show you the difference,' answered Doris. 'But why are you so bothered about it? You've seen my hairy bits millions of times?'

'I know I have,' said Fred, 'But the rest of the darts team hadn't!'

****

This couple had been married for 25 years and they decided to go to the same place as they had done for their honeymoon 25 years ago. As they were driving through the country the old man said: 'My love, I want to touch you the same way as I did 25 years ago.'

'You may, you old devil,' the old lady said and he touched her on the knee. A couple of miles later he touched her on the arm, and said, 'Let's do the same thing we did 25 years ago.' He stopped the car and the two old-timers got out the car and made love passionately up against a wire fence. When they were finished they resumed their journey.

'My love,' said the old boy, '25 years ago you didn't move like you've just moved!'

'25 years ago,' said the woman, 'the fence wasn't electrified.'

****

An older woman was doing her exercises in front of the mirror, admiring her figure.

'What are you looking at?' asked her husband.

'I'll have you know that my aerobics instructor says I have the chest of a 23-year-old woman!' she replied.

'Yeah?' said her husband. 'Well, did he say anything about your 60-year-old arse?'

'Why, no, dear,' she said, 'we never talk about you.'

****

Two cannibals sat beside a large fire, after eating the best meal they'd had in ages.

'Your wife sure makes a great roast,' said the first cannibal.

'Yeah,' replied the second cannibal. 'I'm really going to miss her...'

****

It was a dark, stormy night and the young soldier was on his first guard duty. A general was out walking his dog, and as he approached the sentry box, the nervous young private snapped to attention, made a perfect salute and called out 'Sir, good evening, sir!'

The general, out for some relaxation, returned the salute and said, 'Good evening, soldier; nice night, isn't it?'

Even though it was a horrible night, the private wasn't about to disagree with a general, so he saluted again and replied, 'Sir, yes, sir!'

The general continued, 'You know, there's something about a stormy night that I find soothing, it's really relaxing. Don't you agree?'

The private didn't agree, but then he was just a private, and so he said, ' Sir, yes, sir!'

The general, then pointed at his dog and said, 'This is a Golden Retriever, the best type of dog to train.'

The private glanced at the dog, saluted yet again and said, 'Sir, yes, sir!'

The General continued, 'I got this dog for my wife.'

'Yes, sir!' said the private. 'Good swap, sir!'

****

A keen huntsman, who just got a rise at work, decides to buy a new sight for his rifle. He goes to a rifle shop, and asks the clerk to show him a sight. The shopkeeper takes out a sight and says to the man, 'This sight is so good, you can see my house all the way up on that hill.'

The huntsman takes a look through the telescope and starts laughing. 'What's so funny?' asks the shopkeeper.

'I see a naked man and a naked woman running around in the house', the man replies.

The shopkeeper grabs the sight from the man, and looks at his house. Then he hands two bullets to the man and says, 'I'll give you this sight for nothing if you take these two bullets, shoot my wife's head off and shoot the guy's dick off.'

The man takes another look through the sight and says, 'You know what? I think I can do that with one shot!'

****

While on holiday at a beautiful island getaway, a man discovers a lamp while walking on the beach. As these stories always go, he rubs the lamp and out pops a genie. The genie grants him three wishes, but adds one stipulation; 'Whatever you wish for, your wife will get double.'

This really upsets the man who's in the middle of a nasty divorce. He decides on his three wishes and tells the genie, 'First, I want to have £1 million.'

'Done,' says the genie. And, as promised, his wife receives £2 million.

'For my second wish,' says the man, 'I want a huge mansion.' Again it is done and his wife receives a house twice as large.

'So,' says the man, 'let me get this straight. I have a £1 million and my wife has £2 million. I have a huge mansion and my wife has one twice that size.'

'Correct,' says the genie. 'What do you want for your third wish?'

The man ponders momentarily and replies, 'I want you to scare me half to death.'

****

It was George the postman's last day on the job after 35 years of carrying the post through all kinds of weather in the same neighbourhood. When he arrived at the first house on his route he was greeted by the whole family, who roundly and soundly congratulated him and sent him on his way with a few quid. At the second house they presented him with a box of fine cigars. The folks at the third house handed him a selection of great golf clubs. At the fourth house he was met at the door by a strikingly beautiful woman in a revealing negligée. She took him by the hand, gently led him through the door, which she closed behind him, and led him up the stairs to the bedroom where she blew his mind with the most fantastic sex he'd ever had. When he'd had enough they went downstairs, where she fixed him a giant breakfast of eggs, bacon, sausages, chips, mushroom, beans and freshly-squeezed orange juice. When he was truly satisfied she poured him a cup of steaming coffee and gave him 50p.

George was baffled. 'All this was just too wonderful for words,' he said, 'but what's the 50 pence for?'

'Well,' she said, 'last night, I told my husband that today would be your last day, and that we should do something special for you. I asked him what to give you and he said, "Fuck him. Give him 50p." The breakfast was my idea.'

****

After her husband dies, a woman goes to the newspaper offices to place an obituary. Being short of money she decides on, 'Fred Dead, Funeral Monday.' Feeling sorry for her, the editor says she can have a few more words for free, so she changes it to, 'Fred Dead, Funeral Monday, Ford Escort for Sale.'

****

A husband and wife were having some problems with their marriage, so they bought a water bed to try to spice things up a bit. It did them no good, though. They started drifting apart.

****

After being examined by the doctor Ted's left to get dressed while the doctor takes his wife to one side to have a quiet word with her.

'To be honest,' he tells her, 'things aren't looking great for Ted. He's under a lot of pressure and if things don't ease up he could well suffer a heart attack soon. You can help by making his life at home as stress-free as possible. Bring him breakfast in bed in the morning, have his clothes ready, pressed and waiting for him, and in the evening when he comes home make him sit down, take his shoes off, run him a bath and gently massage his neck while he's in it. Anything like that will help with the stress.'

After Ted's got dressed, he's leaving the surgery with his wife when he turns to her and says, 'I noticed you were having quite a long chat with the doctor. What did he say to you?'

'He said you're going to die,' replied his wife.

****

One guy to another: 'I married Miss Right. I just didn't know that her first name was Always'.

****

Q: Did you hear about the new 'Divorced Barbie?'
A: Yeah, it comes with all of Ken's stuff!

****

An old farmer's having trouble with his prize bull. It won't breed with the cows, and he's lamenting the fact to a few of his friends down at his local.

One of them says, 'You know, I used to have the same trouble with my bull, but I got it fixed really quick.'

'How did you get it fixed?' asked the old farmer.

'Well I just dipped my finger in the cow's vagina and rubbed it all over the bull's nose and he got right after her,' explains his friend.

When the old boy goes home to the farm, he decides to try it. He grabs a cow, dips his fingers in her vagina and rubs it all around the bull's nose. The bull gets a rip-roaring boner and jumps on the cow immediately.

That night, the old farmer gets into bed with his wife and can't get the effect on the bull out of his mind. As she lies sleeping, he dips his fingers into his wife's vagina and feeling that it's nice and wet, he rubs it all around his nose and – hey presto! – he gets a rip-roaring hard on.

He quickly shakes his wife awake and cries out, 'Darling! Look at this!'

She rolls over, turns on the light and says, 'You mean you woke me up in the middle of the night just to show me that you have a nose-bleed?

****

Husband: Fancy a quickie?
Wife: As opposed to what?

****

There was once a lion-tamer who worked at the circus. His bunch of lions were well known for being the most ferocious lot around, but he never thought twice about going in with them.

After a show one night he'd been out for a few beers and, reckoning on a right bollocking from the missus, decided not to go home. He wandered around looking for somewhere to kip and eventually decided on going into the lion's cage where, resting his head on a particularly large beast, he fell asleep.

The following morning his wife woke up alone and, annoyed, came to look for him. After wandering around for some time she spied him, still dozing, in the lion's cage.

'Oi!' she shouted at him. 'Wake up, you bleedin' coward!'

****

A wife was having a go at her husband. 'Look at Mr Barnes across the road,' she moaned. 'Every morning when he goes to works, he kisses his wife goodbye. Why don't you do that?'

'Because I haven't been introduced to her yet,' replied her old man.

✳✳✳✳

A man and a woman had been together for a few months. The woman was extremely wealthy and the man was very poor and they both knew that their relationship was a bit of fun, but one night the man took the woman out for a romantic meal with all the trimmings.

'Will you marry me?' he asked her.

'No,' replied the woman.

'I didn't think you would,' said the man.

'Well, why did you ask me then?' inquired the woman.

'Because I just wanted to know what it felt like to lose millions,' said the man.

✳✳✳✳

A big Hollywood star fired his personal assistant one day because she hadn't been very good at keeping his personal records straight. According to her he'd had one more divorce than he'd had marriages.

✳✳✳✳

On a particularly warm day one summer, a man decided to sunbathe naked in his back garden. Having recently built a large fence he was confident that no one would be able to see him.

'I wonder,' he mused to his wife, 'what the neighbours would say if they could see me.'

'They'd probably say that I must have married you for you money,' replied his wife.

✳✳✳✳

Barry Davies was a very henpecked husband. In fact the only time he managed to get away from it all was at the annual school reunion where, each year, a trophy was awarded to the man who told the funniest story about making love to his wife. This particular year Barry won it and proudly took the trophy home.

'What did you get that for?' demanded his wife.

'Er, it was, er… it was for telling a story about when we played golf on holiday last summer, dear,' Barry stammered in reply.

'Hummmph,' grunted his missus and wandered off. The next day Barry's wife was chatting to the wife of another man who had been at the dinner.

'Hello, Mrs Davies,' said the woman. 'I gather that your Barry won a prize for telling the best story at the do last night.'

'Yes, but I've no idea why,' replied Mrs Davies. 'We only did it once. His cap blew off, he couldn't get it in the hole and he lost a ball.'

****

A husband goes up in the loft and notices an eggbox containing no eggs but £5,000 in used notes. He says to his wife, 'What's all this money doing in this eggbox?'

She instantly breaks down and cries: 'I can't lie any more, I've been unfaithful. Every time I slept with another man, I took six eggs in payment.'

'Well that explains the eggbox,' says the husband. 'But how about the £5,000?'

'Well,' says his wife,. 'every time I collected a dozen eggs I sold them.'

****

On their ruby wedding anniversary Janet turned to Jack and said, 'Do you know, Jack, we've been married for 60 years and I've been by your side all that time.'

'Yes,' said Jack. 'When I took a bayonet in the leg in the First World War you nursed me back to health. Then in the Second World War, after I was shot, you did the same. After the war when I was out of work, there you were for me. Then, when I did get a job and had to work all hours of the day just to make ends meet, you were by my side. When I was sacked and spent three years on the dole you never left me. When I developed kidney trouble and had to have an operation, there you were. And now that we're living in a B&B and I'm too old to work, you're still here. You know what Janet? You're a bloody jinx.'

****

After his beautiful wife died, John was understandably upset. 'I can feel your pain,' the local vicar told him. 'But it's good to grieve. And believe me, in time things will get better and you'll meet someone else.'

'I know,' said John, 'but what am I going to do tonight?'

****

A newly-married couple were getting ready for their wedding night but they both had a painful secret. He had terribly smelly feet and she had bad breath. To hide things he'd thrown his socks in the bath and she'd sprayed herself with breath freshener. They met in the middle of the room…

'Darling,' said the husband, 'I think there's something you should know. I've got very smelly feet.'

'That's OK,' said the wife. 'I've got something to tell you, too.'

'I know what you're going to tell me,' said the husband. 'You've eaten my socks.'

****

A woman is reading the ads in the local newspaper when she spots one that upsets her. 'Can you believe this?' she says to her husband. 'Some guy has put an advert in the paper offering to swap his wife for tickets to the Cup Final. You'd never do anything like that would you dear?'

'Course not, love,' says her husband. 'I've already got tickets for the game.'

****

On returning from the newsagent one morning a husband says to his wife, 'I've just heard a rumour that our postman's slept with every woman in this street except one. Can you believe that?'

'Hah,' says his wife, 'I bet it's that snobby, stuck-up cow at number 12.'

****

Two women are chatting. 'Dennis asked me to make him the happiest man in the world and marry him,' said the first one.

'Ooh, that's a tough one,' said the other. 'Which one did you choose?'

****

A woman was telling her friend about the tragic and sudden death of her husband.

'One minute he was with me and then he went out into the garden to pick some peas for our tea and he dropped dead,' she said.

'That's terrible,' said her friend. 'What did you do?'

'Opened a tin of beans instead,' she replied.

****

Two blokes were arguing about the merits of a particular actress.

'Look,' said the first one, 'take away her beautiful eyes, her great breasts, her fantastic figure and her lovely long hair, and what have you got?'

'My wife,' said the other sadly.

****

Two expectant fathers were waiting in the maternity ward.

'This is our first,' said one. 'Is it your first?'

'Oh no,' said the other, 'this is our fifth.'

'Really?' said the first bloke. 'Tell me something. Erm, how long before... well, you know? I mean, well... when can you have sex with your wife again after the birth?'

'Well,' said the other bloke. 'That all depends on whether she's on a ward or in a private room.'

****

A husband caught his wife in bed with another man and in a fury pulled out a gun ready to shoot him.

'No, no, don't kill him,' pleaded the wife. 'Who do you think paid for the new car? And that holiday? And who do you think paid for Kevin to go to that private school?'

'Was that you?' said the husband to the man.

'Yes,' spluttered the man, nodding. 'Well, get your clothes on then,' said the husband. 'You don't want to catch cold now, do you?'

****

A father came home one day and told his three kids that he had a surprise for them. 'Now,' he said to them, 'I've got some sweets and I'm going to give them to the person who never answers mummy back and always does what they're told. So who's going to get them?'

In unison the kids said, 'You are, Daddy!'

****

A beautiful woman was at the airport waiting for her husband to return from a long overseas trip. She spotted him at customs and waved, at which the husband waved back and shouted, 'F.F.'

'E.F.,' woman shouted back the.

'F.F.' came the reply, to which the woman again shouted, 'E.F.' This went on for a while until eventually the customs officer's curiosity got the better of him and he asked, 'Is that a special code that you have with that lady?'

'Sort of,' said the man. 'She's my wife and she's just saying that she wants to eat first.'

****

An actor who'd been out of work for some time finally landed a part. Excitedly, he phoned his dad with the news. 'Dad, dad,' he said, 'Guess what? I've landed a really challenging role in the new Ken Branagh film. I'm playing a guy who's been married for 30 years.'

'That's great news son,' said his Dad. 'Soon you'll be able to move on to speaking parts.'

****

Tom and Sally had been married for 40 years. After Tom died Sally missed him terribly so she went to a medium and made contact with him on the other side. 'Tom, Tom,' she said. 'Is that really you?'

'Yes, it is,' said Tom.

'Tell me,' she asked, 'are you happy on the other side?'

'Oh yes, very,' replied Tom.

'Happier than when you were alive and with me?' asked Sally.'

'Yes Sally, I'm very much happier than when I was alive and with you,' said Tom.

'Gosh,' said Sally. 'Heaven must be such a wonderful place.'

'Who said anything about heaven?' said Tom.

****

A man rushed home excitedly one day with some great news.

'Darling, darling,' he shouted. 'I've found a fantastic job. £25,000 a year, company car, five weeks holiday a year and flexible hours.'

'That's brilliant news,' said his wife.

'Yes, I knew you'd be pleased,' he said, 'you start tomorrow.'

****

The bellboy had carried the couple's luggage up to a room on the sixth floor of the hotel and was rewarded with a large tip.

'Thank you sir,' he said. 'Can I get you anything else?'

'No, thank you,' said the man.

'What about something for your wife, sir?' asked the boy.

'That's a good idea,' said the man. 'Bring me a postcard to send to her.'

****

Two businessmen were having lunch one day when two women entered the restaurant. 'Shit,' said one. 'My wife and my lover have just walked in.'

'Fuck,' said the other one. 'So have mine.'

****

Gary was down the local with his mate Ted. 'Do you know, Ted,' said Gary. 'I never slept with my wife before we were married. What about you?'

'I don't know,' replied Ted. 'What was her maiden name?'

****

'Where are you going on holiday?' John asked Trevor.

'We're off to Thailand this year,' Trevor replied.

'Oh; aren't you worried that the very hot weather might disagree with your wife?' asked John.

'It wouldn't dare,' said Trevor.

****

'Darling,' said Joan to her husband Clive. 'Every day you come in from work and I ask you how your day was and I sit patiently and listen as you tell me. You never ask me how my day was, here with the children and all the washing, ironing, cleaning and shopping to do.'

'OK, OK,' said Clive. 'How was your day, dear?'

'Terrible,' replied Joan. 'Don't ask.'

****

A husband and wife were talking about their dog. 'You know, dear,' said the wife. 'I think Fido's getting a bit old.'

'What makes you say that?' said the husband.

'Well, I think he's going a bit deaf. I often have to whistle two or three times before he comes,' said the woman.

'Nonsense,' said the man. 'Look at this. Fido! Sit!'

'I told you, dear, didn't I?' said the wife. 'Shall I get the disinfectant and the shovel?'

****

A honeymooning couple are about to get into bed when the woman bangs her foot on the bathroom door. 'Oh dear, darling,' says the man. 'Come here and I'll kiss it better.' She does so and before long they're shagging away. After a good session the woman gets up to go to the bathroom and once again she bangs her foot on the door.

'Can't you watch where you're going, you clumsy cow?' says the man.

****

Goldstein, the man with the biggest dick in Britain, dies. At the funeral an American tourist puts in a huge offer for his penis. After some discussion the relatives decide to sell the organ to the tourist. Back in the States the American rushes home and shouts to his wife, 'darling, darling. Come and see what I've got for you.'

The woman comes in, has a look and says, 'Oh my God! Goldstein's dead!'

****

An Italian woman has just got married and is about to have sex for the first time. After her husband takes off his shirt she rushes downstairs and says to her mother, 'Mama, mama! He's got scars all the way up his arm.'

'Don't worry, bambina,' says her mother. 'It's OK. You go back up there and I'll carry on making the spaghetti.'

So she goes back upstairs, but after her husband has taken off his vest she runs down again. 'Mama, mama!' she shouts. 'He's got hairs all over his chest.'

'Don't worry, bambina, it's OK,' says her mother. 'Go back up there while I finish the spaghetti.'

So she goes back upstairs, but after her husband has taken off his shoes, socks and trousers she's down again. 'Mama, Mama!' she shouts. 'He's got half a foot.'

'Here, bambina,' says her mother. 'You make the spaghetti.'

****

A rich geezer rings home and when the butler picks up the phone he asks to speak to his wife.

'I'm sorry sir,' says the butler, 'but she can't speak to you at the moment.'

'Why not?' asks the rich geezer.

'Well, sir, she's busy,' says the butler.

'Doing what? asks the rich geezer.

'She's in the bedroom, sir,' the butler informs him.

'What's she doing in the bedroom?' asks the rich geezer becoming more irate by the second.

'I don't know sir, but she's with a man,' says the butler.

'Right,' says the rich geezer. 'Here's what I want you to do. Go and get the shotgun I use for hunting, go to the bedroom and shoot both of them.'

So the butler puts the phone down and goes about the task. After hearing two loud bangs down the phone the man hears the butler returning to the phone.

'Are they dead?' he asks the butler. 'Yes sir,' says the butler.

'Right,' says the rich geezer, 'I want you to take the gun into the garden and throw it into the fishpond at the bottom.'

'But sir,' exclaims the butler, 'we don't have a fishpond.'

'That is 454 7234, isn't it?' says the rich geezer.

✱✱✱✱

A couple celebrating their 60th wedding anniversary decide to spice things up a little by sitting down to supper stark naked.

'Oh, Herbert,' says the woman, 'this is so lovely. I can feel my heart warming already.'

'I'm not surprised, Lily,' says Herbert, 'one of your tits is in the soup.'

✱✱✱✱

A couple of American tourists are visiting London Zoo. When they get to the skunk cage the husband is so enchanted by the creatures that he sneaks in and steals one. He hides it in his bag, but as they approach the exit he becomes increasingly nervous and passes it to his wife telling her to hide it up her skirt.

'But what about the smell?' says the anxious wife.

'Don't worry,' says the man. 'If it dies I'll go back and get another one.'

✱✱✱✱

A policeman gets home very late at night and so as not to disturb his wife creeps into their bedroom without turning on the light. Unfortunately, as he's slipping into bed his wife wakes up.

'Oh, darling,' she says, 'I've got a terrible headache. Please can you pop to the all-night garage and get me some aspirin?'

So the copper gets dressed again and goes to the shop.

'Hey,' says the assistant when he gets there. 'I thought you were a policeman.'

'I am,' says the copper.

'Then why are you wearing a fireman's uniform?' asks the shop assistant.

****

A woman who lived on a main road was having trouble with her bedroom closet. Every time a bus went past, its doors would fly open. So she called a carpenter who came round to look at it. He couldn't see any problem on the outside, so he climbed into it. Just then the woman's husband came home and sensing something was up ran straight into the bedroom and flung open the closet doors.

'What the hell are you doing in here?' he demanded.

'Would you believe I'm waiting for a bus?' said the carpenter.

****

Jane entered the kitchen one morning, reached to turn on the light, and found it didn't work. After replacing the bulb, there was still no light. When John, her husband, came home, she said, 'Darling, the light switch is broken. Could you fix it for me, please?'

To which John replied – while proudly displaying the front of his T-shirt – 'Do you see the word "Electrician" written on the front of this shirt?'

Jane said nothing.

Next day John came home and Jane said, 'Darling, the cabinet door fell off today. Could you put it back on for me, please?'

To which John replied, 'Do you see the word "Carpenter" written anywhere on the front of this shirt?'

Next day John came home and Jane said, 'Darling, the water pipe under the sink is leaking. Could you fix it for me, please?'

'Look,' John replied, 'Do you see the word "Plumber" written anywhere on the front of this shirt?'

Next day John came home and the light switch was working, the cabinet door had been replaced, and the pipe wasn't leaking. John said, 'I see you found some good repairmen'.

To which Jane replied, 'No, I just called the neighbour next door.'

'Oh, really?' said John. 'And how much did he charge?'

Jane laughed and said, 'He didn't charge anything. He said I could just bake him some "goodies" or we could trade it out in sex.'

To which, of course, John asked, 'Well, what kind of "goodies" did you bake for him?'

And Jane said proudly, while displaying the front of her shirt, 'Do you see the words "Delia Smith" written on here anywhere?'

****

All men who hope to enter heaven have to queue at one of two gates: one marked, 'For Henpecked Men,' and one marked, 'For Men Who Have Not Been Henpecked.'

One morning the Angel Gabriel turns up for work and is amazed to see, along with the usual very long line at the first gate, one little geezer standing by the second. 'Hello,' said the Archangel, 'are you sure you're in the right line, mate?'

'Well, I don't really know,' said the little bloke, 'my wife told me to come and stand here.'

****

Two married couples were playing bridge one night. Unfortunately, the husband of one of the couples was a bloody awful player and he and his wife were getting a drubbing. Eventually the husband decided he had to go and take a leak. After he'd left, his wife said, 'That's the only time this evening when I've known what's in his hand.'

****

A middle-aged woman goes to visit a fortune teller.

'I see only good for you,' says the fortune teller. 'You will meet a tall, dark, handsome stranger who will sweep you off your feet and make you incredibly happy.'

'That's fantastic,' says the woman. 'But I do have one small question.'

'And what may that be?' says the fortune teller.

'What happens to my husband?' she asks.

✱✱✱✱

A posh newly-wed woman was telling her friends all the intimate details of her recent honeymoon. 'It was truly marvellous,' she exclaimed. 'No sooner had we arrived in the hotel than Sebastian rushed me upstairs and we had a performance. Then just after lunch we had another performance, in the middle of the afternoon we had another and before dinner we had another. And then after dinner we had a dress rehearsal.'

'What is a dress rehearsal?' enquired one of her friends.

'It's the same as a performance,' said the posh woman, 'only nobody comes.'

✱✱✱✱

Not long after he'd been brought into existence, Adam couldn't help noticing that the animals would pop off into the forest in pairs and return some time later with wide, contented grins on their faces. Bemused, he asked God what it was all about.

'It's called reproduction,' said the Lord. 'Why don't you take Eve into the forest and find out about it?'

Adam did as the Lord had suggested, but returned to him the next day with another question. 'Lord,' asked Adam, 'What's a headache?'

✱✱✱✱

A husband and wife take their young son along with them when they go on holiday to a nudist camp. The boy can't help noticing that some men have, 'big ones' and some have 'little ones,' so he asks his dad about it.

His dad doesn't want to get into the whole thing, so quickly says, 'Oh, those with big ones are smart and those with small ones are stupid; now run along and find something to do.'

'Later on the family are having supper and the dad asks the little boy what he's been doing.

'Oh, I wandered around the woods and saw a lot of men getting much smarter,' said the boy.

****

There was a butler who worked for a wealthy couple. The husband was old, and the wife young and beautiful. One night the couple went out to dinner. The young wife returned home earlier than the husband, and she called the butler, Sam, into her room.

She told him: 'Sam, I want you to take my shoes off.' So Sam took her shoes off. Next she said, 'Sam, now I want you to take my stockings off.' so Sam took her stockings off. 'Now, Sam, take my dress off. Now my bra, and now my panties. And Sam, if I ever catch you wearing my clothes again…'

****

Two pairs of newly-weds went on honeymoon together. After the first week they got a bit fed up with their partners and agreed to swap to liven things up a bit. The next morning one of the husbands turned to his new partner and said, 'That was great. Shall we see how the girls are getting on?'

****

Two mates are chatting over a few beers when one of them says something that would be considered a Freudian slip. He also recalls the last slip he had when he asked a gorgeous, big-breasted travel agent for two 'Pickets to Titsburgh'. His friend says, 'Yeah, I know what you mean. Last week I was having breakfast with my wife and I meant to say, "Could you please pass the milk, dear?' but what came out of my mouth was, "You fucking bitch, you ruined my life"'.

****

A bloke is having marital problems. He and the wife aren't communicating at all and he's lonely, so he goes to a pet shop thinking a pet might help.

The shop happens to specialise in parrots and as he wanders down the rows of parrots he notices one with no feet. Surprised, he mutters to himself, 'That's strange, I wonder how he hangs on to the perch?'

To which the parrot replies: 'With my prick, you thick bastard.'

The bloke's startled and says, 'You talk really well for a parrot.'

To which the parrot replies: 'Of course I do, I'm a very well educated parrot. I can discuss politics, sports, religion – any subject you like.'

The guy says 'Blimey, you sound like just what I was looking for.'

The parrot says: 'There's not much of a market for maimed parrots. If you offer the proprietor £20 for me, I'll bet he'll sell me.'

The bloke buys the parrot and for three months things go great. When he comes home from work the parrot tells him how Tony Blair's done something new, or that Tim Henman won again, or how badly England lost the Test Match by and so and so, until one day when he comes home from work and the parrot waves a wing at him and says, 'Come in and shut the door.'

'What's up?' says the bloke.

The parrot says, 'I don't know how to tell you this but the postman came today. Your wife answered the door in her negligée and he kissed her right on the lips.'

The bloke says, 'Oh, it must have been a momentary flight of passion.'

Then the parrot says, 'Then he fondled her breasts.'

The bloke says, 'He did?'

The parrot says, 'Then he pulled her negligée down and started sucking on her tits.'

The guy says, 'My God, what happened next?'
The parrot says, 'I don't know I fell off my perch.'

****

It's a beautiful, warm spring day and a man and his wife are at the zoo. She's wearing a cute, loose-fitting, pink spring dress, sleeveless with straps. As they are walking through the monkey house and pass in front of a very large gorilla, the gorilla goes apeshit. He jumps up on the bars, holding on with one hand (and two feet), grunting, and pounding his chest with the free hand – obviously excited at the pretty lady in the pink dress.

The husband noticing the excitement, suggests that his wife tease the poor fellow. The husband suggests she pucker her lips, wiggle her bum, and play along. She does and the gorilla gets even more excited making noises that would wake the dead. Then the husband suggests that she let one of her straps fall. She does, and the gorilla is just about ready to tear the bars down. 'Now, try lifting your dress up your thighs,' says the husband. This drives the gorilla bananas. Suddenly, the husband grabs his wife by the hair, rips open the door to the cage, slings her in with the gorilla and says, 'Now, tell *him* you've got a headache!'

****

A married couple went to the hospital to have their baby delivered. Upon arrival, the doctor said he'd invented a new machine that would transfer a portion of the mother's labour pain to the father. He asked if they were willing to try it out.

They were both very much in favour of it, so the doctor set the knob to 10 per cent for starters, explaining that even 10 per cent was probably more pain than the father had ever experienced before.

As the labour progressed, however, the husband felt fine, so he asked the doctor to go ahead and bump it up a notch. The doctor then adjusted the machine to 20 per cent pain transfer. After a while, though, the husband was still feeling fine. The doctor checked his blood pressure and pulse and was amazed at how well he was doing. At this, they decided to try for 50 per cent. The husband continued to feel quite well.

Since it was obviously helping out his wife considerably, he encouraged the doctor to transfer ALL the pain to him and the wife delivered a healthy baby with virtually no pain. She and her husband were ecstatic and they were allowed to leave the hospital that evening. When they arrived home they found the milkman dead on their doorstep.

****

Bill worked in a pickle factory. He had been employed there for a number of years when he came home one day to confess to his wife that he had a terrible compulsion. He had an urge to stick his penis into the pickle slicer. His wife suggested that he should see a sex therapist to talk about it, but Bill indicated that he'd be too embarrassed. He vowed to overcome the compulsion on his own.

One day, a few weeks later, Bill came home absolutely ashen. His wife could see at once that something was seriously wrong. 'What's wrong, Bill?" she asked.

'Do you remember I told you how I had this tremendous urge to put my penis into the pickle slicer?'

'Oh, Bill, you didn't!'

'Yes, I did.'

'My God, Bill, what happened?'

'I got fired.'

'No, Bill. I mean, what happened with the pickle slicer?'

'Oh... she got fired too.'

****

Mark and Sharon decide they don't want to discuss sex in front of their four- and six-year-old children, so they decide to talk in code. One day Mark is feeling a little bit turned on and says to Katie, 'Tell your mother I would really like to type a letter.'

Katie runs off to find her mum. 'Mummy, mummy', shouts Katie, 'Daddy would like to type a letter.'

Sharon replies slightly sheepishly, 'Katie, go and tell your daddy that he can't type a letter today as there's a red ribbon in the typewriter.'

Katie tears off to her dad and says, 'Daddy, daddy, mummy says you can't type a letter today as there's a red ribbon in the typewriter.'

A few days later Sharon remembers that Mark was keen for a bit of nookie and so she called Katie, 'Katie, tell your daddy that he can type that letter today.'

So Katie runs off to look for her dad and when she finds him she says, 'Daddy, mummy says you can type that letter today.'

'That's OK, Katie,' Mark says, 'You can tell your mummy that I don't need the typewriter any more. I wrote the letter by hand.'

✶✶✶✶

Fred's boss told him that he had to work overtime. 'OK,' said Fred, 'but we've only just moved into our new home and the phone ain't connected – how can I let my old lady know I'll be late home?'

'I know where you live,' says the boss. It's not far from my house. I'll pop in and tell her on my way home.'

When the boss arrived at Fred's house, his wife comes to the door.

'I just popped round to let you know that Fred will be late home tonight,' says the boss.

'Oh, OK,' says Fred's wife. 'Can I get you a cup of tea?'

'Well, that would be nice,' said the boss, 'but how about taking me upstairs and letting me fuck you instead?'

'I've never heard such cheek,' said the wife.

'What about if I give you 50 quid?' says the boss.

'No! Fred would be furious,' said the wife.

'How about £100?' says the boss.

'No!' says the wife.'

'Alright,' says the boss. '£150.'

'OK, then,' says the wife and she takes him upstairs and screws him. Later that day, Fred arrived home.

'I'm sorry I'm late, darling. Did the boss call round and tell you about the overtime?'

'Yes he did, darling,' replied his wife.

'Oh yeah,' said Fred remembering something else. 'He said he'd drop my wages off as well. Did he give them to you?'

****

A young couple was invited to a swanky masked Hallowe'en party. The wife came down with a terrible headache and told her husband to go to the party and have a good time. Being the devoted husband, he protested, but she argued and said she was going to take some aspirin and go to bed. She told him there was no need for him to miss the fun. So he took his costume and away he went.

The wife, after sleeping soundly for an hour, woke up feeling normal and, as it was still early, decided to go to the party. Because hubby didn't know what her costume was, she thought she'd have a bit of a laugh watching her husband and seeing how he acted when she was not around.

She joined the party and soon spotted her husband cavorting around on the dance floor. He was dancing with every nice woman he could, and copping a feel here and stealing a kiss there. His wife sidled up to him and being a rather seductive babe herself, he left the partner he was with and devoted his time to the new 'action'.

She let him go as far as he wished, naturally, since he was her husband, and when he whispered a little proposition in her ear she agreed to go off with him to one of the bedrooms for a bunk-up.

Afterwards they went back to the party and, just before the unmasking at midnight, she slipped out, went home, put the costume away and got into bed. She was sitting up reading when he came in, and she asked him what he had done.

He said, 'Oh, the same old thing. You know I never have a good time when you're not there.'

Then she asked him if he danced much and he said: 'I never even danced one dance. When I got to the party, I met Pete, Bill and some other guys so we went into the kitchen and got a poker school going. But I'll tell you... the guy I loaned my costume to, he told me what he'd been up to and he had one a hell of a time...'

****

Two women were standing at a funeral. 'I blame myself for his death,' said the wife.

'Why?' said her friend.'

''Cos I shot him,' said the wife.

****

A married couple had jet-black hair, so when their daughter was born a redhead, the husband was a bit suspicious. He went to the doctor and explained the situation.

The doctor said, 'Well how often do you have sex?'

'Oh, about once every two years,' said the husband.'

'Well, that explains it,' said the doctor. 'You're a bit rusty.'

****

'You never cry out when you orgasm,' said the husband.

'How would you know?' replied his wife, 'you're never there.'

****

A very old millionaire goes for a check-up. The doctor looks him over and pronounces him in fine physical shape.

'I'm curious,' says the doctor. 'Why did you decide to have a physical now?'

''Cos I'm just about to marry an 18-year-old and we're planning on having children.'

The doctor tries not to look too astonished.

'Is there anything you think I should do to help things along?' asks the old man.

The doctor thinks about this for a while and says, 'I think you should get a young lodger.'

'OK,' says the old man and leaves. A year later, the doctor sees the old man in the street and asks how things are going.

'My wife's pregnant,' says the old man.

'That's great,' says the doctor. 'And how's the lodger?'

'Oh, she's pregnant, too,' replies the old man.

✱✱✱✱

Two bricklayers were chatting at work. 'Are you going to the match on Saturday?' said one. 'Arsenal are playing Spurs.'

'No,' said the other. 'My wife won't let me.'

'What?' said the first. 'It's easy to get out of that. About an hour before the game, what you do is pick her up, take her to the bedroom, rip off her clothes and make mad, passionate love to her. Then she'll let you do anything you want.'

'I'll try that,' said the other man.

The following Monday the two men meet on the building site. 'How come you didn't make it to the game?'' asked the first man.'

'Well, I'll tell you what happened,' said the second man. 'About an hour before kick off, I did as you said. I picked her up, took her to the bedroom and ripped off her clothes. And then I thought, Spurs haven't been playing that well recently.'

✱✱✱✱

This poor old couple were sitting in a flat. 'We've completely run out of money,' said the husband. 'You're going to have to go out and sell your body.'

'You can't be serious,' said his wife.

'Yes, I am,' said the husband.

So off she goes and comes back 12 hours later with £5 and 10 pence.

'Who gave you the 10 pence?' asked the husband.

'Everybody,' she replied.

****

This man went to the doctor because he wanted to kill his wife. The doctor said to him, 'I've got the perfect solution. Take these pills every day and you'll be able to make love to your wife 15 times a day. In a month, she'll be dead.'

The man was very grateful and rushed off with the pills. Four weeks later, the doctor was walking down the street and saw his patient, in a wheelchair, moving very slowly towards him.

'What happened?' said the doctor.

'Two more days,' said the man. 'Just two more days…'

****

There was this man who had just got married and was spending his wedding night with his new wife in a very posh hotel. It was to be the first time that he had ever had sex with her; indeed, he had never even seen her naked.

As they were both undressing, he looked up from taking his socks off to notice that she had huge breasts and even went so far as to compliment her on them.

Unfortunately, the poor girl had always had a bit of a complex about them and got very distraught at this. So much so that she sent him with a blanket out into the corridor to sleep. The man was pretty upset at this, but not wishing to fuel her anger further, did as he was told.

Just as he was getting off to sleep another man came into the corridor to join him. The first man asked the second why he was out there, to which he replied that he was also on his wedding night and had never had the pleasure of seeing his new wife's body before. When she was undressing, he had suddenly exclaimed out loud what an absolutely enormous bum she had. She hadn't really been very impressed with this outburst, and had ordered him to go and sleep in the corridor.

Before long jilted honeymooner number three sulkily sauntered out to join the other two.

'What's wrong with you?' asked the first, 'did you put your foot in it as well?'

'No,' replied the third, 'but I bloody well could have.'

✳✳✳✳

An architect, an artist and a computer programmer were discussing whether it was better to have a wife or a mistress. The architect said he enjoyed time with his wife, building a solid foundation for an enduring relationship. The artist said he enjoyed time with his mistress, because of the passion and mystery he found there. The computer programmer, meanwhile, said, 'I prefer to have both.'

'Both?' said his friends incredulously.

'Yeah,' said the programmer. 'If you have a wife and a mistress, they'll each assume you're spending time with the other woman, leaving you plenty of time to mess about on the computer.'

✳✳✳✳

A young couple hadn't been married for very long when, one morning, the man came up behind his wife as she was getting out of the shower and grabbed her by the buttocks. 'Y'know love, if you firmed these up a bit you wouldn't have to keep using your girdle.'

Her feelings were so hurt that she refused to speak to him for the rest of the day. A week or two later she was again stepping out of the shower when he grabbed both her breasts and said, 'Y'know what love? If you firmed these up a bit you wouldn't have to wear a bra.'

The young wife was infuriated, but had to wait 'til the next morning to get her revenge. Waiting until her husband stepped out of the shower she grabbed him by his dick and hissed, 'Y'know what love, if you firmed this up a little bit, I wouldn't have to use your brother.'

****

Two old men are comparing their sex lives:
Man 1: I can still do it twice!
Man 2: Which time do you enjoy the most?
Man 1: I think the winter.

****

Ten things a woman will never say:
10. Could we be more physical? I'm tired of just being friends.
9. I think you should have another beer.
8. I think hairy arses are really sexy.
7. Hey, I just farted. Phew! get a whiff of that one!
6. Don't throw that smelly, old t-shirt out… it's really cute!
5. This diamond is far too big!
4. I won't even put my lips on that thing unless you let me swallow!
3. My God! It really is 14 inches.
2. Does this make my bum look too small?
1. I'm wrong. You must be right again.

Ten things a man will never say:
10. I think Peter Andre is a really cool bloke!
9. While I'm up could I get you a beer?
8. I think hairy arses are sexy.
7. Her tits are far too big.
6. Sometimes I just want to be held.
5. Why don't we invite your mother?
4. Of course! I'd love to wear a condom!
3. Hey, let's go shopping and why don't you drive!
2. Fuck the football, let's watch your 'Cagney and Lacey' videos.
1. It looks like we're lost, better pull over for some directions.

Chapter 3
Don't Mix Your Drinks

It's an age-old adage and it is as true today as it ever was, mix your drinks and come a cropper: a bit of cider; a few beers; a gin and tonic; a whiskey; a chocolate milkshake; another glass of wine; some Guinness; a flaming Sambuca; an Irish Coffee... stick it all in your belly, dance like a king and spend the next few days wondering what on Earth could be the matter with you. Thankfully, the same cannot be said of mixing jokes, so, here is a mighty selection of all the jokes that we couldn't crowbar into the other sections all laid out for your enjoyment and edification.

****

A woman goes into a clothes shop. 'Can I try that dress on in the window, please?' she asks.

'I'm sorry, madam,' replies the shop assistant, 'but you'll have to use the changing-rooms like everyone else.'

****

At the top-secret army HQ, two generals were testing the new computer. They asked it to answer the question: 'How long is a piece of string?'

After a few moments '5,000,' came up on the computer screen.

'5,000 what?' said one of the generals. '5,000 sir!' flashed up on the screen.

****

Van Gogh goes in to a pub and his mate asks him if he wants a drink. 'No thanks,' said Vincent, 'I've got one ear.'

****

Q: What was the first thing Dick Turpin said on completing his epic ride from London to York?
A: 'Woah!'

****

The orchestra had hired a new conductor from Russia. He started off on the first day by shouting at the orchestra, 'You bunch of lazy bastards. You don't practice enough! From now on you get here three hours before practice every day to work with your section head. Only once you are sufficiently warmed up will I grace you with my genius. You are so bad you need to practice every day!'

This really annoyed the musicians, especially the man who played the kettle drums, and he banged them – BOOM BA-DA BOOM! BOOOOOM! – in frustration.

The new conductor glared at the orchestra, 'Right, who did that?'

****

In the old Soviet Union, the secret police discovered a man who looked exactly like Stalin. This was obviously dangerous as he could impersonate the Leader so Beria, the secret police chief, reported the discovery to Stalin, and asked him for instructions.

'Why, shoot him,' said Stalin.

'Certainly, comrade Stalin – that's a great idea,' says Beria, 'but... '

'BUT?' says Stalin. 'But what?'

'Well, I just thought, if we shaved off his moustache he wouldn't be a problem... ' says Beria.

'A valuable suggestion, comrade Beria!' says Stalin. 'Give him a shave and then shoot him!'

****

One cold morning two Russian border guards, Ivan and Vladimir, are looking across the border. Ivan is smiling to himself when he notices that Vladimir is also smiling.

Ivan (suspiciously): 'What are you thinking about?'

Vladimir: 'Same thing as you, comrade.'

Ivan: 'Then it is my duty to arrest you.'

****

A nerd walks into a chemist's and says: 'I need a box of tampons.'

The sales assistant is surprised and says, 'Young man, what do you want with tampons?'

'Well,' says the nerd, 'My sister says that if you use them, you can run, go horseback riding, and take part in all kinds of dangerous sports.'

****

This traveller is driving past a psychiatric hospital in the middle of nowhere when the front wheel comes off his van. Looking into the problem he finds that all four of the wheel's nuts have come off and he hasn't got any to replace them. In despair, he sits down by the side of a road to think things out.

All this is watched by one of the mental patients from a window. After a while the mental patient calls out to the traveller and beckons him over.

The traveller looks at him and decides that the last thing he needs right now is a conversation with a nutter, and so ignores him. The mental patient, however, is insistent and keeps calling out to the traveller until, in the end, the traveller gives in and goes over to talk.

When he approaches the window the mental patient tells him to take one nut out of each of his other wheels and use it temporarily on the wheel that's come off. This way he could get to the next town and buy four more. The traveller looks at him in disbelief; this had never occurred to him. Totally blown away by this, he apologises for his previous rude behaviour and asks him why he's in a nut house when he obviously has so much common sense. To this he gets the reply, 'I may be mad but I'm not STUPID.'

****

Two old men were walking down the street when they came across a frog. The frog looked up at them and said, 'Hey, if you pick me up and kiss me I'll turn into a beautiful princess and you can have your wicked way with me.'

One old man reached down and picked the frog up and put it in his pocket. The other man said, 'Hey, aren't you gonna kiss that frog?'

The first old man says, 'No way, at my age I'll have more fun with a talking frog!'

****

Three months after having sold a fridge to an Eskimo, the world's greatest salesman decided to check up on his new customer.

'How you getting on with the fridge?' he asked the Eskimo.

'Oh, not too bad,' replied the Eskimo, 'but it's a real pain cutting the ice into squares so it will fit into the tray.'

****

A bloke walked into a posh block of flats one day and saw the following sign; PLEASE RING BELL FOR DOORMAN. So he rang the bell and the doorman appeared. 'Yes, sir?' said the doorman, 'can I help you?'

'Yes you can,'' came the reply. 'I just wanted to know why you can't ring the bell yourself?'

****

Two old boys are sitting on the top deck of a bus talking.

'I'm telling you my friend, it's spelt w-o-o-o-o-o-o-m-m-m-m-b, wooooommmmmb!" said one.'

'No, no, no. It's spelt, w-o-o-o-m-m-m-m-m-m-m-b-b-b-b-b, wooom-mmmmmmmbbbbb!' said the other.

This went on for a while until a nurse sitting behind them leant over and said, 'I'm sorry, I couldn't help overhearing your discussion and I can tell you that it's spelt, w-o-m-b, womb.'

'I'm sorry, madam,' said the one old boy, 'but have you ever *heard* an elephant fart under water?'

****

Two sperms are swimming along and one is starting to get tired. He asks his mate, 'How far do you think is it to the uterus? I'm getting pretty tired!'

His mate says, 'I'm not sure, but I think it must be still a long way – we've only just passed the oesophagus!'

****

A horse and a chicken are playing in a meadow. The horse falls into a mud hole and is sinking. He calls to the chicken to go and get the farmer to help pull him out to safety. The chicken runs to the farm but the farmer can't be found. So he drives the farmer's Mercedes back to the mud hole and ties some rope around the bumper. He then throws the other end of the rope to his friend, the horse, and drives the car forward and saves him.

A few days later, the chicken and horse are playing in the meadow again and this time the chicken falls into the mud hole. The chicken yells to the horse to go and get some help from the farmer. The horse says, 'I think I can stand over the hole!' So he stretches over the width of the hole and said, 'Grab my love pump and pull yourself up.' The chicken does and hauls himself to safety.

The moral of the story? If you're hung like a horse, you don't need a Mercedes to pick up chicks.

****

One day, Pinocchio and his girlfriend were in bed doing what girls and wooden boys do. As they were having a cuddle afterwards, Pinocchio could tell that something was bothering his girlfriend. So, he asked her, 'What's the matter, baby?'

Pinocchio's girlfriend gave a big sigh and replied, 'You're probably the best bloke I've ever met, but every time we make love you give me splinters.'

This remark bothered Pinocchio a great deal, so the next day he went to seek some advice form his creator, Gepetto. When Pinocchio arrived, Gepetto could tell something was bothering Pinocchio, and asked him what was the matter. As Pinocchio revealed his dilemma to Gepetto, Gepetto searched up and down for a solution.

Eventually, he suggested that sandpaper might be able to 'smooth' out Pinocchio's relationship with his girlfriend. Pinocchio thanked Gepetto and went on his way.

When Gepetto didn't hear from Pinocchio for a while, he assumed that the sandpaper had solved all Pinocchio's problems. A couple of weeks later, Gepetto was in town to have some blades sharpened at the hardware store when he ran into Pinocchio. When he saw Pinocchio buying all the packs of sandpaper the store had in stock, Gepetto remarked, 'So, Pinocchio, things must be going pretty damn good with the girls.'

Pinocchio looked at him with a grin and said, 'Girls? who needs girls?'

****

Ahmed Al-Mohammed was in the bazaar when he felt terrible stomach cramps. Unable to control himself, he let out a long and noisy fart. People all around stared and Ahmed felt his face redden. He ran home, packed up his few belongings and journeyed to the far side of the world vowing never to return. But over the years, he missed his home and finally, at the age of 83, he felt he could return safely, his aged face concealing his true identity.

So, Ahmed returned to his home. He walked around the bazaar feeling happier than he had for years. He was browsing in one shop and asked the trader when the paving stones had been relaid so neatly.

'By the grace of Allah,' said the trader, 'that was four years and two months after Ahmed Allah Mohammed farted.'

****

An elderly man stands in line for hours at a Warsaw meat store during the last days of Communism. When the butcher comes out at the end of the day and announces that there's no meat left, the man flies into a rage.

'What is this?' he shouts. 'I fought against the Nazis, I worked hard all my life, I've been a loyal citizen, and now you tell me I can't even buy a piece of meat? This rotten system stinks!'

Suddenly a thuggish man in a black leather coat sidles up and murmurs, 'Take it easy, comrade. Remember what would have happened if you had made an outburst like that only a few years ago,' and he points an imaginary gun to his head and pulls the trigger.

The old man goes home, and his wife says, 'So they're out of meat again?'

'It's worse than that,' he replies. 'They're out of bullets.'

✱✱✱✱

A Chinese man goes for a job on a building site. 'Can you lay bricks?' asks the foreman.

'No,' says the Chinaman.'

'Can you paint?'' asks the foreman.

'No,' says the Chinaman.

'Can you plaster?' asks the foreman.

'No,' says the Chinaman. The foreman's a bit exasperated by all this, but after a bit he says, 'OK, you can work on supplies.'

Three months later, the foreman's walking around the site. 'Has anyone seen that Chinaman we took on a few months ago,' he asks. Just then, the Chinaman jumps out from behind some boxes and shouts, 'Suplise!'

✱✱✱✱

A farmer sent his 15-year-old son to town. He gave him a duck and said, 'I want you to come back a man. Use the duck to get what is needed.'

The son walked off into town and came across a prostitute. 'Would you sleep with me for this duck?' asked the boy.'

'Yes, I would,' said the prostitute. 'I've always liked animals.'

When they were finished, the prostitute was very impressed. 'I'll tell you what,' she said. 'If you can do it again, I'll give you the duck back.' So they did it again and the boy got his duck back.

He was walking home later that day when the duck flew out of his hands and into the path of an oncoming truck. The truck driver was very upset and came over to the boy. 'I'm very sorry about your duck,' gave him £5 and drove off.

When the boy got home, the father asked his son how the day had gone.

'Pretty good,' said the boy. 'I got a fuck for a duck, a duck for a fuck and £5 for a fucked-up duck.'

****

Jim and John, two drunks, are lying next to a hot-dog stand in the street.

'We've only get 50p and I need another drink,' said Jim.

'I know how we can drink all day for that,' said John.

John buys a hot dog and sticks it in his fly. Next, they walk into a pub, order drinks and knock them back in one. When the publican asks them to pay up, Jim gets down on the floor and started sucking the hot dog. The publican throws them out.

They do this scene 12 more times until John calls a halt.

'You must be getting tired kneeling down and standing up again and again'

'Well, I don't feel too bad,' says Jim, 'but I think you dropped the hot dog after the second pub.'

****

What's the difference between a working-class woman and a rich woman? The working-class woman has real orgasms and fake pearls.

****

What do you get when you cross LSD and the Pill? A trip without the kids.

****

Why did the Siamese twins move to France? So the other one could learn to drive.

****

What's the difference between a woman in church and a woman in a bathtub? One has hope in her soul...

****

What has six balls and fucks you twice a week?
The National Lottery!

****

What's the difference between a tyre and 365 condoms?
One's a Goodyear, and the other's a fucking excellent year!

****

Two little old ladies with very weak eyesight go shopping one day. After shopping a while, they decide to go to the toilet. Mistakenly, they walk into the Gents instead of the Ladies. Inside, two men who are equally desperate to take a leak are standing at the urinals, about to begin. When the two ladies walk in, the men not knowing what else to do, put their backs against the wall and pretend they're part of the toilet fixtures.

The first lady, mistaking one of the men for the sink, walks up to him and pulls his penis a couple of times. The man looses control and lets go.

She then turns to the other one and says, 'Oooh, you should try this one Gladys. It has lovely warm water!

To which Gladys replies, 'No dear, I think I'll stick with this one. It not only has warm water, it dispenses liquid soap as well!'

****

A frog telephones the Psychic Hotline and his Personal Psychic Advisor tells him: 'You're going to meet a beautiful young girl who will want to know everything about you.'

The frog is thrilled, 'This is great! Will I meet her at a party?'

'No,' says his Advisor, 'in her biology class.'

****

A ventriloquist cowboy walked into a little town in Texas and saw a rancher sitting on his porch with his dog.

Cowboy: Hey, cool dog. Mind if I speak to him?

Rancher: Dawgs cain't talk.

Cowboy: Hey dog, how's it going?

Dog: Doin' alright.

Rancher: (Extreme look of shock)

Cowboy: Is this your owner? (Pointing at rancher)

Dog: Yep.

Cowboy: How's he treat you?

Dog: Real good. He walks me twice a day, feeds me great food and takes me to the lake once a week to play.

Rancher: (Look of disbelief)

Cowboy: Mind if I talk to your horse?

Rancher: Horses cain't talk.

Cowboy: Hey horse, how's it goin?

Horse: Cool.

Rancher: (An even wilder look of shock)

Cowboy: Is this your owner? (Pointing at the rancher)

Horse: Yep.

Cowboy: How's he treat you?

Horse: Pretty good, thanks for asking. He rides me regularly, brushes me down often and keeps me in the barn to protect me from the elements.

Rancher: (Total look of amazement)

Cowboy: Mind if I talk to your sheep?

Rancher (Gesturing wildly and hardly able to talk): Them sheep ain't nothing but liars!

****

A man stood before the judge.

'I sentence you to three years for breaking and entering,' said the judge.

'But your honour, I didn't do anything !' said the man.

'You were caught with your burglar tools in your possession,' said the judge.

'In that case you can put me in jail for rape,' said the man.

'Did you really rape somebody?' asked the judge.

'No, your honour, but I had the equipment on me.'

****

A woman living in a rural area wanted to have an outside lav. that wouldn't stink. She advertised in the local papers for a contractor that could build such a structure. After some time, a contractor applied for the job and guaranteed that the outside lav. would not have any odour. He got the job.

Some time after completing the construction, the man got a frantic phone call from the woman.

'You better get here fast. That outside lav you built has a terrible smell.'

He rushed over, went to the lav, poked his head through the door, and exclaimed, 'No wonder it stinks – you took a shit in it!'

****

This big, rough-looking cowboy walks into the bar. He orders up bottle after bottle of rot-gut whisky and proceeds to get really wasted. In the process of doing so, he manages to anger just about everyone in the bar with offensive and obnoxious remarks.

Finally he finishes up his fifth bottle and decides he's had enough. He proceeds to get up and swagger out of the bar. He gets outside to untie his horse from the post and he notices someone's painted his horse's balls a real bright shade of yellow. This pisses him off immensely, so he rolls back into the bar, slamming the doors open and yelling out at the top of his lungs. 'JUST WHO IN THE SAM-HILL PAINTED MY HORSES BALLS YELLAH!!'

After everyone in the bar rustles around a bit, this bloke at the back of the bar stands up. He's six feet tall and built like a brick shit house. He says to the cowboy, 'I did. What you got to say about it, boy?'

The cowboy looks back at this guy and says, 'Oh, I just was going to let you know that the first coat of paint is dry.'

****

There were two church-going women gossiping in front of the store when a dusty old cowboy rode up. He tied up in front of the saloon, walked around behind his horse, lifted its tail and kissed the horse full on its rectum. Repulsed, one of the women asked, 'That's disgusting; why did you do that?'

To which the cowboy replied, 'I've got chapped lips.'

Confused, the other woman asked, 'Does that make them feel better?'

'No,' replied the cowboy, 'but it stops me from licking them!'

****

A pony walks into a pub. The publican says, 'What's the matter with you?'

'Oh it's nothing,' says the Pony. 'I'm just a little horse!'

****

One night, the Potato family sat down to dinner: Mother Potato and her three daughters. Midway through the meal, the eldest daughter spoke up. 'Mother Potato?' she said, 'I have an announcement to make.'

'And what might that be?' said Mother Potato, seeing the obvious excitement in her eldest daughter's eyes.

'Well,' replied the daughter, with a proud but sheepish grin, 'I'm getting married!'

The other daughters squealed with surprise as Mother Potato exclaimed, 'Married? That's wonderful! And who are you marrying, eldest daughter?'

'I'm marrying a King Edward!'

'A King Edward!'' replied Mother Potato with pride. 'Oh, a King Edward is a fine tater, a fine tater indeed!'

As the family shared in the eldest daughter's joy, the middle daughter spoke up. 'Mother? I, too, have an announcement.'

'And what might that be?' encouraged Mother Potato.

Not knowing quite how to begin, the middle daughter paused, then said with conviction, 'I, too, am getting married!'

'You, too!' Mother Potato said with joy. 'That's wonderful! Twice the good news in one evening! And who are you marrying, middle daughter?'

'I'm marrying a Jersey!' beamed the middle daughter.

'A Jersey!' said Mother Potato with joy. 'Oh, a Jersey is a fine tater, a fine tater!'

Once again, the room came alive with laughter and excited plans for the future, when the youngest Potato daughter interrupted. 'Mother? Mother Potato? Um, I, too, have an announcement to make.'

'Yes?' said Mother Potato with great anticipation.

'Well,' began the youngest Potato daughter with the same sheepish grin as her eldest sister before her, 'I hope this doesn't come as a shock to you, but I am getting married, as well!'

'Really?'' said Mother Potato with sincere excitement. 'All of my lovely daughters married! What wonderful news! And who, pray tell, are you marrying, Youngest Daughter?'

'I'm marrying David Coleman!'

'DAVID COLEMAN?!' Mother Potato scowled suddenly. 'But he's just a common tater!'

****

An old lady is rocking away the last of her days in front of the fire, reflecting on her long life, when all of a sudden a fairy godmother appears and informs her that she will be granted three wishes.

'Well, now,' says the old lady, 'I guess I'd like to be really rich.'

POUF! her rocking chair turns to solid gold.

'And I'd like to be a young and beautiful princess.'

POUF! she turns into a beautiful young woman.

'And your third wish?' asked the fairy godmother. Just then the old woman's cat wanders across the porch in front of them.

'Ooh – can you change him into a handsome prince?' she asks.

POUF! there before her stands a young man more handsome than anyone could possibly imagine. She stares at him, smitten. With a smile that makes her knees weak, he saunters across the porch and whispers in her ear: 'Bet you wish you'd never had me neutered.'

****

There was this bloke and he suffered from terrible headaches. Finally he went to the doctor, who gave him a thorough examination.

'Well, I'm not sure exactly what's causing the problem,' said the doctor, 'but we've found a cure. You'll have to be castrated.'

The man, needless to say, was horrified. 'No, doctor, I prefer to suffer the headaches.' But as time passed, they got worse and worse and finally he was driven back to the doctor's surgery.

'OK,' he said to the doctor, 'I can't stand it any longer. I'll have the operation.' And so he was castrated.

Afterwards the man was very depressed and his doctor told him, 'I recommend you begin a new life – start afresh from this point.'

Taking the doctor's advice, the man went to a men's shop for new clothes. The salesman said, 'Let's start with the suit. Looks like you're a 38 regular.'

'That's right,' said the man. 'How did you know?'

'Well, when you've been in the business as long as I have, you get pretty good at sizing a man up,' said the salesman. 'Now for the shirt. Looks like a 15 long.'

'Exactly!' said the man.

'And for underpants, I'd say a size 36,' guessed the salesman.

'Well, there's your first mistake,' said the man. 'I've worn 34s for years.'

'No, you're a size 36 if ever I've seen one,' said the salesman.

'I ought to know,' the man replied, becoming irritable.

'Well, OK, if you insist,' said the salesman. 'But they're going to pinch your balls and give you terrible headaches.'

****

An Englishman, Frenchman, Mexican, and Texan were flying across country in a small plane when the pilot comes on the loudspeaker and says, 'We're having mechanical problems and the only way we can make it to the next airport is for three of you to open the door and jump; then at least one of you can survive. The four open the door and look at the passing countryside below. The Englishman takes a deep breath and with a shout of 'God Save The Queen!' jumps.

The Frenchman, inspired by the Englishman's bravery, shouts 'Vivé la France!' and he also jumps. This really pumps up the Texan, so he shouts out, 'Remember the Alamo!' and pushes the Mexican out of the plane.

****

A military cargo plane, flying over a populated area, suddenly loses power and starts to nose down. The pilot tries to pull up, but with all their cargo, the plane is too heavy. So he shouts to the soldiers in back to throw things out to make the plane lighter. They throw out a pistol.

'Throw out more!' shouts the pilot. So they throw out a rifle.

'More!' cries the pilot. So they heave out a missile, and the pilot regains control. He pulls out of the dive and manages to lands safely at an air base. The soldiers meanwhile get into a jeep and drive off.

Pretty soon they meet a boy on the side of the road who's crying. They ask him why he's crying and he says, 'A pistol hit me on the head!' They drive on until they meet another boy who's crying even harder. Again they ask why he's crying and the boy says, 'A rifle hit me on the head!'

Feeling severely guilty they drive on until they meet a boy who's laughing hysterically. 'Hey kid, what's so funny?' they ask him. 'What's so funny?'

The boy replies, 'You won't believe this, but I just farted and a house blew up!'

****

On reaching his plane seat a man is surprised to see a parrot strapped in next to him. He asks the stewardess for a coffee, whereupon the parrot squawks, 'And get me a whisky, you stupid cow!'

The stewardess, flustered, brings back a whisky for the parrot and forgets the coffee. When this omission is pointed out to her the parrot drains its glass and bawls, 'And get me another whisky, you slapper.'

Quite upset, the girl comes back shaking with another whisky but still no coffee. Unaccustomed to such slackness the man tries the parrot's approach. 'I've asked you twice for a coffee, go and get it now, you thick bitch,' he shouts at the stewardess.

Next moment both he and the parrot have been wrenched up and thrown out of the emergency exit by two burly stewards. As they land on the runway the parrot turns to the man and says, 'Blimey, you've got a lip for someone who can't fly!'

****

This young lady walks into a pet store to buy a parrot. The shop keeper tells her he only has one and that it's a real smart-arse, with vulgar vocabulary and rude temperament. The woman says, 'That's OK, I know how to handle arseholes like that – I want the parrot anyhow.'

So the woman gets the bird home, puts it in her room, and starts to get ready for bed. Just as she gets her skirt off the parrot says: 'AWK… NICE LEGS, BABY.' Well, the the woman isn't going take this shit, so she takes the bird out of the cage and puts it in the freezer for three minutes. While the parrot's in the freezer, he comes to the realisation that this was the wrong thing to say, and makes a mental note not to say it again.

The next night, the woman is getting ready for bed and this time the parrot knows not to say any thing about her legs, but after she removes her blouse, and then her bra, the parrot just can't resist any longer. He blurts out: 'AWK… GREAT TITS BABY! GIVE 'EM A SHAKE!'. Once again this pisses the woman right off and she decides that instead of three minutes in the freezer, she's going to keep the parrot in for five minutes.

Well, the parrot has lots of time to think this time, and remorse gives way to desperation and then anger. Finally, the woman opens the freezer door, takes out the near frozen parrot and asks, 'Well, have you learned your lesson?'

The parrot still shivering and barely able to speak says, 'AWK... YEAH, YEAH, BUT I CAN I ASK JUST ONE QUESTION?'

'Fire away,' says the woman.

'AWK... WHAT THE FUCK DID THE TURKEY DO? ASK FOR A BLOW-JOB?'

****

A man walks into a pub and says, 'Landlord, give me two single whiskys.'

The landlord says, 'You want them both now or one at a time?'

'Oh, I want them both now,' the man says. 'One's for me and one's for my mate here,' and he pulls a three-inch man out of his pocket.

'Can he drink?' the landlord asks.

'Oh, sure. He can drink,' says the man. So the landlord pours the drinks and sure enough, the tiny man drinks it all up.

'That's amazing,' says the landlord. 'What else can he do – can he walk?'

The man flicks a 10p piece down to the end of the bar and says, 'Hey, Jake. Go get that.' The tiny man runs down to the end of the bar, picks up the coin, then runs back down and gives it to the man.

The landlord is in total shock. 'That's amazing,' he says. 'What else can he do? Can he talk?'

'Of course,' says the man. 'Hey, Jake, tell him about that time we were in Africa and you called that witch-doctor a wanker...'

****

A bloke walks into a pub and sits on a stool. In front of him he sees a big jar full of fivers and a little card which reads: 'Hello, if you'd like to win all of this money you have to make the horse at the end of the bar laugh. Entry fee: £5.'

'I'll have a crack at that,' thinks the bloke, sticks five quid in the jar and takes the horse into the bathroom. Two minutes later they come out and the horse is laughing so hard that he pisses on the floor. So the guy takes the money and leaves.

The very next day the same guy walks into the pub again and sees the horse and the jar, this time full of tenners, with a sign stating, 'You can win all of this if you make the horse cry. Entry fee: £10. So the bloke puts in his tenner and takes the horse into the bathroom. Two minutes later they come out and the horse is crying like a baby. So the guy takes the jar, but before he can leave the landlord asks, 'How did you do that?'

'Well, says the bloke, 'the first time I told him my dick was bigger than his and the second time I showed him!'

****

A pirate was talking to a 'land-lubber' in a pub. The land-lubber noticed that, like any self-respecting pirate, this fella had a peg leg, a hook in place of one of his hands and a patch over one eye. The land-lubber just had to find out how the pirate got in such bad shape, so he asked the pirate, 'How did you lose your leg?'

The pirate responded, 'I lost me leg in a battle off the coast of Jamaica!'

His new acquaintance was still curious so he asked, 'What about your hand. Did you lose that at the same time?'

'No,' answered the pirate. 'I lost it to the sharks off the Florida Keys.'

Finally, the land-lubber asked, 'I notice you also have an eye-patch. How did you lose your eye?'

The pirate answered, 'I was sleeping on a beach when a seagull flew over and shat right in me eye.'

'But how could a little bird-shit make you loose your eye?' the land-lubber asked.

'It was the day after I got me hook!' the pirate snapped.

****

A newly-wed couple were on their honeymoon. Before hopping into bed, the bride said to the groom, 'Darling, please be careful… you know I'm a virgin.'

The groom was shocked and replied, 'What are you talking about? I'm your third husband, for Christ's sake!'

'Well,' the bride replied, 'my first husband was a psychologist and all he wanted to do was talk about it, and my second husband was a gynaecologist and all he wanted to do was look at it. I know you'll screw me, though; that's why I married a lawyer.'

****

A guy walks into a drug store in America and asks for a pack of condoms. 'That'll be $5 with the tax,' says the shopkeeper.

'Tacks?' the guy exclaims, 'I thought you rolled them on!'

****

These three geezers went to the top of the Empire State Building to show off the length of their manhoods. The first one opened his fly and let it out. It flopped down 20 storeys.

'Top that,' he said.

So the second geezer opened his fly and let it out. It flopped down 25 storeys. 'Top that,' he said.

The last guy opened his fly and let his out. Down it went, on and on until, suddenly, he started to shift from side to side in jerky movements.'

'What's the matter? You OK?' his friends asked.

'Yeah, no problem. I'm just dodging traffic!' he replied.

****

A young man went to a chemist and asked if he could speak with the pharmacist.

'I am the pharmacist,' a little old lady informed him.

'Oh, in that case, forget it,' he replied and started to leave.

'Young man,' the old lady said to him, 'my sister and I have been pharmacists for 40 years and there's nothing we haven't seen or heard of, so come on, what's your problem?'

'Well,' the young man said reluctantly, 'I have a problem with erections. Once I get hard, it won't go down for hours and hours, no matter how much I masturbate or how many times I have intercourse! Please, can you give me something for it?'

'I'll have to go in the back and talk to my sister,' she told him.

About ten minutes later she came back out. 'Young man, I have consulted with my sister and the best we can give you is £100 a week and a third interest in the business.'

****

Mr Evans had been retired for a year when his wife of 50 years said to him one day, 'Why don't we take a cruise for a week and make wild passionate love like we did when we were young?'

He thought it over and agreed. He put on his hat and coat and went down to the corner shop. He stepped up to the counter and asked for a bottle of seasick pills and a box of condoms. Upon returning home his wife greeted him at the door saying, 'You know dear, I've been thinking it over and I see no reason why we couldn't manage a month-long cruise so we could relax and make wild passionate love like we did when we were young.'

He smiled, turned around and went back to the shop. He stepped up and ordered 12 bottles of seasick pills and a dozen boxes of condoms.

Upon returning back home his wife met him on the porch with a big smile on her face. 'Arthur, I have a marvellous idea. You know, now that our children are all grown up, there's nothing to stop us from cruising around the world for years on end.'

'I'll be right back,' he said. Back to the corner shop he went. When he approached the counter the shop keeper looked up with a puzzled grin. Mr Evans sheepishly ordered 297 bottles of seasick pills and the same number of boxes of condoms.

The startled shop keeper busied himself filling the order, then passed the wrapped package across the counter saying, 'You know, Mr Evans, you've been coming in here for over 30 years. I certainly don't mean to pry, but if it makes you that sick, why do you do it?'

✱✱✱✱

There was an old man whose family could no longer afford to take care of him. So the family decided that a nursing home for the aged would be appropriate. Of course the old man rejected the idea, but soon he was convinced that it was the right thing to do.

On his first day at the home, he spent most of his time lying in bed reflecting on life and feeling lonely. A while later, an orderly stopped by to see how the old man's first day was going.

'How you doing today?' she asked the old man. 'First day, I see.'

The old man replied with a nod. In no time the two began talking up a storm. As the conversation began to drag on, the orderly was eyeing the room filled with fresh flowers, cards and balloons from friends and relatives. She noticed a bowl full of peanuts sitting on top of the table next to the bed, and helped herself to a handful. As the two continued to converse with each other, the orderly kept eating more helpings of the peanuts.

After two hours she looked at her watch and said, 'My goodness, the time's gone by quickly. I have to tend to other people here, too.'

'That's OK,' said the old man, 'I feel so much better being able to talk to someone.'

Looking into the bowl the orderly said, 'I feel awful! I ate almost all of your peanuts!'

'That's OK,' the old man responded. 'Ever since I got these false teeth, all I could do was suck the chocolate off of them anyhow.'

✻✻✻✻

Elvis, Liberace, and River Phoenix were sitting around in heaven, bored of their heavenly lives. They went to see Gabriel and asked him if there was any way they could get out. He apprehensively decided to let them go back to earth for a short while, but told them if they even thought of sin, they would go straight to hell. So zap, there they are on Hollywood Boulevard.

As they are walking, Elvis sees a bar. He thinks for a moment and heads toward the door; the moment he touches it, POUF!, he's gone. The others think, 'Hmm, Gabriel was serious'.

A little while later River Pheonix sees a dollar bag of coke in the gutter. He thinks for a moment and bends over to pick up the bag and POUF!, Liberace disappears.

✻✻✻✻

A newspaper photographer, reporter and editor are walking down the beach. They see a bottle in the sand. The reporter grabs it, rubs it and a genie pops out. So grateful is the genie he grants them each one wish.

The photographer says, 'I want to be on a mountain-top with the wisest of the wise, soaking up wisdom.' And POUF! he's gone.

The reporter says, 'I want to be on a tropical paradise being served pina coladas and bon-bons all day long.' and POUF! she's gone. And the editor says, 'I want those two hacks back here, right now!'

****

It was time for an elderly gentleman to be put into a nursing home, as his grown-up children could no longer care for him. After a week, the children went to visit their father at the nursing home. During the visit, the father leaned to the right, and a nurse quickly came over and propped him up with a pillow.

A little while later, he leaned to the left, and a nurse came and propped him up with another pillow. The man's children were amazed at how attentive the home staff seemed to be, and questioned their father on how he liked it there.

'I've been treated well,' he tells them, 'but I've got to tell you – they sure don't want you to fart round here.'

****

Two old women were sitting on a bench waiting for their bus. The buses were running late, and a lot of time passed. Finally, one woman turned to the other and said, 'You know, I've been sitting here so long, my bum has fallen asleep!'

'I know!" said the other woman. 'I heard it snoring!'

****

One morning, a teacher asked her class which part of the body went to heaven first. One little girl raised her hand and said, 'I think your mind goes to heaven first because you have to have a mind in order to believe in God.'

'Very good,' said the teacher.

Then a little boy raises his hand and said, 'I think your heart goes to heaven first because God is all about love.'

'Very good,' said the teacher. She then looked up and saw that little Johnny's hand was up. 'Johnny,' she said, 'which part of the body do you think goes to heaven first?'

Johnny thought for a minute and then said, 'Your feet.'

'What makes you think your feet go to heaven first?' the teacher asked him.

'Well,' he replied. 'I was walking past my parent's bedroom last night and my mum had her feet up in the air and she was shouting, 'Oh God, oh God, I'm coming!'

****

Little Johnny's next door neighbours had a baby. Unfortunately, the little baby was born with no ears. When they arrived home from the hospital, the parents invited Johnny's family to come over and see their new baby. Johnny's parents were very afraid that their son would say something embarrassing about the baby, so his dad had a long talk with him before they left.

'Now, son,' he said, 'that poor baby was born without any ears. I want you to be on your best behaviour and not say a word about his ears or I promise you I'll give you a good hiding when we get back home.'

'I promise not to mention his ears at all,' said Johnny.

At the neighbours home, Johnny leaned over in the cot and touched the baby's hand. He looked at its mother and said 'Oh what a beautiful little baby'.

'Thank you very much, Johnny,' said the mother. 'This baby has perfect little hands and perfect little feet,' said Johnny. 'Just look at his pretty little eyes. Did his doctor say that he had good sight?'

'Yes,' said the mother. 'In fact, his doctor said he had perfect 20/20 vision.'

'Well, thank God for that,' said Johnny, 'because there's no way he could wear glasses.'

****

An after-dinner speaker was in such a hurry to get to his engagement that when he arrived and sat down at the table, he suddenly realised that he'd forgotten his false teeth. Turning to the man next to him he said, 'I forgot my teeth.'

'No problem,' said the man and with that he reached into his pocket and pulled out a pair of false teeth. 'Try these,' he said.

The speaker tried them. 'Too loose,' he said.

'I've got another pair,' the man said, 'try these.'

The speaker tried them but they were too tight, so the man said, 'I've got just one more pair… try these.'

The speaker said, 'Wow, these fit perfectly.' With that he ate his meal and gave his address. After the dinner was over, the speaker went over to thank the man who'd helped him. 'I want to thank you for coming to my aid and I wouldn't mind putting a bit of business your way, too.' he said. 'Where's your office? I've been looking for a good dentist.'

'I'm not a dentist,' replied the man, 'I'm the local undertaker.'

****

A man who is not qualified keeps pestering this tailor about giving him a job selling suits. Finally, the tailor tells him if he can sell this one green suit he'll give him a job. Another employee points out to the tailor that they've had that suit on the rack for four years, and that it's such an ugly, green suit that no one will ever buy it.

'Yes, I know,' the tailor tells the employee, 'that's my way of getting rid of that pest.'

Two hours later the new bloke calls his boss for his next assignment. The tailor can't believe it and heads down to the shop to find out how he managed to sell the suit.

Upon his arrival he finds the new salesman bleeding, scratched and his clothes torn in several places, but smiling.

'Congratulations, the job is yours,' he says to the man. 'Nobody has come close to selling that old, ugly, green suit. But what in the world happened to you?'

'Thank you for the job,' says the man. 'The man who bought it loved the suit, but he had a very sensitive guide-dog.'

****

This woman goes into a restaurant and orders a scoop of vanilla ice-cream, a scoop of strawberry ice-cream and a scoop of chocolate ice-cream. The waiter who takes her order, however, apologises and tells her that they don't have any chocolate.

'OK,' says the woman, I'll have a vanilla milk shake, a strawberry milk shake and a chocolate milk shake.' Once again, however, the waiter tells her there isn't any chocolate!

The woman changes her order for the third time. 'OK. I'll have vanilla cake, strawberry cake, and chocolate cake.'

This time the waiter is very annoyed and shouts, 'Madam, we have no chocolate. Let me try to explain this to you. Do you see the word 'van' in the word 'vanilla'?'

The woman replies, 'Yes.' So the waiter asks her if she sees the word 'straw' in the word 'strawberry' and once again she replies, 'Yes'. Then he asks her if she sees the word 'fuck' in the word 'chocolate' and the woman says, 'There's no fuck in chocolate.'

And the waiter screams, 'That's what I've been trying to tell you.'

****

A man returning from a overseas business trip decides to bring his son a young puppy as a present. Unfortunately, he doesn't have time to sort out the paperwork and he doesn't want the puppy to get stuck in quarantine at Heathrow for six months, so he hides the puppy down the front of his trousers and gets on the plane.

About 30 minutes into the flight a stewardess notices the man shaking and quivering. 'Are you OK, sir?' she asks him.

'Yes, I'm fine,' says the man.

Sometime later the stewardess noticed the man moaning, and shaking again. 'Are you sure you're all right sir?' she asks him again.

'Yes,' says the man, 'but I have a confession to make. I didn't have time to get the paperwork done to bring a puppy on board, so I hid him down the front of my trousers.'

'Oh dear,' says the stewardess, 'I guess he's not house-trained yet, eh?' she adds with a knowing smile.

'Oh no, that's not the problem,' says the man. 'The real problem is he's not weaned yet!'

****

An army major is visiting sick soldiers. He goes up to one private and asks, 'What's your problem, soldier?'

'Chronic syphilis, sir,' says the soldier.

'What treatment are you getting?' asks the major.

'Five minutes with the wire brush each day, sir, ' replies the soldier.

'What's your ambition, soldier?' asks the major.

'To get back to the front, sir,' says the soldier.

'Good man,' says the major. He goes to the next bed and says, 'And what's your problem, soldier?'

'Chronic piles, sir,' comes the reply.

'What treatment are you getting?' asks the major.

'Five minutes with the wire brush each day, sir' replies the soldier.

'And what's your ambition, soldier?' asks the major.

'To get back to the front, sir,' replies the soldier.

'Good man,' says the major. He goes to the next bed. 'What's your problem, soldier?" he asks.

'Chronic gum disease, sir," is the reply.'

'What treatment are you getting?' asks the major.

'Five minutes with the wire brush each day, sir' says the soldier.

'And what's your ambition, soldier?" asks the major.

'To get the wire brush before the other two, sir,' replies the soldier.

****

A lawyer named Strange died, and his friend asked the tombstone maker to inscribe on his tombstone, 'Here lies Strange, an honest man, and a lawyer.'

The inscriber insisted that such an inscription would be confusing, for passers-by would tend to think that three men were buried under the stone. However, he suggested an alternative: he would inscribe, 'Here lies a man who was both honest and a lawyer.' That way, whenever anyone walked by the tombstone and read it, they would be certain to remark: 'That's Strange!'

****

Did you hear about the fat bloke who tried every diet in the world in an attempt to lose weight? He tried them all but none worked. Then, one day, he was reading the paper when he noticed a small ad that read: 'Lose weight Only £1 a pound. Call 018556785-0238.'

The fat bloke decided to give it a try and called the number. A voice on the other end asked, 'How much weight do you want to lose?'

'Ten pounds,' the fat bloke replied.

'Very well,' replied the voice, 'give me your credit card number and we'll have a representative over to your house in the morning.'

About 9am the next day the fat bloke heared a knock on the door. When he opened it, there was a beautiful redhead standing on his doorstep, completely starkers except for a sign around her neck stating, 'If you catch me, you can have me.'

Well, the fat bloke chased her upstairs, downstairs, over sofas, through the kitchen, all around the house until finally, panting and wheezing like a dog, he caught her.

When he'd had his way with her she said to him, 'Quick, go into the bathroom and weigh yourself.'

He did just that and was amazed to find that he'd lost 10 pounds, right to the ounce!

That evening he called the number again. The voice on the other end asked, 'How much weight do you want to lose?' to which the not-so-fat bloke man replied, '20 pounds.'

'Very well,' the voice on the phone told him, 'Give me your credit card number and we'll have a representative over at your house in the morning.'

At about 8am the next day there was a knock on the not-so-fat bloke's door and when he opened it he saw a beautiful blonde dressed only in track shoes and a sign around her neck stating, 'If you catch me, you can have me.'

The chase took a good while longer this time and the man nearly passed out, but he finally caught her. When he was done she told him, 'Quick, run into the bathroom and weigh yourself.'

He ran to the bathroom and found he'd lost another 20 pounds! 'This is fantastic!' he thought to himself.

Later that evening he called the number again and the voice at the other end asked, 'How much weight do you want to lose?'

'Fifty pounds!' the man exclaimed.

'Fifty pounds?' the voice asked, 'That's an awful lot of weight to lose at one time.'

'Listen mate,' the man replied. 'Here's my credit card number, you just have your representative over here in the morning!'' and he hung up.

About 6am the next morning the man got out of bed, splashed on some cologne and got all ready for the next representative. At about 7am he got a knock on the door. When he opened the door, he saw this huge gorilla with a sign around his neck saying, 'IF I CATCH YOU, I'M GOING TO FUCK YOU.'

****

A rather posh lady is showing her small daughter around Rome in the back of a taxi. They pass a railway station and the daughter asks, 'Mummy, what are all those ladies doing standing around in very short dresses?'

The mother realises that she's referring to the prostitute dayshift, but hedges. 'I expect they're waiting for their friends, or looking at the Roman architecture, dear,' she tells her daughter.

The taxi driver flips back the partition and says, 'Go on, don't lie to the kid. Tell your daughter they're prostitutes!'

'Mummy, what are "prostitutes"?' asks the little girl.

With a sigh, the mother explains all. The little girl is very interested: 'But Mummy,' she says, 'don't they sometimes have babies?'

'Well, yes dear, I'm afraid they do,' replies her mother.

'But Mummy, what happens to the babies?' the little girl asks.

'Well, dear, that's the interesting thing about it,' explains her mother, 'they almost invariably turn out to be taxi-drivers.'

****

A teacher asks a class of kids if their skin could be made out of anything other than skin, what they would choose. One kid puts his hand up and says, 'Gold, Miss.'

'Why?' asks the teacher.

'Because then I'd go to a car showroom, give them a few shavings and drive off in a new car.'

Another child puts his hand up and says, 'Platinum, Miss.'

'Why?' asks the teacher. 'Because then I'd go to the car showroom, give them a few shavings and drive off in an even better car.'

A third child puts his hand up and says, 'Pubic hair miss.'

'Why pubic hair?' asks the teacher.

'Because my sister's only got a little bit, but you should see the cars outside our place.'

****

A guy goes to his local supermarket to buy some dog food. When he gets to the check-out with a couple of tins the cashier asks him where his dog is.

'He's at home,' replies the man.

'Well I'm sorry,' replies the cashier, 'but the rules state that unless you have the dog with you I can't sell you the dog food.'

The next day the same bloke is in buying cat food. When he gets to the cashier he's asked where his cat is.

'She's at home,' he replies.'

'Sorry, rules are rules,' says the cashier. 'I can't sell you the cat food unless your cat is with you.'

The next day the bloke goes into the supermarket with a brown paper bag. When he gets to the check-out he asks the cashier to put his hand in.

'What is it?' asks the cashier. 'It feels soft and warm.'

'I'd like three rolls of toilet paper,' replies the man.

****

It is the wedding day of Prince Charles and Lady Di. Charles has been up late the night before boozing with his old Navy buddies. He wakes up late, throws on his clothes, rushes to the Royal Coach and sets off.

In the coach, he notices that he's forgotten his shoes, so he borrows the ones his valet's wearing. Only problem is, they're two sizes too small. Charles makes it through the ceremony, then through the reception with his feet in agony the whole time, and finally with great relief, goes upstairs with his new bride.

Their departure, however, is noticed by the Queen and Queen Mother who follows them up and listen at the the door. First they hear, 'Ohhh, ohhh, that feels so goood, that was sooo tight.'

'I told you she was,' said the Queen to the Queen Mother. Then they hear, 'Ohhh, ohhh, ohhh, ahhhh, that feels even better, that one's so much tighter.'

'Tsk tsk tsk,' said the Queen Mother. 'Once a sailor, always a sailor.'

****

A Tory MP woke up in a hospital bed after a complicated operation, and found that the curtains were drawn around him. 'Why are the curtains closed,' he asked. 'Is it night?'

A nurse replied, 'No, it's just that there's a fire across the street, and we didn't want you waking up and thinking that the operation was unsuccessful.'

****

An airplane lands at an airport with great difficulty, stopping just short of an accident. When they arrive at the gate, the captain wipes his brow and says, 'My God, that's the shortest runway I've ever seen!'

'You're not kidding,' says his co-pilot, looking out the window. 'But it sure is wide.'

****

Q: What's the difference between a small blue whale and a great white whale?
A: Size and colour.

****

Q: What's black and white, black and brown, black and black?
A: A nun on a spit

****

Q: What's black and white and walks sideways down corridors?
A: A nun with a javelin through her head

****

Q: What green and red and races at 100 mph?
A: A frog in a blender

****

Q: What goes black and white, black and white, black and white?
A: A nun falling downstairs

****

Q: What's grey and comes in half-pints?
A: An elephant.

****

Q: What's the ultimate in trust?
A: Two cannibals doing 69.

****

Mother Superior is recounting her days as she lies on her deathbed when another aged Sister asks her a question.
'Mother Superior do you remember going to the Zoo in the 1920s?'
'Yes I do.'
'And Mother Superior do you remember the gorillas?"
'Yes I do.'
'And do you remember one gorilla in particular?'
'Yes I do.'
'And do you remember this gorilla... grabbed you... a-and raped you?'
'Yes I do Sister, now what is the point of all this!' snapped the dying nun.
'Mother Superior, did it hurt?'
'Hurt? You ask did it hurt! He never wrote, he never called...'

****

Q: What's the difference between an Essex girl and a 747?
A: The 747 stops whining when it gets to Majorca

****

Q: Why do Essex girls only get half an hour for lunch?
A: So they don't need to be retrained when they get
back

Chapter 4
The Lock-In

So there you are at about quarter to eleven when the bell goes for last orders leaving you thinking, 'Shit, I've only had 17 pints and four double whisky chasers, I'm not even vaguely pissed yet.' So you're just fumbling for the car keys, resigned to the fact that a promising night has been cut off in its prime, when the landlord, God bless him, sticks a proverbial two fingers up at the ridiculous licensing laws in this country by dimming the lights, ushering in the two local coppers who've been lumbered with the night beat, and locks the door.

There's a joyous feeling of camaraderie all round, probably a bit like a black-out during the war only with a lot more booze and a lot less bombs. It's time for the serious drinking to begin, and of course the serious drinking jokes…

****

A drunken man gets on the bus late one night, staggers up the aisle, and sits next to an elderly woman. She looks the man up and down and says, 'I've got news for you; you're going straight to hell!'

The man jumps up out of his seat and shouts, 'Good heavens, I'm on the wrong bus!'

****

A man comes home very late one night, pissed out of his mind, to find his wife waiting for him at the door.

'WHERE HAVE YOU BEEN?' she screams, 'It's FOUR IN THE MORNING !'

He says, 'Aww, I just stopped at this pub, I was only going to have one pint... but this pub, it was incredible. Everything in it was gold-plated. They had a gold rail under the bar, gold ashtrays, they served the drinks in gold pint glasses, the table posts were all gold-plated, even the mirror behind the bar was gold. The cash register was gold. I was so amazed by all this gold, I just kept on ordering pints, so I could stay in the pub and look at it. Hell, even when I went to the Gents, they had gold-plated urinals… it was wonderful.'

'I don't believe that story for one minute,' his wife said. 'What was this place called?'

'Fucked if I can remember,' he replies, 'I'm far too pissed up.'

'You'll have to prove it to me tomorrow then, when you sober up, or else I'm going to divorce you!' said his wife.

The next day, the man looks through The Yellow Pages under PUBS, but none of the names ring a bell. He decides that he'll call all the boozers listed, and ask the landlords about the decor in their establishments.

He's called about 50 pubs, and still no luck. Finally he calls one pub, asks his question, and the landlord says 'Yes, this is the pub with all the gold-plated stuff.

'Here,' the man says, handing the phone to his wife. 'Ask the landlord if I'm lying!'

The wife gets on the line, and begins to ask the landlord about all the things her husband had told her about on the previous night… the rail, the pint glasses, the mirrors, the table posts and the cash register. Finally, she says, 'Now, this may seem like a strange question, but my husband says you even have gold-plated urinals, do you?'

The landlord puts the phone down on the bar, and she hears him yell, 'Hey Frankie! I think I know who pissed in your saxophone last night.'

****

A man stumbles out of a pub and is spied by a copper. The copper approaches and says, 'Can I help you, lad?'

'Yeah,' says the man, 'ssssomebody ssstole my car!'

'Well,' says the copper, 'where was your car last time you saw it?'

'It was at the end of this key!' says the man holding up a key. Suddenly the copper notices the man has his manhood out.

'Are you aware that you are exposing yourself?' he asks.

'Oh God,' says the man. 'They got me girl, too!'

****

An Irishman walks into a pub in Dublin, orders three pints of Guinness and sits in the back of the room, drinking a sip out of each one in turn. When he finishes them, he comes back to the bar and orders three more. The landlord says to him, 'You know, a pint goes flat after I draw it; it would taste better if you bought one at a time.'

The Irishman replies, 'Well, you see, I have two brothers. One is in America, the other in Australia, and I'm here in Dublin. When we all left home, we promised that we'd drink this way to remember the days when we drank together.'

The landlord admits that this is a nice custom, and leaves it there. The Irishman becomes a regular in the pub, and always drinks the same way: he orders three pints and drinks them in turn. One day, he comes in and orders two pints. All the other regulars notice and fall silent.

When he comes back to the bar for the second round, the bartender says, 'I don't want to intrude on your grief, but I wanted to offer my condolences on your great loss.'

The Irishman looks confused for a moment, then a light dawns in his eye and he laughs. 'Oh, no,' he says, 'everyone's fine. I'm just off the liquor.'

****

A white horse walks into a pub, pulls up a stool, and orders a pint. The landlord pours him a tall, frothy mug and says, 'You know, we have a drink named after you.'

To which the white horse replies, 'What, Eric?'

****

A gorilla walks into a pub, pulls up a stool, and orders a pint. The landlord pours him a tall, frothy mug and says, 'That'll be five quid.'

As the gorilla's paying for his pint, the landlord adds, 'You know, we don't get many gorillas in here.'

To which the gorilla replies, 'At five quid a pint, I'm not fucking surprised.'

****

A guy walks into a pub and says to the landlord, 'I want you to give me 12-year old Scotch, and don't try to fool me because I can tell the difference.'

The landlord is sceptical and decides to try to trick the man with five-year scotch. The man takes a sip, scowls and says, 'Oi, landlord, this crap is five-year old Scotch. I told you I want 12-year old Scotch.'

The landlord tries once more with eight-year old Scotch. The man takes a sip, grimaces and says, 'Oi, landlord, I don't want eight-year old Scotch like this filth. Give me 12-year old Scotch!'

Impressed, the landlord gets the 12-year old Scotch, the man takes a sip and sighs, 'Ah, now that's the real thing.'

A disgusting, grimy, stinking drunk has been watching all this with great interest. He stumbles over and sets a glass down in front of the man and says, 'Hey, I think that's really amazing what you can do. Try this one.'

The man takes a sip and immediately spits out the liquid and cries, 'Yechhh! This stuff tastes like piss!'

The drunk's eyes light up and he says, 'Yeah, now how old am I?'

****

On the top of a tall building in a large city, there was a bar. In this bar, a man was drinking heavily. He would ask the bartender for a tequila shot, then walk out to the balcony and jump off. Minutes later, he would appear in the lift and repeat the whole process. This one bloke watched this happen a number of times until curiosity got the better of him.

Finally, he went up to the man and asked, 'Hey, you keep drinking, then jumping off the balcony. And yet, minutes later, you're back again. How do you do it?'

'Well, the shot of tequila provides so much buoyancy that when I get near the ground, I slow down and land gently. It's great fun. You should try it.'

The bloke, who was also quite pissed thought to himself, 'Hey, why not?' So he went to the bar, drank a shot of tequila, then walked out to the balcony, jumped off, and whoooooooooooooooshSPLAT! The bartender shakes his head, looked over at the first bloke and said, 'Superman, you're a such an arsehole when you're pissed.'

****

A drunk is standing pissing into a fountain in the middle of town, so a copper comes up to him and says, 'Stop that and put it away!' The drunk shoves his dick into his trousers and does up his zip. As the cop turns to go, the drunk starts laughing. 'OK,' asks the copper, 'what's so funny?'

'Fooled you,' says the drunk, 'I may have put it away, but I didn't stop.'

****

Steve and Ollie are good friends. Each day, they get together after work and have a pint down the local. This is a tradition that goes on for some time. One day, Ollie says, 'Steve, if I die before you, promise me that you'll have a pint for me, each day.'

Steve considers this and agrees. Well, sure enough, Ollie dies, and sure enough, Steve has an extra pint for him every day after work. This goes on for some time, and the barmaid is quite familiar with the ritual and the reason.

One day, Steve comes in and only orders one drink. Well, the barmaid is in shock, and says, 'But, Steve, aren't you going to have another drink for your friend, as usual?'

And Steve says, 'Well, you see, I joined Alcoholics Anonymous, but I don't think that Ollie should be punished for that.'

****

Two geezers were in a pub partying like mad. They were drinking doubles and triples, buying rounds and generally having a great time. When asked why they were celebrating, they boasted that they'd just finished a jigsaw puzzle and it had only taken them two months!

'TWO MONTHS?!" cried the landlord. 'That's ridiculous. It shouldn't take that long!!'

'Well,' says one guy, 'the box said two to four years!'

****

A man drinks a shot of whisky every night before bed. After years of this his wife wants him to quit, so she gets two shot glasses, fills one with water, the other with whisky. She gets him to the table with the glasses and makes him fetch his fishing bait-box. 'I want you to see this,' she says and puts a worm in the water and it swims around. She then takes the worm out and puts it in the whisky where it dies. 'So,' she says. 'What do you have to say about this experiment?' '

'Well,' he says. 'If I drink whisky I won't get worms.'

****

A drunk man was casually taking a piss into a drinking fountain in the park. A police officer comes up to him and yells frantically, 'What the hell do you think you're doing? There's a public toilet 20 metres from here!'

The man, amazed, yells back, 'What do you think I have here between my legs? A hose?'

****

A drunk walks into a pub and says loudly, 'Landlord, a round for the house, and have one yourself, too!' The crowd cheers, the landlord pours and passes out the drinks, then knocks back a shot himself.

That'll be £80 for the round,' says the landlord, to which the man replies, 'I don't have a penny on me.'

The landlord is furious and drags the man to the door and roughly throws him into the street.

The next night, the drunk again walks in and says, 'Landlord, a round for the house, and have one yourself, too!' As the crowd cheers, the landlord reasons to himself that no one would come in and do that twice, and that the man probably has the money for the previous night, so he passes out the shots and knocks one back himself.

'OK, that's £80 for last night, and £63 for tonight,' he says to which the man again replies, 'I don't have a pot to piss in or a window to throw it out of, I'm sorry to say.'

The landlord, enraged at this, smashes the man in the head over and over again as he drags him to the door and again throws him roughly into the street.

The next night, amazingly, the landlord hears over his shoulder as he's working, 'Landlord, a round for the house.' Turning around, he can't believe the drunk is back for a third time.

'What, nothing for me this time?' says the landlord.

'You gotta be joking,' says the drunk. 'You get really shitty when you drink!'

****

This bloke goes into a pub to find only two men at opposite ends of the bar and the landlord. He orders his drink and listens in on the conversation. One fellow says: 'Live here?'

'Yeah, over on Miller Road,' says the other.

'I live on Miller Road too,' says the first.

'Is that right,' replies the other, 'I live over the corner shop and have a brown and white dog.'

The first responds, 'I live over the corner shop and I have a brown and white dog. I was born there on April 23, 1947.'

From the other end of the bar comes, 'I was born on April 23, 1947, too. Ain't this a small world?'

Suddenly the telephone rings and it's the landlord's wife who wants to know if anything's going on.

'Same old thing,' replies the landlord, 'the Johnson twins are drunk again!'

****

One very cold night, a young man dropped into the local brothel and the Madam said, 'You'll have to wait.'

'But there's lots of girls that aren't busy right now,' insists the man.

'Yes, but several of the rooms are closed for repairs,' the Madam informs him.

'Listen,' he says, 'I'm pretty desperate. I don't need a room.'

So she takes his money and he goes upstairs with one of the staff and, after looking for a place to consummate the transaction, they decide to do it on the roof. But it's a very, very cold night, and the two of them freeze to death and fall to the pavement below, where a passing drunk looks them over, staggers to the door and knocks.

'Go away!' says the Madam. 'We don't allow drunks in here!'

'I don't want in,' says the drunk. 'I just wanted to tell you that your sign fell down.'

****

A lad walks into a pub and orders 12 shots of the best whisky in the house. The landlord proceeds to fill 12 shot glasses and stares, puzzled, at the guy as he begins to drink them down, one by one.

As the lad's finishing the 11th shot, the landlord asks, 'What's the occasion, mate?'

'I'm celebrating my first blow-job!' says the lad as he finishes off the last shot. '

'Well,' says the bartender, 'in that case, have one on the house,' and he fills another shot glass.

'No thanks,' says the guy, 'If 12 didn't get the taste out of my mouth, one more won't!'

****

A drunk walks into a crowded pub and takes the last barstool next to an older woman. After a while, the woman starts to smell this horrible odour coming from the direction of the drunk. She turns to him and says, 'Excuse me, but did you just shit yourself?'

The drunk replied, 'Yes, I have indeed shit myself.'

'Well, why don't you go somewhere and clean yourself up?' shouts the woman.

''Cos I'm not finished yet,' says the drunk.

****

This bloke walks into a pub. He walks up to the landlord and asks for a rum and coke. The landlord puts an apple on the table. The bloke looks at it and says, 'I'm sorry, I said I wanted a rum and Coke.'

'Just try the apple,' says the landlord. So the guy bites into the apple.

'Wow,' he says. 'This tastes like rum. The landlord tells him to turn it around and bite it again. 'Wow, this bit tastes like Coke.'

A minute later another bloke walks into the pub and asks the landlord for a gin and tonic. The landlord puts an apple on the bar leaving this bloke just as confused as the first, but the first bloke urges him to try it, so the guy bites into it.

'Wow!' he exclaims, 'it tastes like gin.' The first bloke tells him to turn it around and bites it again.

'Wow it tastes like tonic,' says the second bloke.

Later that night a third bloke walks in and joins the two blokes at the bar. The first two are so excited about these apples that they tell this third bloke that the landlord has an apple for whichever taste you want. So the guy asks for an apple that taste like a vagina. The landlord puts the apple on the table and the guy bites into it .

'Urggh,' he shouts. 'This tastes like SHIT!!!'

'Turn it around,' says the landlord.

****

This geezer dies and is sent to Hell. Satan meets him and shows him the doors to three rooms and says he must choose one of the rooms to spend eternity in. Satan opens the first door. In the room there are people standing in shit up to their necks.

'No thanks,' says the geezer. 'Can I see the the next room?

Satan shows him the next room and this has people with shit up to their noses. And so he says 'No' again. Finally Satan shows him the third and final room. This time there are people in there with shit up to their knees drinking cups of tea and eating cakes.

'I'll choose this room please,' says the geezer. So he goes in and is standing in there eating his cake and drinking his tea thinking, 'Well it could be worse,' when the door opens and Satan pops his head around.

'Okay,' says Satan. 'Tea-break's over. Back on your heads!'

****

There was this drunk who said to the landlord at his local, 'I want a woman!' So the landlord gave him directions to a place, but the drunk was so messed up that he couldn't remember where he had been told to go and accidentally walks into a chiropodist's office.

'Can I help you?' asks the receptionist.

'Yes,' replies the drunk. 'I want some service.'

'OK, sir,' says the receptionist. 'Go in the other room and put it on the table and someone will be with you shortly.'

So the drunk goes in the other room and puts his todger on the table. When the chiropodist comes in she screams, 'That's not a foot!'

'Give it time, lady,' said the drunk, 'give it time.'

****

This man who stutters badly, walks into a pub, and says, 'S-say! B-b-b-arman, g-g-g-imme a b-b-beer'. The barman, who is badly humpbacked, serves him a beer and says, 'That'll be £2.50 please!'

The guy thinks that's pretty expensive and says, 'D-d-d-amn! T-t-that's a high price!'

'Yes,' says the barman, 'but that's our price and that's what we get!'.
So the stutterer pays him and drinks it down.

'S-s-say! B-b-barman,' he says, 'g-g-gimme a w-whisky p-p-please!''
The barman serves him a shot of whisky and says, 'That will be £5 please!'

'D-d-d-damn!' says the stutterer. 'T-t-that's a high price!'

'Yes,' says the barman, 'but that's our price and that's what we get!'

The stutterer pays him, drinks his whisky and, before leaving he says,
'B-b-barman t-thanks for n-not m-m-making f-f-fun of my st-st-st-stuttering
w-w-while I w-was in h-h-here!'

'Oh, that's OK,' says the barman, 'I want to thank you for not making
fun of my hump while you were in here.'

'Oh, t-t-that's OK,'' says the stutterer, 'e-everything else in t-this p-p-
place w-was so h-h-high, I th-th-thought it w-was y-your ARSE!'

****

There was a bloke in a theatre, sprawled out over three seats. The usher
came by and told the bloke to move. The bloke mumbled, but didn't answer,
so the usher went to get the manager.

'Sir,' the manager said to the man, 'if you don't move, I'll call the police
and have you removed.' Again, the bloke mumbled, but didn't answer. So
the manager called the police and a copper came over.

'Excuse me, sir,' the copper said to the bloke, 'what's your name?'

'Pete,' said the bloke.

'And where are you from, Pete?' asked the policeman.

'The balcony!'' replied Pete.

****

One day at the end of class, little Billy's teacher has the class go home and
think of a story and then infer the moral of that story. The following day the
teacher asks for the first volunteer to tell their story; little Suzy raises her hand.

'My dad owns a farm and every Sunday we load the chicken eggs on the
truck and drive into town to sell them at the market. Well, one Sunday we

hit a big bump and all the eggs flew out of the basket and on to the road.'

The teacher asks for the moral of the story and Suzy replies, 'Don't put all your eggs in one basket.'

Next is little Lucy ... 'Well, my dad owns a farm, too, and every weekend we take the chicken eggs and put them in the incubator. Last weekend only eight of the 12 eggs hatched.'

The teacher asks for the moral of the story and Lucy replied, 'Don't count your chickens before they're hatched.'

Last is little Billy ... 'My uncle Ted fought in the Second World War, his plane was shot down over enemy territory, but he jumped out before it crashed with only a case of beer, a machine-gun and a machete. On the way down he drank the case of beer. Unfortunately, he landed right in the middle of 100 German soldiers. He shot 70 with his machine-gun, but ran out of bullets, so he pulled out his machete and killed 20 more. The blade on his machete broke, so he killed the last 10 with his bare hands.'

The Teacher looks in shock at Billy and asks if there is possibly any moral to his story. 'Of course there is,' Billy replies, 'Don't fuck with uncle Ted when he's been drinking.'

****

There are these two pissed geezers in a pub. One says to the other, 'Does your watch tell the time?'

The other replies, 'No, mate. You have to look at it.'

****

A man goes into a pub with a newt sitting on his shoulder.

'That's a nice newt,' says the landlord, 'what's he called?'

'Tiny,' replies the man.

'Why's that?' asks the landlord.

'Because he's my newt,' says the man.

****

A bloke goes into a pub and orders a double. The landlord says, 'You look terrible, mate. What's the problem?'

The guy says, 'I just caught my girlfriend in bed with my best friend.'

Landlord: 'That's awful. What did you do?'

Bloke: 'I threw her out on to the front lawn, threw her clothes out after her and told her that we were finished and I never wanted to see her again.'

Landlord: 'Good for you, mate – that was pretty tough. What did you do to your best friend?'

Bloke: 'I shook my finger at him and said, 'BAD DOG!'

****

A group of men were having a few drinks in a pub. They were swapping stories about the dogs they used to own. One man said, 'I used to have a Labrador that killed a Bull Terrier'

Another man said, 'That's nothing, I had a Poodle that killed a German Shepherd.'

Another man said, 'Well, I had a little Yorkshire Terrier that killed an American Pit Bull'.

All the men cracked up laughing. 'Bullshit,' said one man. 'How can a Yorkshire Terrier kill a Pit Bull?'

'Quite easily,' said the man, 'if the Pit Bull chokes on him.'

****

A horse walks into a bar. The barman says to him, 'Hey, why the long face?'

****

I had 18 bottles of whisky in my cellar and was told by my wife to empty the contents of each and every bottle down the sink, or else... I said I would and began to pour.

I removed the lid from the first bottle and poured the contents down the sink with the exception of one glass, which I drank.

I then removed the lid from the second bottle and did the same, with the exception of one glass, which I drank.

I then removed the lid from the third bottle and poured the whisky down the sink which I drank.

I pulled the lid from the fourth bottle down the sink and poured the bottle down the glass, which I drank.

I pulled the bottle from the lid of the next and drank one sink out of it, and threw the rest down the glass.

I pulled the sink out of the next glass and poured the lid down the bottle.

Then I lidded the sink with the glass, bottled the drink and drank the pour.

When I had everything emptied, I steadied the house with one hand, counted the glasses, lids, bottles, and sinks with the other, which were 29, and as the houses came by I counted them again, and finally I had all the houses in one bottle, which I drank.

I'm not under the affluence of incohol as some thinkle peep I am. I'm not half as thunk as you might drink.

I fool so feelish I don't know who is me, and the drunker I stand here, the longer I get.

✱✱✱✱

A Russian is strolling down the street in Moscow and kicks a bottle laying in the street. Suddenly out of the bottle comes a genie.

The Russian is stunned and the genie says, 'Hello, master, I will grant you one wish – anything you want.'

The Russian begins thinking, 'Well, I really like drinking vodka.' and so finally says, 'I wish to drink vodka whenever I want, so make me piss vodka.'

The Genie grants him his wish. When the Russian gets home he gets a glass out of the cupboard and pisses in it. He looks at the glass and it's clear. Looks like vodka. Then he smells the liquid. Smells like vodka. So he takes a taste and it is the best vodka he has ever tasted.

The Russian yells to his wife, 'Natasha, Natasha, come quickly!' She comes running down the hall and the Russian takes another glass out of the cupboard and pisses into it. He tells her to drink, it is vodka. Natasha reluctant antlt takes a sip. It's the best vodka she has ever tasted.

The two drink and party all night.The next night the Russian comes home from work and tells his wife to get two glasses out of the cupboard. He proceeds to piss in the two glasses. The result is the same, the vodka is excellent and the couple drink until the sun comes up.

Finally, Friday night comes and the Russian comes home and tells his wife, 'Natasha grab one glass from the cupboard and we will drink vodka.'

His wife gets the glass from the cupboard and sets it on the table. The Russian begins to piss in the glass and when he fills it his wife asks him, 'But Boris, why do we need only one glass?'

Boris raises the glass and says, 'Because tonight, my love, you drink from the bottle.'

****

Q: Why do elephants wear small green hats?
A: So they can sneak across snooker tables unobserved.

****

Q: How is being at a singles bar different from going to the circus?
A: At the circus the clowns don't talk.

****

Q: How does a man show he's planning for the future?
A: He buys two crates of beer instead of one.

****

Q: How does a blonde give a high-5 sign?
A: Smacks herself in the forehead.

Chapter 5
Medicinal Purposes

If you're going to spend hours in the pub, you've got to feel it's doing you some good. 'Booze agrees with me', you'll say. The fact that it only agrees that you're a sad alcoholic who's looking for excuses to justify his excess consumption of booze has nothing to do with it.

Worse still, is the excuse that 'it's for medicinal purposes'. Not only is it not doing you any harm, but it's actually promoting a healthier lifestyle. You may end up with your head down the toilet at two in the morning but that's a small price to pay for fitness and well-being.

In short, booze is only really for medicinal purposes in the sense that if you get really pissed, you could end up in hospital. If you do end up there, you might hear some of these jokes…

✳✳✳✳

A woman went to the doctor wanting to find out about the latest weight-loss programme.

'Well,' said the doctor, 'there's a new one that you can lose a lot of weight with. All you have to do is ingest everything anally.'

So the woman decided to follow this course of treatment. After about six weeks, she walked back into the doc's office for a follow-up. It was obvious that she'd lost an awful lot of weight, but she was walking a bit bent over, and was swaying her behind from side to side.

'Wow,'' said the doc, 'you look wonderful!'

'Thanks,' said the woman. 'I've lost four stone!'

'Great!' said the doctor, 'Now let me see if I can do something about that limp of yours.'

'Limp?' said the woman. 'I'm chewing a piece of gum!'

✳✳✳✳

Doctor: I have some bad news and some very bad news.
Patient: Well, you might as well give me the bad news first.
Doctor: The lab called with your test results. They said you have 24 hours to live.

Patient: 24 HOURS! That's terrible!! WHAT could be WORSE? What's the very bad news?

Doctor: I've been trying to reach you since yesterday.

****

Patient: I'm in a hospital! Why am I in here?

Doctor: You've had an accident involving a train.

Patient: What happened?

Doctor: Well, I've got some good news and some bad news. Which would you like to hear first?

Patient: Well… The bad news first…

Doctor: Your legs were injured so badly that we had to amputate both of them.

Patient: That's terrible! What's the good news?

Doctor: There's a guy in the next ward who made a very good offer for your slippers.

****

A doctor on his rounds in a mental hospital sees a couple of patients behaving rather strangely. The first man is sitting on the edge of his bed clutching an imaginary steering wheel and making loud noises, 'VRROOOOM, VRRROOOOMM… SCREEEECH…' he's going.

'What are you doing?' asks the doctor.

'I'm taking this juggernaut down to Barcelona,' replies the ex-trucker.

Somewhat taken aback, the doctor moves on to the next bed where he can see some very energetic activity going on underneath the covers. On pulling them back he finds a man totally naked, face down on the mattress.

'And what are you doing?' asks the doctor, a little perplexed.

'Well,' pants the man, 'While he's in Barcelona, I'm fucking his wife.'

****

An elderly man and his wife go to the doctor so he can get a check-up. The doctor examines him thoroughly in the presence of his wife.

'You're in perfect health!' said the doctor, 'what do you attribute this to?'

'It is the help of God,' says the old geezer. 'Even when I wake in the night and go to the bathroom, God turns the light on for me so I will not stumble, and when I leave, he turns it off again.'

'That is totally amazing!' says the doc.

'No, it isn't!' says the old geezer's wife. 'He pisses in the refrigerator!'

****

Doctor, doctor, I keep thinking I'm a set of curtains!
Pull yourself together, man!

****

Doctor, doctor, I keep thinking I'm a bell.
Well, just go home and if the feeling persists, give me a ring.

****

Doctor, doctor, I've only got 59 seconds to live.
Wait a minute, please.

****

Doctor, doctor, I keep thinking I'm invisible.
Who said that?

****

Doctor, doctor, I keep trying to get into fights.
And how long have you had this complaint?

Who wants to know?

****

Doctor, doctor, people keep ignoring me!
Next!

****

Doctor, doctor, I can't concentrate, one minute I'm OK, and the next minute, I'm blank!
And how long have you had this complaint?
What complaint?

****

Doctor, doctor, no one believes a word I say.
Tell me the truth now, what's your REAL problem?

****

A surgeon came to see his patient on the morning after her operation. The young woman asked him, somewhat hesitantly, how long it would be before she could resume her sex life.

'I really haven't thought about it,' gulped the stunned surgeon. 'You're the first patient who's asked me that question after a tonsilectomy!'

****

An artist asked the gallery owner if there had been any interest in his paintings which were on display at that time.

'I have good news and bad news,' the owner replied. 'The good news is that a gentleman enquired about your work and wondered if it would appreciate in value after your death. When I told him it would, he bought all

15 of your paintings.'

'That's wonderful,' the artist exclaimed. 'What's the bad news?'

'The guy was your doctor…'

****

A woman goes to her doctor and says, 'I'd like to have bigger breasts.'

The doctor tells her to take a piece of toilet tissue and rub it between her breasts every day.

'That will make make my breasts bigger?' she asks, amazed.'

'Well, just look what it did for your arse!' said the doc.

****

A woman rushes into the vet's surgery carrying her ailing pet.

'Please,' she begs, 'You've got to do something for my dog!'

The vet leads her to the examining room where she gently lays the animal on the table. After a brief check of the body, the vet declares, 'Madam, I'm afraid your dog is dead.'

'Oh, no,' sobs the woman, 'He can't be! Please, I beg you, there must be something you can do to help him!'

So the vet takes a closer look. He lifts one of the dog's eyes, feels its nose, feels the chest for a pulse, but there is nothing, the corpse is cold and lifeless.

'I really am sorry, madam, but your dog is gone,' the vet says.

The woman begins to sob, 'Oh, please! Isn't there something you can do to help him? ANYTHING?'

The vet sighs, then says, 'Well, there is one more thing I can try.'

He goes into the next room for a moment, and returns with a live cat. Grasping the cat firmly in one hand, he waves the hissing feline in the dog's face, all around the dog's body, then in the dog's face again. But the dog just lies there, so the vet returns the cat to the next room.

'I'm really sorry, madam," says the vet on his return, 'but your dog is really dead, and nobody can bring him back.'

Regaining her composure, the woman sniffs, wipes away a tear, and asks the vet, 'Well, thank you for at least trying. How much do I owe you?'

'That'll be £500,' says the vet.

Shocked, the woman exclaims, 'What?! But you didn't really do anything!'

'Standard fee,' says the vet. '£20 for the examination, and £480 for the cat scan.'

****

A bloke was suffering from constipation, so his doctor prescribed suppositories. A week later he was back at the doctor's complaining his constipation was worse, not better. The doctor asked, 'Have you been taking the suppositories regularly?'

'What do you think I've been doing?' said the bloke. 'Shoving them up my arse?'

****

There was once a very prim and proper older lady who had a problem with passing wind. Since she came from a generation when people didn't even talk about this kind of problem it took a long time for her to seek help.

Finally, however, she was persuaded to consult her family doctor. After she filled out all the proper forms and had waited about 20 minutes in the waiting room, the doctor called her into his office, leaned back in his chair, folded his hands into a steeple and asked her how he could help.

'Doctor,' she said, 'I have a very bad wind problem.'

'A wind problem?' replied the doctor.

'Yes. Yesterday afternoon I had lunch with the Secretary of State and his wife and had six, um, er, ahhh... silent wind emissions. Last night I had dinner with the governor and his wife and had four silent wind emissions. Then, while sitting in your waiting room I had five silent wind emissions! Doctor, you've got to help me! What can we do?'

'Well,' said the doctor thoughtfully, 'I think the first thing we're going to do is give you a hearing test.'

****

This lad went into a doctor's office and tells the nurse, 'I have a problem with my dick.'

The nurse, half horrified, says, 'I am amazed that you the audacity to use that language in here. I will not help you until you call it something else.'

A little embarrassed, the lad leaves. A few minutes later, he comes back in and says, 'I have something wrong with my ear.'

So the nurse says, 'That's better. Now what's wrong with your ear?'

'I can't piss out of it,' the lad replies.

****

While his wife is away, this man decides to paint the toilet seat. The wife comes home sooner than expected, sits, and gets the seat stuck to her arse. She's understandably distraught about this and asks her husband to drive her to the doctor.

She puts on a large overcoat so as to cover the frozen seat, and they go. When they get to the doctor's, the man lifts his wife's coat to show their predicament.

'Doctor,' the man asks, 'have you ever seen anything like this before?'

'Well, yes,' the doctor replies, 'but never framed.'

****

Mrs May was suffering from exhaustion and went to the doctor.

'Tell me, Mrs May,' said the doctor. 'How often do you have sex?'

'Oh, four times a week,' replied Mrs May. 'On Sunday, Tuesday, Friday and Saturday nights.'

'Well you're going to have to cut out the Sunday nights,' said the doctor.

'I can't do that,' exclaimed Mrs May. 'That's the night I'm with my husband.'

****

In the middle of the night, Karen awoke screaming in pain. 'Quick, quick,' she screamed to her husband Dave. 'Ring the doctor, I think it's my appendix.'

So Dave got on the blower. 'Doctor, it's my wife,' said Dave. 'She's screaming in pain and thinks it's her appendix.'

'Dave, Dave,' said the Doctor, 'calm down and go back to sleep. I took out your wife's appendix four years ago and in all my years as a doctor I've never heard of anyone having another one.'

'Fine,' replied Dave dryly, 'but have you ever heard of anyone having another wife?'

****

A plastic bag goes to the doctor. After a thorough examination the doctor says, 'I'm very sorry, but you've got AIDS.'

'That's impossible,' says the plastic bag. 'I've never even had sex.'

'Well,' says the doctor, 'your mother must be a carrier.'

****

A bloke working in a brewery died one day after falling into a vat of beer. The managing director and some colleagues went to tell his widow.

'Tell me, did he suffer much?' cried the widow.

'I don't think so,' replied the MD, 'he got out to go to the bog three times.'

****

This woman goes to the dentist. As he leans over to begin working on her, she grabs his balls. The dentist says, 'Madam, I believe you've got a hold of my privates.'

The woman replies, 'Yes. We're going to be very careful not to hurt each other, aren't we?'

****

An 80-year-old woman married an 85-year-old man. After about six months together the woman wasn't feeling well and she went to her doctor. The doctor examined her and said, 'Congratulations, Mrs Jones, you're going to be a mother.'

'Get serious Doctor, I'm 80!' she replied.

'I know,' said the Doctor, 'this morning I would have said it was impossible, but this afternoon you are a medical miracle.'

'Well, I'll be blowed,' said the old woman and stormed out of the office. She walked down the hall and around the corner to where the phones were. In a rage, she called her husband.

'Hello,' she heard his familiar halting voice.

'You bastard,' she screamed, 'you got me pregnant!'

There was a pause on the line. Finally her husband answered:

'Who's calling, please?'

****

One day John's tennis elbow was acting up so he decided to stop in and see a doctor. When he got to the doctor's office the nurse told him he could see the doctor in 15 minutes but first he'd have to give a urine sample.

John said that this was absurd but the nurse insisted and John complied. 15 minutes later, John was ushered in to see the doctor.

'So that tennis elbow is really acting up, huh?' the doctor said.

'The nurse must have told you,' said John, wondering how the Doctor knew.

'No. It was in your urinalysis,' and the doctor continued to say that he had just purchased this new urology machine that could diagnose every physical condition with total accuracy.

John didn't believe a word of this but he did agree to provide another urine sample on a check-up visit. Two days later, John was sitting at the kitchen table with his wife and his teenage daughter. He was telling them about this ridiculous machine, when he decided to have a little fun with the doctor. John pissed in the bottle as did his wife and teenage daughter. Then John had a brainstorm. He added a few drops of motor oil to the jar and finally had a wank and put a few drops of semen in with it too. He went to the doctors office, shook the bottle, then handed it to the nurse.

This time his urinalysis took half an hour. Finally, John was ushered in to see the doctor. The doctor looked at him and said, 'I've got some bad news. Your daughter's pregnant, your wife's got clap, your car's about to break down and if you don't stop wanking that tennis elbow's gonna get worse!'

****

This geezer was in the pub when he spotted someone he thought he knew. 'Are you Derek Maygrove?' he asked.

'No,' came the reply.

'That's weird,' said the geezer, 'you look just like him. You must have a double.'

'Thanks very much,' said the bloke, 'I'll have it on the rocks, please.'

****

A day-tripper goes up to a local and says, 'Excuse me, I'm not from round here, can you tell me where I'll find the nearest boozer?'

'You're looking at him,' says the local.

****

A very wealthy, very classy lady goes to see her doctor. 'Doctor, I have this MOST disgraceful and EMBARRASSING problem. I have VERY loud, VERY frequent flatulence. Thank HEAVENS it is COMPLETELY odourless.'

The doctor tells her, 'Well, I don't think it's likely to be anything serious but, just in case, I'll give you a thorough examination.'

So the lady takes off her clothes, lays down on the examining table and put her feet up in the stirrups. The doctor bends over to examine her when all of a sudden she lets one rip BAAAAAARRRRRR-RUUUUUUMPPPPPPPP!!!!!!

The doctor stands up immediately and says, 'This is serious. Just stay still. I'm going to call an ambulance and check you into the hospital immediately. We'll have to do exploratory surgery.'

The woman was terrified at this. She said, 'Oh my God. Is it... CANCER?'

The doctor said, 'That's a distinct possibility.'

The woman said, 'How treatable is CANCER of the BOWELS?'

The doctor said, 'Christ, woman, your bowels are fine. I'm worried about your nose.'

****

Why has Guinness got a white head on it?
So when you're drunk you know which end to drink first.

****

Two blokes are chatting in a pub one day.
'How did you get those scars on your nose?' said one.
'From glasses,' said the other.
'Well why don't you try contact lenses?' asked the first.
'Because they don't hold as much beer,' said the second.

****

A heavy drinker is warned by his doctor that if he doesn't reduce his consumption he'll be dead in five years.

'You've got to cut down to only three drinks a day,' said the doc. The drinker nods in agreement and goes off. A couple of weeks later the doctor comes across the bloke in a terrible state.

'Hey, I thought you agreed to only three drinks a day?' fumed the doctor.

'Yes I did,' said the drinker, 'but I went to five other doctors for second opinions and they all prescribed the same.'

****

A drunk bloke came upon a geezer looking under the bonnet of his car.

'What's the matter?' mumbled the drunk. 'Oh, piston broke,' replied the motorist.'

'Yeah, me too,' replied the drunk.

****

Two guys were staggering home one night after a particularly excessive bout of drinking.

'Ish thas the shum or the moon up shere?' asked one.

'Don't know,' came the reply, 'I'm not from around here.'

****

'After another night on the ale John comes home to find his wife is somewhat annoyed.

'So, what's your excuse this time?' she demands.

'Well, there I was in front of a blazing fire with a drink in me hand. It was very difficult to leave,' says John.

'Well, why didn't you just get up and walk away?' asks the wife.'

'It's not that easy when you've got to get past all those firemen and their equipment,' explains John.

****

Why did the farmer feed his chickens whisky?
Because he was hoping they would lay scotch eggs.

****

Two terrorists were driving to a bombing mission when they decided to stop for a few stiff ones along the way. On getting back into the car, the passenger put the bomb in his lap.

'I'd better drive carefully,' said the driver, 'we don't want it going off too soon.'

'Oh, don't worry about that,' said the passenger, 'there's another one in the boot.'

****

This bloke was tottering along the road much the worse for wear, booting old cans and litter all over the place.

'What do you think you're up to?' asked a passing copper.

'I'm on my works outing,' replied the bloke.

'So where's everyone else?' asked the copper.

'There isn't anyone else,' came the reply, 'I'm self-employed.'

****

A man goes to the doctor. 'Doctor, doctor, I keep thinking I'm a bottle of gin.'

'I think you need a little tonic,' advises the doc.

****

A woman is laying naked, except for a sheet, on a bed out in a hospital corridor waiting to go into surgery. As she lays there, a man in a white coat comes by, lifts up the sheet and then leaves. This happens a second time. The third time this happens she says, 'Doctor, am I going into surgery soon?'

The man replied, 'Don't ask me lady. I'm just a painter!'

****

Three geezers have been drinking all evening when one of them passes out on the floor. One of the others goes to the bar to buy the next round. 'What's he having?'' asks the landlord pointing to the bloke on the floor.

'Oh he'd better not have any more,' comes the reply, 'he's driving.'

****

A woman was asleep at home when she was woken up by the sound of a terrible crash. Rushing downstairs, she sees her husband sitting in the car in the living room.

'How the fuck did you get into the living room?' she shouts.

'Well, I took a left at the front door, passed through the kitchen and then made a right,' came the reply.

****

A ghost went into a pub after closing time. To the terrified barmaid he asked, 'Do you serve spirits at this time of night?'

****

A man walks into a pub and asks, 'Do you serve women in this pub?'

'No,' replies the landlord, ' you've got to bring your own.'

****

A bloke walks into a pub at 11 o'clock one morning and asks the landlord, 'Was I in here last night?'

'Yes, mate,' goes the landlord.

'And did I spend a lot of money?' asks the bloke.

'Yes mate, you did,' replies the landlord, 'about £80.'

'Thank God for that,' says the bloke, 'I thought I'd wasted it.'

****

A man went to the doctor. 'Look, doc,' he said, 'I can't stop my hands from shaking.'

'Do you drink much?' asked the doctor.'

'No,' replied the man, 'I spill most of it.'

****

A stuttering man finally decides to go to the doctor to see if his speech impediment can be cured. The doctor thoroughly examines the man and finally asks him to drop his pants. Out comes this gigantic dick and the doctor pronounces the root of the problem to be strain on the vocal chords from the effects of gravity being transmitted up to the neck area.

The patient then asks, 'Wh-wh-at c-c-ca-an b-b-e d-d-done ab-b-bout- t-t i-it?'

To which the doctor replies, 'modern surgery can work miracles. We can replace your dick with one of normal size and the stuttering will disappear right after the operation.'

The patient eagerly agrees to the surgery, and as promised his stuttering disappears. About three months later the man returns to the doctor and complains, 'Doctor, I'm grateful to you for having cured me, but my wife really misses a big dick, and rather than lose her I've decided to get my old dick back and live with stuttering for the rest of my life.'

The doctor then looks straight at the man and replies, 'A d-d-de-deal's a d-d-deal.'

****

Q: What's so great about being a test tube baby?

A: You get a womb with a view.

****

Pissed and confused, this bloke is staggering home one night when he stops to ask someone the time. On getting his reply he says, 'I don't get it. That's the fourth person I've asked and I get a different answer each time.'

****

On his way home from the pub, a drunk decides to go and see a late-night film. After buying a ticket he staggers into the cinema, only to return two minutes later to buy another ticket and stagger in again. Two minutes later he's back again buying a third ticket.

'Do you realise,' says the girl in the ticket office, 'that's the third time you've bought a ticket?'

'Yes,' replies the drunk,' but every time I get to the cinema some bloke takes it from me and tears it in half.'

****

Two women are in a wine bar. They order a couple of glasses of white wine.

'And make sure my glass is clean,' says one woman. 'Last time I was here I got a dirty one.'

The waiter goes off and returns later with their wine. 'Now then,' he says, 'who was it who wanted the clean glass?'

****

The Sally Army were collecting outside a pub one day when a slightly pissed geezer wandered out of the pub and said to one of the girls collecting, 'Do you save fallen women?'

'Why yes, we do,' replied the girl.

'Well, can you save me one for Friday night, then?' asked the bloke.

****

Man goes to the doctor. 'Doctor, doctor, I keep seeing fish everywhere.'
'Have you seen an optician?' asks the doctor.
'Look I told you,' snapped the patient, 'it's fish that I see.'

****

A charity worker knocked on Mrs Smith's door and said, 'Hello, I'm collecting for a home for drunkards. Can you donate anything?'
'Yes,' replied Mrs Smith, 'if you come back after closing time you can have my husband.'

****

In desperation the alcoholic tried drinking varnish. Sadly he he came to a terrible end... but a beautiful finish.

****

A guy rang up Alcoholics Anonymous in the middle of the night.
'I need help,' he said. 'I'm currently sitting in a room with 50 bottles of wine.'
'I see,' came the reply. 'And how can we help?'
'I just wondered if you could put me in touch with one of your clients with a corkscrew they don't need any more?' said the man.

****

After sinking a good eight pints, a worse-for-wear tough guy slammed his fists down on the bar and shouted, 'Right, everyone on the left side of the pub is a bastard.'

Getting no reaction, the guy tried again with, 'Everyone on the right of the pub is a homosexual.'

On hearing this, one chap got up. 'Right,' said the tough guy,' do you want some, then?'

'No,' said the chap, 'it's just that I'm on the wrong side of the pub.'

****

An old pisshead was staggering along the road pulling a piece of string along behind him.

'Why are you pulling that piece of string along?' asked a passing policeman.

''Cos it's a damn sight easier than pushing it,' replied the pisshead.

****

The wife of a friend of mine was in an accident and is now in hospital in a coma. She's on monitors and the nurses noticed that when they bathed her, her brain waves would elevate. So the doctors called in the husband and suggested he come in everyday to wash and massage her. They even suggested having oral sex, as this would keep her mind active.

So the next day as the husband was washing her, the doctors where delighted to see the brain waves go so high. Then everything went flat-line. They rushed in to inquire as to what had happened. The husband replied, 'I did everything you told me, I guess she choked to death.'

****

Two doctors and an NHS Trust manager died and lined up at the Pearly Gates for admission to heaven. St Peter asked them to identify themselves. One doctor stepped forward and said: 'I was a pediatric spine surgeon and helped kids overcome their deformities.'

St Peter said, 'You can enter.'

The second doctor said: 'I was a psychiatrist. I helped people rehabilitate themselves.' St Peter also invited him in.

The third applicant stepped forward and said, 'I was a NHS Trust manager, I helped people get cost-effective health care.'

St Peter said, 'You can come in too.' But as the NHS Trust manager walked by, he added, 'But you can only stay three days. After that you can go to hell.'

****

A mad fan of Michelle Pfeiffer wins a date with her in a competition. Naturally, he's very nervous when they meet, but she turns out to look even better than she does on the big screen, beautifully turned out in a designer dress, with her blue eyes sparkling in the light.

Clearing his throat, the fan offers Michelle a drink. 'Erm, would you like a port or a Martini, Michelle?'

'Oh, a port,' says Michelle. 'Port to me is like a deep sunset over a forest of blazing russet trees. It makes me glow and shimmer like a ray of light bouncing off an icy lake in winter. Martini, on the other hand, makes me fart.'

****

Q: Why did the blonde have a sore navel?
A: Because her boyfriend was also blonde!

****

Q: Why do black widow spiders kill their males after mating?
A: To stop the snoring before it starts.

****

Q: How do you get a man to do situps?
A: Glue the TV remote control between his ankles.

Chapter 6
One For The Road

OK, so we all know that drink driving is a big no no, unless of course you live in the country where in order to get your license you have to pass a special drink driving test, but that doesn't stop people going on about how they reckon they actually drive better after a few stiff ones.

It's bloody ridiculous. You don't get people claiming to play a better game of chess after 10 pints, or thinking they could scale Mount Everest that bit more smoothly after a couple of bottles of gin, do you?

Actually after a couple of bottles of gin you'd probably reckon you could scale Everest whilst playing chess, but fortunately we're not dealing with the real world here, rather the world of jokedom and gaggery in which getting into the car as pissed as a newt is almost bleedin' obligatory. And, in a strange life-imitates-art sort of way, after seven pints you'll find that even though you start thinking that your delivery of the gags is getting better, it is in fact a whole lot worse. Weird…

✳✳✳✳

A copper sees a car weaving all over the road and pulls it over. He walks up to the car and sees a nice-looking woman is driving and smells booze on her breath.

He says, 'I'm going to have to give you the breathalyser test to determine if you are under the influence of alcohol.'

She blows into the bag and he walks over to the police car. After a couple of minutes he comes back and says, 'It looks like you've had a couple of stiff ones.'

'You mean it shows that, too?' she replies.

✳✳✳✳

A young couple are out driving down the motorway. The lad says to the girl, 'If I go at 100 miles an hour, will you take off your clothes?'

She agrees and he begins to speed up. When the speedometer hits 100 she starts to strip. When she gets all her clothes off he's so busy staring at her that he drives off the road and flips the car. The girl is thrown clear without a scratch, but her clothes and her boyfriend are trapped in the car.

'Get help!' he pleads.

'I can't, I'm naked,' she says.

He points to his shoe that has been thrown clear and says, 'Cover yourself with that and get help.'

She takes the shoe, covers herself, and runs to the service station down the road. When she arrives she's frantic and calls to the attendant, 'HELP! HELP! My boyfriend's stuck!'

The attendant looks down at the shoe covering her crotch and replies, 'I'm sorry Miss. He's too far in.'

✶✶✶✶

After a car crash one of the drivers was lying injured on the pavement.

'Don't worry,' said a policeman who's first on the scene, 'a Red Cross nurse is coming.'

'Oh shit,' moaned the victim, 'couldn't I have a blonde, cheerful one?'

✶✶✶✶

A middle-aged businessman took a young woman, half his age, as his wife. The fantasy of having a young woman in his bed soon became a nightmare when he found that he could not last long enough to satisfy his young bride.

His wife, as understanding as she was exciting, told him that all was well even if he was quick to get out of the saddle.

Determined to satisfy this sweet young thing, the man visited the doctor to get some advice. 'Doctor,' he said, 'I can't seem to hold back for very long when I make love to my young wife and I can't satisfy her. What can I do?'

The doctor smiled, patted him on the shoulder, and said in a professional manner, 'Try a bit of self-stimulation before having intercourse with your wife and you'll find that you'll last longer and ultimately satisfy her.'

'OK, Doctor,' said the man. 'If you think that will help.'

Later that afternoon, his young bride called him at work to let him know that she would be attacking him at the front door when he arrived home.

'Be prepared, my darling. I'm going to ravish you,' she cooed over the phone. Undaunted, the man decided to follow the doctor's advice. But where? In the office? The toilet? What if someone walked in on him? So eventually he got in his car and began the journey home. Soon he decided he would find a spot on the road to pull over, climb underneath the car and, pretending to be inspecting the rear axle, do the deed there.

A moment later, he pulled over, crawled beneath the car, closed his eyes tightly, and fantasising about his young wife, began his 'therapy'.

A few minutes later, just as he was about to complete his therapy session, he felt someone tugging on his trouser leg. Keeping his eyes tightly shut to avoid ruining the fantasy he was enjoying, he said, 'Yes?'

'Sir, I'm a policeman. Could you tell me what you are doing, please?' said the copper.

'Yes, officer, I'm inspecting my car's rear axle,' he replied confidently.

'Well, why don't you check the brakes while you're down there. Your car rolled down the hill ten minutes ago.'

****

A policeman walked over to a parked car and asked the driver if the car was licensed. 'Of course it is,' said the driver.

'Great, I'll have a pint then,' said the policeman.

****

One day while on patrol, a policeman pulled over a car for speeding. He went up to the car and asked the driver to roll down her window. The first thing he noticed, besides the nice red sports car, was how attractive the driver was! Drop-dead gorgeous blonde, the works.

'I've pulled you over for speeding, madam... could I see your licence?' said the copper.

'What's a licence?' replied the blonde, instantly giving away the fact that she was as dumb as a stump.

'It's usually in your wallet,' replied the officer. After fumbling for a few minutes, the driver managed to find it.

'Now may I see your insurance details?' asks the copper.'

'Insurance details? What's that?' asked the blonde.

'It's usually in your glove compartment,' said the copper, impatiently. After some more fumbling, she found her insurance details.

'I'll be back in a minute,' said the copper and walked back to his car. He radioed in to run a check on the woman's details and after a few moments, the control room came back to him.

'Ummm… is this woman driving a red sports car?'

'Yes,' said the copper.

'Is she a drop-dead gorgeous blonde?'

'Uh, yes,' replied the copper.

'In that case, give her the stuff back and drop your trousers.'

'WHAT!? I can't do that,' shrieked the copper.

'Trust me, just do it…'' said the copper in the control room.

So the cop goes back to the car, gives the woman back her documents and drops his trousers. The blonde looks down and sighs, 'Oh no… not ANOTHER breathalyser.'

****

Late one night the police were following a car. The driver of the car was driving immaculately, never going over the speed limit, giving the correct signals and even being courteous to other drivers.

Eventually the police car pulled alongside and an officer said to the driver, 'Excuse me sir, you're not in trouble, we just wanted to compliment you on your exemplary driving.'

'Thank you, officer,' replied the driver, 'I always make a point of driving especially carefully when I've had a few pints.'

****

The Pope arrives at Heathrow Airport and gets straight into a chauffeur-driven car.

'I'm rather late for a very important meeting, my good man,' he tells the driver, 'so I would appreciate it if we could go as fast as possible.'

The driver agrees, but being a law-abiding fellow, doesn't do more than 70 miles per hour on the motorway. This infuriates the Pope, who badgers the driver to go faster, but with no success.

Eventually the Pope says, 'Look, I really do have to get to this meeting. It's extremely important. You sit in the back and I'll drive.'

Being a good Catholic lad the driver feels he can't refuse His Holiness, so they change places and set off. The Pope really puts his foot down and before long they're doing well over 100. Inevitably, though, a few miles down the road they get pulled over by the police.

The officer comes over to the car, looks in and then walks away to radio his boss.

'Chief, chief,' he says into his radio, 'I think I might have just pulled over someone really, really important.'

'Is it the Prime Minister?' asks the chief.

'No,' says the officer, 'more important than him.'

'Well, is it the Queen?' asks the chief.

'No sir,' replies the copper. 'More important than her.'

'Well, who on earth is it then?' asks the chief.

'I don't know, sir,' says the officer, 'but he's got the Pope driving him around.'

****

A rabbi and a priest get into a car accident and it's a bad one. Both cars are totally demolished but, amazingly, neither of the holy men is hurt. After they crawl out of their cars, the rabbi sees the priest's collar and says, 'So you're a priest. I'm a rabbi. Just look at our cars. There's nothing left, but we are unhurt. This must be a sign from God. God must have meant that we should meet and be friends and live together in peace the rest of our days.'

The priest replies, 'I agree with you completely. This must be a sign from God.'

'And look at this,' the rabbi says, 'here's another miracle. My car is completely demolished but this bottle of kosher wine didn't break. Surely God wants us to drink this wine and celebrate our good fortune.'

So he hands the bottle to the priest who takes a few big swigs, and hands the bottle back to the rabbi. The rabbi takes the bottle, immediately puts the cap on, and hands it back to the priest. 'Aren't you having any?' asks the priest.

'No,' replies the rabbi, 'I think I'll wait for the police.'

****

The elderly man entered the car showroom together with his young wife. The owner of the showroom spotted the couple and went over to wait upon them himself, but he could not help staring at the lady, which, of course, the elderly man noticed.

'May I propose a wager?' he said. 'If you can do everything to my wife that I can do and still end up the same way as I do, I will pay you double for the car. But if you cannot, you will give it to me for free!'

'OK, agreed!' said the owner.

The elderly man gave his wife a passionate kiss and the agency owner did the same. Then the man unbuttoned her blouse and kissed her breasts. So did the agency owner. Then the husband opened his fly, pulled out his pecker and bent it in half.

'What colour car do you want?' asked the showroom owner.

****

A policeman stops a woman and asks for her licence.

'Madam,' he says, 'it says here that you should be wearing glasses.'

'Well,' replies the woman, 'I have contacts.'

'Listen, love,' says the copper, 'I don't care who you know; You're nicked!'

****

Three cowboys were hanging out in the bunkhouse. 'I know that smart alec Tex,' said the first. 'He's going to start bragging about that new foreign car he bought as soon as he gets back.'

'Not Tex,' the second cowboy replied. 'He'll always be just a good ol' boy. When he walks in, I'm sure all he'll say is hello.'

'I know Tex better than either of you,' said the third. 'He's so smart, he'll figure out a way to do both. Here he comes now.'

Tex swung open the bunkhouse door and shouted, 'Audi, partners!'

****

A motorist parked outside the Bank of England was approached by a plain-clothes policeman.

'Will you be staying long?' inquired the officer.

'What's it got to do with you?' asked the motorist.

'I'm a policeman, sir,' replied the officer.

'Get out of it,' said the motorist, 'you're wearing an ordinary jacket.'

'That's right, sir. This is a routine check,' the officer told him.

****

A man goes out and buys a 1998 Turbo BeepBeep. It's the best and most expensive car in the world, and it costs him £750,000. He takes it out for a spin and, while doing so, stops at a red light. An old man on an even older looking moped pulls up next to him. The old man looks over the sleek, shiny surface of the car and asks, 'What kind of car's that, sonny?'

The geezer replies, 'A 1998 Turbo BeepBeep. They cost £750,000.'

'That's a lot of money!' says the old man, shocked. 'Why does it cost so much?'

' 'Cos this car can do up to 320 miles per hour!' says the geezer proudly.

'Can I take a look inside?' the old man asks.

'Sure,' replies the owner. So the old man pokes his head in the window and looks around. Leaning back on his moped, the old man says. 'That's a nice car, all right.'

Just then the lights change, so the geezer decides to show the old man what his car can do. He floors it, and within 30 seconds the speedometer reads 320 mph.

Suddenly, the geezer notices a dot in his rear-view mirror. It seems to be getting closer! Whhhoooooooooosssssshhhhhh! Something flies by him! Going maybe three times as fast! The guy wonders what on earth could be going faster than his Turbo BeepBeep. Then, ahead of him, he sees a dot coming toward him. Whooooooooooosh! Goes by again! And, it looks distinctly like the old man on the moped!

'It couldn't be,' thinks the geezer. 'How could a moped outrun a Turbo BeepBeep?' But again, he sees a dot in his rear-view mirror! WhoooooooshhhhhhhhhKa-BbbbblaMMMMM! It ploughs into the back of his car, demolishing the rear end.

The geezer jumps out and is amazed to discover it is the old man. He's in a bad way so the geezer says to him, 'Is there anything I can do for you?'

'Yeah,' says the old man. 'You could unhook my braces from your near-side mirror.'

****

A yuppie opened the door of his BMW when suddenly a car came along and hit the door, ripping it off completely. When the police arrived at the scene, the yuppie was complaining bitterly about the damage to his precious BMW.

'Officer, look what they've done to my Beeeeemer!' he whined.

'You yuppies are so materialistic, you make me sick!' retorted the officer. 'You're so worried about your stupid BMW that you didn't even notice that your left arm was ripped off!'

'Oh my gaaawd…' replied the yuppie, finally noticing the bloody stump where his left arm once was. 'My Rolex!'

****

There was a young lad who was quite inventive and was always trying out new things. One day he thought he'd see just how fast a bicycle could go before it became uncontrollable. He asked his friend, who owned a Porsche, if he could tie his bike to the bumper of his car to test his theory. 'Sure,' his friend said.

So the young lad tied his bike to the back of the car and said to his friend, 'I'll ring my bike bell once if I want you to go faster, twice if I want you to maintain speed, and repeatedly if I want you to slow down.'

With that, off they went. Things were going pretty well, with the car driver slowly speeding up to well over 60 miles per hour. The young lad on the bike was handling the speed just fine until, all of sudden, a Ferrari came up beside them and before you knew it the bloke driving the Porsche forgot all about the lad on the bike and started to race the Ferrari.

A little further down the road sat Constable Pigg in his police car. As the racing cars passed him he radioed in saying, 'Hey, lads. You aren't going to believe this, but there's a Porsche and a Ferrari racing out here on the M1, and there's a bloke on a bike ringing his bell and waving his arms trying to pass them!'

****

A police officer had just pulled a car over. When he walked up to the car the man rolled down the window and said, 'What's the problem, officer?'

To which the policeman responded, 'I stopped you for going through that red light back there.'

Just then, the man's wife leaned forward from the passenger seat and said with a very loud voice, 'I told him to stop at that light. But did he listen? No. He just kept right on going.'

The man then turned to his wife and shouted, 'Shut up, bitch!'

'And just before the red light,' continued the policeman, 'I clocked you doing 50 miles per hour and the speed limit is only 30.'

His wife then leaned forward again and squawked, 'I told him to slow down. But did he listen to me? No! He never listens to me.'

And again the man shouted at his wife, 'Listen, bitch, I told you to SHUT UP!'

The policeman then looked at the woman and said, 'Does he always talk to you this way?'

'Oh no, officer,' replied the woman, 'Only when he's been drinking.'

****

Leaving the pub a bit worse for wear, this guy got into his car and decided that the best thing for him to do would be to follow the rear lights of another car that was just pulling out. Everything was fine for about five miles until the lights of the car in front went out and the drunk driver smashed into the back of it.

'Hey, what the hell do you think you're doing turing your lights off? It's pitch black,' shouted the drunk driver.

'What the hell do you expect me to do?' came the reply, 'I'm in my own garage.'

****

Two judges were booked for speeding and being friends they agreed to try each other. The next day one of them sat on the bench and the other entered the dock. He pleaded not guilty and after all the evidence was heard the case was dismissed and the judges changed places.

The second judge also pleaded not guilty, but after hearing the evidence his friend pronounced him guilty and fined him £250.

The second judge was amazed, but before he could say anything his friend said, 'This is the second case of speeding we've had this morning and I'm determined to stamp it out.'

****

A man driving down a country road was flagged down by a policeman on a motorcycle.

'Excuse me, sir, but there's a lady about a mile back who says she's your wife and she fell out of the car when you went over a bump in the road.'

'Thank God for that,' said the man, 'I thought I'd gone deaf.'

****

A flash geezer in a Porsche bombed through a quiet village at 90 miles an hour. At the other side of town he was stopped by the local bobby who asked him if he hadn't seen the, 'Dead Slow,' sign when he came in. 'Of course I did,' said the flash bloke,' but I thought it referred to the villagers.'

****

A policeman stopped a motorist in the centre of town one evening. 'Would you mind blowing into this bag, sir?' asked the policeman.

'Why?' said the driver.

'Because my chips are too hot,' replied the copper.

****

A distraught little boy rang his dad at work one day. 'Dad,' cried the boy, 'Mum was backing the car out of the garage this morning and she ran over my bicycle.'

'Look,' said his dad, 'how many times have I told you not to leave your bike in the middle of the lawn?'

****

An advert in a local paper offered a brand-new Porsche for sale for only £50. On spotting this a keen motorist decided to call round to the address given. He arrived to find a very large house in a wealthy area.

The door was opened by an attractive woman in her late forties who showed him the Porsche which was indeed brand new. Of course he snapped it up and after handing over the £50 asked, 'Why are you selling this car so cheaply? You could probably have got at least £12,000 for it.'

'Well,' explained the woman, 'my husband died recently and in his will he left strict instructions that the proceeds from the sale of his car were to go to his 21-year-old blonde secretary.'

****

A driver came to a stream to discover that the bridge over it was in need of repair. Standing nearby was an old boy, so the driver asked him if he thought the stream was shallow enough for him to drive across.

'Yes, I should think you could do that, sir,' replied the old boy.

So the driver drove into the stream and almost immediately his car sank and he only just managed to scramble out. 'What the hell's the idea of telling me I could drive across,' he shouted at the old boy. 'It must be at least 30 feet deep.'

'I don't understand it,' said the old boy, 'the water only comes halfway up the ducks.'

****

Whizzing round a sharp bend on a country road a motorist ran over a large dog. A distraught farmer's wife ran over to the dead animal.

'I'm so very sorry,' said the driver, 'I'll replace him, of course.'

'Well, I don't know,' said the farmer's wife, 'are you any good at catching rats?'

****

'Why don't you buy a car?' says a salesman to a farmer.

'Well, I'd much rather buy a cow,' replies the farmer.

'You'd look pretty silly riding around on a cow,' says the salesman.

'Not half as silly as I'd look milking a car,' says the farmer.

****

A woman goes to the garage and says, 'I need a longer dip-stick.'

'Why's that?' asks the mechanic.

'Because the one I've got won't reach the oil,' replies the woman.

****

A policeman in a lay-by is amazed when a car whizzes past at 70 miles an hour with a woman calmly knitting at the wheel. He gives chase and on catching her up shouts, 'Pull over!'

'No, pair of socks,' she shouts back.

****

A police officer stopped a car for speeding and saw a dog in the back.

'Does this dog have a licence?' the officer asked the driver.

'Oh no, officer,' said the driver, 'I do all the driving myself.'

****

A copper pulls over a motorist who's been weaving erratically across all three motorway lanes. He approaches the motorist's window carefully, holds out a plastic tube and says, 'Sir, I'll need you to blow into this breathalyser.'

'I'm sorry, officer, I can't do that,' replies the guy, 'I'm an asthmatic, and if I do that I could have a bad asthma attack.'

'OK, sir,' says the policeman. 'Then I'm going to have to ask you to come down to the station with me to give us a blood sample.'

'I can't do that either, officer,' says the driver. 'I suffer from a life-threatening form of haemophilia, and if my skin is punctured in any way, especially by a sharp needle, I could easily bleed to death.'

'No problem, sir,' says the officer, 'then we'll just take a urine sample.'

'I'm awful sorry, officer,' says the motorist, 'I also have diabetes, and if I piss this late at night, I'll get low blood sugar and possibly even go into cardiac arrest.'

'I see sir,' replies the officer calmly, 'then I'll need you to step out of your vehicle and walk a straight line for me right here and now.'

'I can't do that either, officer,' says the guy.

'And why is that, sir?' asks the policeman.

'Because I'm too pissed.'

****

A penguin was driving through the desert when his car broke down. He waddled to the nearest phone to call the AA. His car was quickly towed to the nearest garage where the mechanic told him he would need a couple of hours to check out the car.

The penguin didn't complain but wandered off to find the closest supermarket. He proceeded to the frozen foods section and hung out near the fish sticks. After an hour he got in the freezer next to the vanilla ice cream and, he couldn't help himself, ate several gallons. Then he saw the time and went back to the garage covered in ice cream.

The mechanic walked over to him wiping his hands and shaking his head, saying, 'It looks like you blew a seal.' Blushing, the penguin said, 'Oh no! It's just ice cream.'

****

An MG Midget pulled alongside a Rolls-Royce at a set of traffic light.

'Do you have a car phone?' its driver asked the guy in the Rolls.

'Of course I do,' replied the haughty deluxe-car driver.

'Well, do you have a fax machine?'

The driver in the Rolls sighed. 'I have that too.'

'Do you have a double bed in the back?' the Midget then asked.

Ashen-faced, the Rolls driver sped off. That afternoon, he had a mechanic install a double bed in his motor. A week later, the Rolls driver passes the same MG Midget, which is parked on the side of the road – back windows fogged up and steam pouring out. The arrogant driver pulls over, gets out of the Rolls and bangs on the Midget's back window until the driver sticks his head out.

'I want you to know that I had a double bed installed,' brags the

Rolls driver.

The Midget driver is unimpressed. 'You got me out of the shower to tell me that?'

****

Q: How many mechanics does it take to screw in a light bulb?
A: Two. One to force it with a hammer and one to go out for more bulbs.

****

Q: What do you call a convertible Lada?
A: A skip

****

Q: How do you double the value of your Lada?
A: Fill it up with petrol.

****

Q: Why does a Lada have a heated rear windscreen?
A: To keep your hands warm while you're pushing it.

****

Q: What do you call a Lada at the top of a hill?
A: A miracle.

****

Q: What do you call a Lada going down a hill?
A: An accident waiting to happen.

Chapter 7
On The Pull

Amongst the many and various reasons why people drink the following juxtaposition, as it were, must surely rank highly. Without a drink inside you, you spend about two hours deciding to go over to the member of the opposite sex you've been eyeing up all night and out of you mouth comes the following: 'frmmm greeebly shtrummmp blarllll orgoonnnta.' With a few bevvies inside you, you spend about five minutes making the same decision and out of your mouth comes the following: 'frmmm greeebly shtrummmp blarllll orgoonnnta.'

However, crucially, in the latter example, if the object of your desire has had a few, you might well be on for a shag, whereas in the former example you're probably on for being sectioned.

Now being realistic, all you're really up for is a quick bunk-up without too much discussion, if any, and then you go home hoping never to have to see each other again. Then again, we've all seen *Fatal Attraction*, and if you're really unlucky you may be entering a battle of the sexes that can last an awfully long time…

****

Q: Why can't dumb blondes count to 70?
A: Because 69 is a bit of a mouthful.

****

Q: What do you call a dumb blonde golfer with an IQ of 125?
A: A foursome.

****

Q: Why do dumb blondes get confused in the ladies toilet?
A: They have to pull their own knickers down.

****

Q: What is 68 to a dumb blonde?
A: Where she goes down on you and you owe her one.

****

Q: What is an dumb blonde doing when she holds her hands tightly over her ears?
A: Trying to hold on to a thought.

****

Q: Why did the dumb blonde stare at a carton of orange juice for two hours?
A: Because it said 'concentrate'.

****

Q: Why did the dumb blonde take two acid tabs?
A: She wanted to go on a round trip.

****

Q: What's the definition of a metallurgist?
A: A man who can tell if a platinum blonde is a virgin metal or a common ore.

****

Q: How does a dumb blonde commit suicide?
A: She gathers her clothes into a pile and jumps off.

****

Q: Why did God give dumb blondes two per cent more brains than horses?
A: Because he didn't want them shitting in the streets during parades.

****

Q: Why was the dumb blonde disappointed with her trip to London?
A: She found out Big Ben is only a clock.

****

A newly-wed couple were spending their honeymoon in a remote log cabin resort way up in the Alps. They had registered on Saturday and they had not been seen for five days. An elderly couple ran the resort, and they were getting concerned about the welfare of these newly-weds. The old man decided to go and see if they were all right.

He knocked on the door of the cabin and a weak voice from inside answered. The old man asked if they were OK.

'Yes, we're fine. We're living on the fruits of love.'

The old man replied, 'I thought so... would you mind not throwing the peelings out of the window, 'they're choking my ducks!'

****

The young man had asked for a job with the circus – any job, just so he could travel with the circus. The owner of the circus, thinking he might be able to make an assistant lion-tamer out of the young man, took him out to the practice cage.

The head lion-tamer, a beautiful young woman, was just starting her rehearsal. As she entered the cage, she removed her cape with a flourish and, standing in a gorgeous costume, motioned to one of the lions.

Obediently, the lion crept toward the young woman, licked her elbow, and rolled over twice.

'Well,' said the owner to the young man, 'think you could do that?'

'I'm sure I could, sir,' said the young man, 'but you'll have to get that lion out of there.'

****

A guy is sitting at the pub enjoying a pint when a great-looking young woman sits down beside him and gives him a dynamite smile. Just as he's figuring out his opening line, she says in a loud indignant voice that the whole pub can hear

'Your place? Absolutely not!' and she gets up and stomps off to the other end of the bar.

He sits there in confusion and embarrassment, nursing his pint and wondering how to get out of there. After a while, she comes back, sits next to him again, and says in a low voice. 'Look, I'm sorry about that. I'm a graduate student in psychology and I'm conducting an experiment to see how people react in unexpected stressful situations. Please accept my apologies and let me pay for your beer.'

The guy stands up indignantly and says at the top of his voice, 'a £100! You must be joking!'

****

A bloke walks into a pub and orders a pint. After a couple of sips he looks up and sees a woman sitting at the end of the bar. He calls the landlord over and says he'd like to buy the lady a drink.

The landlord says, 'Listen, pal, let me save you some trouble. She's a lesbian.'

The bloke takes a second, thinks it over, shrugs his shoulders and says, 'That's OK. I'd like to buy her a drink anyway.'

So the landlord brings the woman her drink. The woman lifts her glass and gives the man a nod of thanks. The bloke gets up from his bar stool and saunters over to the woman. As he's sitting down on the stool next to her he says, 'So, what part of Lesbia are you from?'

****

As an airplane is about to crash, a female passenger jumps up frantically and announces, 'If I'm going to die, I want to die feeling like a woman.' She removes all her clothing and asks, 'Is there someone on this plane who is man enough to make me feel like a woman?'

A man stands up, removes his shirt and says, 'Here, iron this.'

****

A businessman boards a flight and is lucky enough to be seated next to an absolutely gorgeous woman. They exchange brief hellos and he notices she's reading a manual about sexual statistics. He asks her about it and she replies, 'This is a very interesting book about sexual statistics. It identifies that American Indians have the longest average penis and Polish men have the biggest average girth. By the way, my name is Jill. What's yours?'

'Tonto Kowalski,' he replies, 'nice to meet you.'

****

A guy is tending the bar at a sophisticated party when two toffee-nosed women approach.

'So, where are you two from?' he asks.

'We,' she answers, 'are from somewhere where people don't end their sentences with prepositions.'

'Oh,' says the bartender. 'So, where are you two from, bitch?'

****

This big geezer meets a woman in a pub, and after a number of drinks, they agree to go back to his place. As they're getting it on in the bedroom, ready for the act, he stands up and starts to undress.

After he takes his shirt off, he flexes his muscular arms and says, 'See there, baby? That's 1,000 pounds of dynamite!.'

She begins to drool. The man drops his pants, and strikes a body-builder's pose, and says, referring to his bulging legs, 'See those, baby? That's 1,000 pounds of dynamite!'. She is aching for action at this point. Finally, he drops his underpants, and she screams and legs it to the front door.

He catches her before she is able to run out the door, and asks, 'Why are you in such a hurry to leave?'

'With 2,000 pounds of dynamite and such a short fuse,' she replies, 'I was afraid you were about to blow!'

****

Each time this bloke visited this pub he had a little white box with him. The barmaid is finally overcome with interest, and asks, 'What's in the box?'

To which he replies, 'The most amazing frog ever. He loves to go down on women and he is really great.' He suggests she might like to find out just how good the frog is, so they go in the back room where she takes off all her clothes, and spreads her legs apart.

The man then takes the frog out of the box and places him between her legs. After several minutes nothing is happening. The man reaches down and picks the frog up, and shaking him says, 'Now listen; I am going to show you just one more time!'

****

Two men are in a disco and both are pretty drunk when one notices a beautiful woman sitting in the corner. 'Wow,' he says, 'I'd really love to dance with that bird.'

'Well, go ahead and ask her, don't be a chicken,' says his mate.

So the man approaches the lovely woman and says, 'Excuse me? Would you be so kind as to dance with me?'

Seeing the man is totally drunk the woman says, 'I'm sorry. Right now I'm concentrating on matrimony and I'd rather sit than dance.'

So the man humbly returns to his friend. 'So what did she say?' he asks.

'She said she's constipated on macaroni and would rather shit in her pants,' says his friend.

****

A rich lonely widow decided that she needed another man in her life so she placed an ad, which read something like this: RICH WIDOW LOOKING FOR MAN TO SHARE LIFE AND FORTUNE WITH. QUALIFICATIONS: 1) WON'T BEAT ME UP 2) WON'T RUN AWAY 3) HAS TO BE GREAT IN BED.

For several months, her phone rang off the hook, her doorbell was buzzing constantly and she received tonnes of post, but all to no avail. No one could meet her qualifications.

Then one day the doorbell rang yet again. She opened the door to find a man with no arms and no legs lying on the welcome mat.

Perplexed, she asked, 'Who are you? And what do you want?'

'Hi,' he said, 'your search is over, for I'm the man of your dreams. I've got no arms so I can't beat you up and no legs so I can't run away.'

'Well then,' she said, 'what makes you think that you're so great in bed?'

To which he replied, 'Well, I rang the doorbell, didn't I?'

****

A young woman was depressed because she was flat-chested. So when her fairy godmother appeared one day and offered to grant her most heart-felt wish, the young woman instantly requested large breasts.

'All right, my dear,' said her fairy godmother. 'From this moment on, every time a man says "Pardon" to you, your breasts will grow.'

So the next day the woman was walking down the street, lost in thought, when she bumped into a policeman. 'Pardon me,' said the copper politely. Instantly her breasts grew an inch. She was ecstatic.

A few days later the young woman was doing her shopping at the supermarket. Leaving with a large bag of groceries, she bumped into a another customer. 'Pardon me,' the man said, bending over to help her collect her groceries, and sure enough the young woman's breasts grew another inch. Very happy, she decided to treat herself to dinner at a Chinese restaurant.

Going in the door, she collided with a waiter, who bowed and said, 'Oh, miss, I beg of you a thousand pardons.'

The following morning the headline in the newspaper read, CHINESE WAITER KILLED BY TWO TORPEDOES.

****

A man walks into a chemist and asks for a pack of condoms. As soon as he's paid for them, he starts laughing and walks out. The next day, there's the same performance, with the man walking out pissing himself. Thinking this a bit odd the chemist asks his assistant to follow the man if he returns.

Sure enough, he comes in the next day, repeating his actions once more. The assistant duly follows and half an hour later, he returns.

'So did you follow him?' asked the chemist.

'I did,' replied the assistant.

'And, where did he go?' asked the chemist.

'Over to your house,' says the assistant.

****

A young man goes into a chemist to buy condoms. The chemist tells him that condoms come in packs of three, nine or 12 and asks which the young man wants.

'Well,' he says, 'I've been seeing this girl for a while and she's really hot. I want the condoms because I think tonight's the night. We're having dinner with her parents, and then we're going out. And I've got a feeling I'm gonna get lucky after that. Once she's had me, she'll want me all the time, so you'd better give me the 12-pack.'

The young man makes his purchase and leaves. Later that evening, he sits down to dinner with his girlfriend and her parents. He asks if he might say grace, and they agree. He begins the prayer, but continues praying for several minutes. The girl leans over and says, 'You never told me that you were such a religious person.'

He leans over to her and says, 'You never told me that your father was a chemist.'

****

A young man wanted to purchase a gift for his new sweetheart's birthday, and as they had not been dating very long, after careful consideration he decided a pair of gloves would strike just the right note – romantic, but not too personal. Accompanied by his sweetheart's younger sister, he went to Harrods and bought a pair of white gloves. The sister purchased a pair of panties for herself. During the wrapping, though, the items got mixed up.

Without checking the contents, the young man sealed the package with the panties in it and sent it to his sweetheart along with the following note: 'I chose these because I noticed that you're not in the habit of wearing any when we go out in the evening. If it had not been for your sister I would have chosen the long ones with the buttons, but she wears the short ones that are easier to remove. These are a delicate shade, but the lady I bought them from showed me the pair she had been wearing for the past three weeks and they were hardly soiled. I had her try yours on for me and she looked really smart. I wish I was there to put them on for you the first time, as no doubt other hands will come in contact with them before I have a chance to see you again. When you take them off, remember to blow in them before putting them away as they will naturally be a little damp from wearing. Just think how many times I will kiss them during the coming year. I hope you will wear them for me on Friday night. P.S. The latest style is to wear them folded down with a little fur showing.'

****

A guy on a date parks his car and gets the girl in the back seat. They make love, but the girl wants it again and the guy complies. She wants more and they do it again. She still wants more and the guy says, 'Excuse me a minute, I have to relieve myself.'

While out of the car he notices a man nearby changing a flat tyre.

'Look,' he says to the man. 'I've got this bird in my car and I've given it to her four or five times and she still wants more. I'll change your flat if you'll take over for me.'

So that's what they do. The second guy gets in the car and starts shagging the bird. Suddenly a copper knocks on the window and shines a light on them.

'What are you doing in there?' asks the copper.

'I'm making love to my wife,' replies the guy.

'Why don't you do that at home?' asks the policeman.

'To tell you the truth,' the guy answers, 'I didn't know it was my wife until you shone the light on her.'

****

A guy is shipwrecked on a celebrity cruise and he wakes up stranded on a desert island with Nicole Kidman. After a few weeks they are having passionate sex which is fine for a bit, but the guy starts getting a bit depressed. Nicole comes up to him on the beach one day and says, 'What's the matter?'

'Well, it's wonderful,' he says, 'I'm on a tropical island with a beautiful woman who I love, but… but… I miss my mates. I miss going down the pub with them.'

'Well, I'm an actress,' says Nicole. 'Maybe if I get dressed in some of those male clothes which were left behind in the trunks, I can pretend to be one of your friends, and you can talk to me as if you were down the pub.'

It sounded a bit weird, but he thought he would give it a try. So she gets into the men's clothing and they sit down next to each other.

'Hey, Joe,' says the man. 'You'll never guess who I've been shagging.'

****

A man and his wife have been stranded on a deserted island for many years. One day a new man washes up on shore. He and the wife are attracted to each other right away, but realise certain protocols must be observed.

The husband, however, is very glad to see the second man there. 'Now we will be able to have three people doing eight-hour shifts in the watchtower, rather than two people doing 12-hour shifts.'

The second man is only too happy to help and in fact volunteers to do the first shift there and then. So up the tower he goes and the husband and wife start placing stones in a circle to make a fire to cook supper.

'Hey, no fucking,' the man yells from the tower.

'We're not fucking,' they shout back. A few minutes later they start to put driftwood into the stone circle.

Again the second man yells down, 'Hey, no fucking,' and again they shout back, 'We're not fucking.'

Later they are putting palm leaves on the roof of their shack to patch leaks. Once again the second man yells down, 'Hey, I said no fucking.'

'We're not fucking!' they shout back.

Finally the shift is over and the second man climbs down from the tower and the husband starts to climb up. He's not even halfway up before the wife and second man are screwing each other's brains out. The husband looks out from the tower and says, 'Blimey, he's right. From up here it really does look like they're fucking'.

****

A man and a woman are riding next to each other in a first-class train carriage. The man sneezes, pulls out his wang and wipes the tip off. The woman can't believe what she just saw and decides she is hallucinating.

A few minutes pass. The man sneezes again. He pulls out his wang and again wipes the tip off. The woman is outraged. She can't believe that such a rude person exists. A few minutes pass. The man sneezes yet again, and he takes his wang out and wipes the tip off.

The woman has finally had enough. She turns to the man and says, 'Three times you've sneezed, and three times you've removed your penis from your pants to wipe it! What kind of degenerate are you?'

'I am sorry to have disturbed you, madam,' says the man. 'I have a very rare condition that causes me to have an orgasm every time I sneeze.'

'Oh, how strange,' says the woman. 'What are you taking for it?'

The man looks at her and says, 'Pepper.'

****

The soldier serving overseas was annoyed and upset when his girl wrote breaking off their engagement and asking for her photograph back. So he went out and collected from his friends all the unwanted photographs of women that he could find, bundled them all together and sent them back with a note saying, 'Regret cannot remember which one is you – please keep your photo and return the others.'

****

Mr Rice got himself a new secretary. Melanie was young, sweet and polite. One day while taking dictation she noticed his fly was open and, on leaving the room, she said, 'Oh, Mr Rice, did you know that your barracks door is open?'

He didn't understand her remark, but later on he happened to look down and saw that his fly was open. He decided to have some fun with his new secretary. Calling her in, he asked, 'By the way, Miss Brown, when you saw my barracks door open this morning, did you see a soldier standing at attention?'

'Why, no, Mr Rice,' she replied. 'All I saw was a disabled veteran sitting on two old duffel bags.'

****

A man mets his girl friend from 25 years ago. She was so happy to see him that she couldn't resist and asked him to come up and see her some time.

'With pleasure!' said the man. So he bought some wine and a bunch of flowers and in the evening he went to see her. When the door opens there she was, stark naked.

'What's this?' – the man was shocked.

She smiles and says, 'I wore my birthday suit for you.'

'That's great,' he says, somewhat embarrassed, 'but couldn't you have pressed it first?'

****

A guy goes to a girl's house for the first time, and she shows him into the living room. She excuses herself to go to the kitchen to make them a few drinks, and as he's standing there alone, he notices a cute little vase on the mantelpiece. He picks it up, and as he's looking at it, she walks back in.

'What's this?' he say.

'Oh,' she says, 'my father's ashes are in there.'

'Ooops... I... don't know what to say,' says the guy.

'Yeah I know, it's shocking,' says the girl. 'He's too lazy to go to the kitchen to get an ashtray.'

****

There was a girl who had one huge goal in life. Her goal was to have a baby. She got a bloke into bed with her and as soon as he was ready, she asked, 'What are we gonna name the baby?' He told her he didn't want a baby and that she was crazy. With that he got out of bed and left.

The next weekend the same thing happened. On the third weekend she finally got someone that was really horny. As he got ready to screw her she asked the question: 'What are we gonna name the baby?' The bloke ignored her and went about his business. About half-way through she asked him again only to get ignored again.

When they finally finish she asked him again. He replied, while taking off his condom and tying it in a knot, 'We'll call him Houdini if he can get out of this.'

****

Derek Rourke rented a flat in a large block, and went to the lobby to put his name on the group letterbox. While there, an attractive young woman came out of the flat next to the boxes, wearing a dressing-gown. Del smiled at the young girl and she struck up a conversation with him. As they talked, her dressing gown slipped open and it was quite obvious that she had nothing on under the robe.

Poor Del broke into a sweat trying to maintain eye contact. After a few minutes, she placed her hand on his arm and said, 'Let's go into my flat, I hear someone coming...'

They went inside and after she closed the door, she leaned against it allowing her robe to fall completely open. She purred at him, 'What would you say is my best feature?'

The flustered, embarrassed Del stammered, cleared his throat several times, and finally squeaked out, 'Oh, it's got to be your ears!'

She was astounded! 'Why my ears? Look at these boobs! They are full, don't sag, and they're all mine! My bum's firm, doesn't sag, and has no cellulite! Look at this skin; no blemishes, or scars! Why in heaven's name would you say my ears are the best part of my body?'

Clearing his throat once again, Del stammered, 'Because when we were outside and you said you heard someone coming – well, that was me'

****

One day God came to Adam to pass on some news. 'I've got some good news and some bad news,' God said.

Adam looked at God and said, 'Well, give me the good news first.'

Smiling, God explained,'I've got two new organs for you. One is called a brain. It will allow you to be very intelligent, create new things, and have intelligent conversations with Eve. The other organ I have for you is called a penis. It will allow you to reproduce your now-intelligent life form and populate this planet. Eve will be very happy that you now have this organ to give her children.'

Adam, very excited, exclaimed, 'These are great gifts you have given to me. What could possibly be bad news after such great tidings?'

God looked upon Adam and said with great sorrow, 'The bad news is that when I created you, I only gave you enough blood to operate one of these organs at a time.'

****

Bill was approaching mid-life and physically he was a mess. Not only was he going bald, but years of office work had given him a large pot-belly. The last straw came when he asked a woman he worked with out on a date, and she all but laughed at him.

'That does it,' thought Bill. 'I'm going to start a whole new regime.' He began attending aerobics classes. He started working out with weights. He changed his diet. And he got an expensive hair transplant. After six months, he was a different man. Again, he asked his female colleague out, and this time she accepted.

So there he was, all dressed up for the date, looking better than he ever had. He stood poised to ring the woman's doorbell, when a bolt of lightning struck him and knocked him off his feet. As he lay there dying, he turned his eyes toward the heavens and said, 'Why, God, why now? After all I've been through, how could you do this to me?'

From up above there came a voice, 'Sorry, I didn't recognise you.'

****

There once was a priest who had to spend the night in a hotel and asked the girl on reception to come up to his room for dinner. After a while he made a pass at her, but she stopped him and reminded him he was a holy man.

'It's OK,' he replied, 'it's written in the Bible.' After a wild night of sex she asked to see where in the Bible it said it was OK, so the priest took the Bible out of the drawer and showed her the first page where someone had written in pencil, 'The girl on reception will shag anybody!'

****

There were three men who died and before God would let them into heaven, he gave them a chance to come back as anything they wanted. The first man said, 'I want to come back as myself, but 100 times brighter.' So God made him 100 times brighter.

The second guy said, 'I want to be better than that bloke, make me 1,000 times brighter.' So God made him 1,000 times brighter.

The last man decided he would be the best. So he said, 'God, make me better than both of them, make me 1,000,000 times brighter.' So God made him a woman.

✱✱✱✱

An old man wanders away from a nursing home. He comes upon a pub that looks friendly enough, and no sooner has he sat down at the bar than a young woman comes up to him.

'Would you like a drink?' she asks him.

'I'd love one,' he replies. So she gets him drink.

'Would you like to dance?' she asks him after he's downed the drink.

'Why of course,' he replies. After a short time on the dance-floor she snuggles up close to him and whispers in his ear, 'Would you like to go home with me?'

'Wow,' says the old man, 'I'd love to!'

The next morning the old man goes to confession. 'I am 85 years old,' he says to the priest, 'and I spent last night with a 28-year-old woman.'

The priest thinks about it and decides that an 85-year-old man couldn't have done much damage.

'Go and say ten Hail Marys,' he says to the man.

'I can't do that,' exclaims the old man, 'I'm Jewish.'

'Well, then what are you doing talking to me?' asks the priest.

'Because I'm 85 years old,' replied the old man. 'I'm telling everybody I can!'

✱✱✱✱

An old man decides to visit a brothel as it's been a long time since he's had any. After paying the madam, he picks out a cute little blonde girl and they go upstairs. After the preliminaries, he climbs on and starts humping away. 'How am I doing, darling? he asks halfway through.

'About three nots,' she replies.

'Three knots?' he says. 'What does that mean?'

'You're not in, you're not hard, and you're not getting your money back!' she says.

****

A guy is walking down the street and enters a clock and watch shop. While looking around, he notices a drop-dead gorgeous female sales assistant behind the counter. He walks up to the counter where she's standing, unzips his fly, and places his dick on the counter.

'What are you doing, sir?' she asks. 'This is a clock shop!'

'I know it is,' he replies. 'And I'd like two hands and a face put on THIS!!'

****

The lovers passionately embraced on her bed, their bodies fused together as they gyrated. Suddenly the woman cocked her ear.

'Quick! It's my husband coming through the front door. Hide in the bathroom!' she cried.

The lover ran into the bathroom. She hid his clothes under the bed and as she turned back, her husband came through the bedroom door.

'What are you doing lying on the bed naked?' he asked.

'Darling, I heard you coming up the drive and got ready to receive you,' she replied with a knowing smile.

'Great,' he said 'I'll just nip into the bathroom and I'll be with you in two shakes.'

Before she could stop him he was into the bathroom where he found the lover clapping his hand in mid-air.

'Who the fuck are you?' the husband demanded.

'I'm from the pest-control company. Your wife called me in to get rid of these moths,' the lover replied.

'But… but you've got no clothes on' stammered the husband.

The lover looked down, jumped backwards in surprise and said, 'Oh! The little bastards!'

****

A missionary is walking through the jungle with the chief of the tribe he is teaching. As they walk, they come across a couple making love.

'What is going on here?' says the chief.

The missionary, embarrassed, says, 'Well, uhhhh, chief, he is riding a bicycle.'

So the chief, grunts, pulls out a blow-gun and shoots a poisoned dart into the man's back.

'Chief, you shouldn't have killed him,' shouts the missionary. 'It was a perfectly natural act they were performing. Why did you have to kill him?'

'He was riding my bicycle!' says the chief.

****

Young Tony was courting Polly, who lived on an adjoining farm. One evening, as they were sitting on Tony's tractor watching the sun go down over the hills, Tony spied his prize bull doing the business on one of his cows. He sighed in contentment at this idyllic rural scene and figured it was a good omen about finally getting to shag Polly.

He leaned in close and whispered in her ear, 'Polly, I'd sure like to be doing what that bull is doing.'

'Well then, why don't you?' Polly whispered back. 'It's your cow.'

****

The elegant young lady was strolling through the zoo and walked all the way around the monkey house. There wasn't an ape or a monkey to be seen, so she sought out the keeper.

'Why are there no monkeys on view?' she asked, her displeasure evident.

'It's mating season,' replied the keeper bluntly. 'They're back in their caves.'

'But I want to see them. Will they come out if I throw them some peanuts?' she asked coolly.

'I dunno, lady,' he answered, looking her over. 'Would you?'

****

This professor had a lie-detecting chair. Whenever anybody sitting on it told a lie, the chair would open up and the person would fall flat on the ground. As a part of his experiment a young brunette came in and sat down. The professor asked her to talk about herself.

'I think,' she began, 'I'm the most beautiful girl in this region, and perhaps even in the whole world!' Immediately after she said that the chair opened up and she landed flat on her arse. She stormed out and a young blonde was invited in to sit on the chair.

She sat down and was invited to talk about herself. 'I think…' she began, and suddenly the chair opened up and she fell flat on her arse!

****

Two dwarfs decide to treat themselves to a vacation in Las Vegas. At the hotel bar, they're dazzled by two women, and wind up taking them to their separate rooms. The first dwarf is disappointed, however, as he's unable to reach a certain physical state that would enable him to shag his bird. His depression is enhanced by the fact that from the next room he hears cries of, 'ONE, TWO, THREE… HUH!' all night long.

The following morning they both meet up. 'How did it go?' his friend asked him.

'It was so embarrassing,' he replied. 'I simply couldn't get an erection.'

The second dwarf shook his head. 'You think that's embarrassing?' he said. 'I couldn't even jump up on the bed!'

****

A shipwreck left three men and one woman on a desert island. They wanted to be fair, and since none of them was promiscuous, they decided that each man would marry the woman for a week at a time and then divorce her. The one-week marriage arrangement went on for about nine weeks and everybody was happy until one day the woman caught a mysterious illness and died. The first week after that was bad; the week after was worse and the week after that was terrible. Then, on the fourth week they buried her.

****

A new recruit arrives in the desert with the Foreign Legion. After a couple of weeks he's feeling in need of some release, so he asks one of his colleagues what they do for sex. The other soldier makes a gesture towards a camel that's tied up nearby and leaves it at that.

The new recruit suddenly loses his sexual appetite, but as the weeks go by it builds up and up and eventually, after two months, he can't control himself any longer and gives the camel the rogering of his life.

The next day he sees the other soldier again and says to him, 'You know that camel? It was one of the best shags of my life.'

'Really?' says the soldier, 'we use it to ride to the brothel in the village.'

****

Very late one night a policeman spotted a lad and a girl sitting in a parked car. The lad was reading and the woman was knitting.

'Excuse me, sir, can you tell what you're doing?' asked the copper.

'Well, I'm reading, officer,' replied the man.

'I see, and what about you, miss, what are you doing?'

'I'm knitting,' said the girl.

'I see,' replied the policeman, 'and can I ask exactly how old you are, madam?'

'Well,' she said glancing at her watch, 'in 15 minutes I shall be 16.'

****

A brunette, a redhead and a blonde all went to see their obstetrician. Trying to make conversation, the brunette said, 'I'm going to have a boy. I'm sure of it because I was on top.'

The redhead said, 'I know I'm going to have a girl. I'm sure because I was on the bottom.'

The blonde suddenly burst into tears. The other women tried to comfort her and asked what was wrong. 'I think I'm going to have puppies,' she sobbed.

****

A computer programmer was on holiday on a cruise ship in the Caribbean for the first time. It was wonderful; the experience of a lifetime. He was being waited on hand and foot. Unfortunately it did not last. A hurricane blew in unexpectedly, and the ship went down almost instantly.

The programmer found himself swept up on the shore of an uncharted island. There was nothing to be seen anywhere: no people, no supplies, nothing. The man foraged around. There were some bananas and coconuts, but that was it. He was desperate and forlorn, but decided to make the best of it. So for the next four months he ate bananas, drank coconut juice and mostly looked out to sea hopefully for a ship to come to his rescue.

One day, as he was lying on the beach stroking his beard and looking for a ship, he spotted movement out of the corner of his eye. Could it be true, was it a ship? No, from around the corner of the island came this rowboat. In it was the most gorgeous woman he had ever seen, or at least seen in four months. She was tall, tanned, and her blonde hair flowing in the sea breeze gave her an almost ethereal quality.

When she saw him waving and yelling and screaming to get her attention, she rowed her boat toward him. Overjoyed, he asked, 'Where did you come from? How did you get here?'

'I rowed from the other side of the island,' she said. 'I landed on this island when my cruise ship sank.'

'Amazing,' he said, 'I didn't know anyone else had survived. How many of you are there? Where did you get the rowboat? You must have been really lucky to have a rowboat wash up with you!'

'It's only me,' she said, 'and the rowboat didn't wash up. Nothing did.'

'Well, then,' said the man, 'how did you get the rowboat?'

'I made it out of raw material I found on the island,' replied the woman. The oars were whittled from gum tree branches, I wove the bottom from Palm branches, and the sides and stern came from a eucalyptus tree.'

'But,' asked the man, 'what about tools and hardware? How did you manage that?'

'Oh, no problem,' replied the woman. 'On the south side of the island there is a very unusual stratum of alluvial rock exposed. I found that if I fired it to a certain temperature in my kiln, it melted into forgeable ductile iron. I used that for tools, and used the tools to make the hardware. But enough of that,' she said. 'Where do you live?' At last the man was forced to confess that he'd been sleeping on the beach.

'Well, let's row over to my place,' she said. So they both got into the rowboat and left for her side of the island. The woman easily rowed them around to a wharf that led to the approach to her place. She tied up the rowboat with a beautifully-woven hemp rope. They walked up a stone walk and around a palm tree, and there stood an exquisite bungalow painted in blue and white.

'It's not much,' she said, 'but I call it home. Sit down, please. Would you like to have a drink?'

'No,' said the man, 'one more coconut juice and I'll puke.'

'It won't be coconut juice,' the woman replied. 'I have a still. How about a Piña Colada?' Trying to hide his continued amazement, the man accepted, and they sat down on her couch to talk.

After a while, having exchanged their stories, the woman asked, 'Tell me, have you always had a beard?'

'No,' the man replied, 'I was clean-shaven all of my life, even on the cruise ship.'

'Well, if you would like to shave, there is a man's razor upstairs in the cabinet in the bathroom.'

So the man, no longer questioning anything, went upstairs to the bathroom. There in the cabinet was a razor made from a bone handle, two shells honed to a hollow-ground edge were fastened on to its end inside of a swivel mechanism. The man shaved, showered and went back downstairs.

'You look great,' said the woman. 'I think I'll go up and slip into something more comfortable.'

While she was gone, the man continued to sip his pina colada. After a short time, the woman returned wearing fig-leaves strategically positioned and smelling faintly of gardenia.

'Tell me,' she said, 'we've both been out here for a very long time with no companionship. You know what I mean. Have you been lonely? Is there anything that you really miss? Something that all men and women need. Something that it would be really nice to have right now?'

'Yes, there is,' the man replied, as he moved closer to the woman while fixing a winsome gaze upon her. 'Tell me… do you happen to have a set of golf clubs?'

****

There was a small bakery shop in a town that had a very attractive female assistant and it became known throughout the town that the pretty woman didn't like to wear panties under her skirt while she was at work.

Men would come in to the store, all day long, to buy a loaf of raisin bread because when they requested raisin bread, the assistant would have to climb a ladder to reach the bread on a high shelf behind the counter which revealed quite a show for the male customers.

As the day went on, the woman became quite exhausted from climbing the ladder to fetch raisin bread and just as she was on the ladder retrieving another loaf of raisin bread for a customer, an elderly gentleman walked into the bakery to purchase a pie for his wife.

The assistant shouted down to the old man, who was pretending not to be looking up and asked, 'Sir, I'll bet yours is raisin, too?'

The old gentleman replied, 'No, it isn't, but it is starting to twitch.'

****

A shy young student had been asked out for a date by a particularly good-looking and intelligent bloke from the college. She was determined not to look stupid and spent much of the time before the evening reading the quality newspapers and brushing up on her political and philosophical viewpoints. The pair met in the Student Union bar.

'Two pints,' ordered the bloke.

Not to be outdone the girl said, 'Two pints for me, too, please.'

****

A bloke's giving head to a woman. 'My word! You've got a large vagina. My word! You've got a large vagina,' he says.

'There's no need to say it twice,' says the woman.

'I didn't,' says the man.

****

A sheep farmer was very concerned because none of his sheep were producing offspring. He was chatting with a neighbouring farmer who told him that he had the horniest ram in the world and would give him a lend of the beast.

'But how will I know if it's worked?' asked the first farmer.

'Well,' said the second, 'if, in the morning, your sheep are at the top of the hill, they're pregnant. If they're at the bottom, they're not.'

So the very next morning the farmer loaded his sheep into his truck and took them round to his neighbour's farm. After leaving them for a good while he took them back home and the next morning looked out of the window. He was dismayed to find his flock at the bottom of the hill, so he loaded them into the truck again and took them back round to his neighbour's. This time he left them even longer, but the following morning when he looked out of the window they were still at the bottom of the hill. Hoping it would be third time lucky, he set off for his neighbour's farm again and this time left the sheep with the ram for what seemed like an age. The following morning he couldn't bring himself to look out of the window so he asked his wife to do so.

'Are the sheep at the bottom of the hill?' he asked her.

'No,' she replied.

'So are they at the top of the hill?' he asked excitedly.

'No,' she replied.

'Well, where are they then?' he said.

'They're in the truck,' said his wife, 'and one of them is honking the horn.'

****

Two fleas are chatting in an airport lounge. 'That's a nasty cold you've got there,' says one.

'Yeah,' says the other. 'I nestled down in a biker's moustache and must have caught it as he was driving along here.'

'Listen,' said the first. 'You should do what I do and find a stewardess. Hole up in her pubic hair and you'll be nice and warm.'

The following week the two fleas meet up again and the one with the cold is no better. 'Why didn't you do what I suggested and find a stewardess?' said the first.

'I did,' said the other, 'but before I knew it I was back in the biker's moustache.'

****

An ant and an elephant get it together and have a fantastic night of non-stop sex. Unfortunately, when the ant wakes up in the morning, the elephant is dead.

'Oh shit,' moaned the ant. 'I get one night of heaven and a life-time digging a grave.'

****

Two guys are driving out in the country when their car breaks down. After a look in the engine one of them decided that if they can get some Vaseline they might just make it to the next garage. So they head off to the farmhouse in the distance.

It just so happens that in the farmhouse the farmer, his wife and two daughters are having an argument about who should hang out the washing. Eventually the father decides that the next person who speaks shall do the chore.

At that moment the two guys arrive and knock on the door. There's no reply, so they go in. They try to introduce themselves to the family but get no response and so, reckoning the family are deaf and dumb, start fooling around with one of the daughters. Before long they've both shagged her and move on to the other daughter and then the mother.

Suddenly one of them remembers why they came to the house in the first place.

'Do you have any Vaseline?' he asks.

'Right, that's it,' says the father. 'I'll hang the washing out.'

****

A Doberman and a poodle are at the vet's. 'What are you here for?' asks the poodle.

'Well,' says the Doberman. 'The other day I got really horny. So I fucked the pillow, I fucked the mattress, I fucked the settee, I fucked the letter box, and then I ran outside and fucked every bitch in the area. Now I'm being neutered. What about you?'

'Well,' says the poodle. 'I also got really horny the other day. I fucked the pillow, I fucked the mattress, I fucked a piece of meat in the kitchen and then I fucked my master's wife who was doing the dishes.'

'So you're going to be neutered, too?' says the Doberman.

'No,' replies the poodle. 'I'm here for a manicure.'

****

A guy goes to a brothel with only a fiver in his pocket.

'I'm sorry, sir,' says the madam. ' The only thing we've got for a fiver is a goat.'

Reluctantly, the guy agrees and goes off to give the kid a damn fine rogering. A week later he's back, but this time he's only got a pound on him.

'I'm sorry, sir,' says the madam, 'but for a pound the only thing we've got is a peep show.'

So he goes in and discovers lots of blokes watching a man toss off a donkey.

'Christ,' says the guy, 'I've never seen anything like this before.'

'You should have been here last week,' says the bloke next to him. 'There was a guy in there shagging a goat.'

****

Dave the lad has struck it lucky with a bit of well posh tottie. They've been going out together for three months when he gets invited round to her parents' house for dinner. He puts on his best clobber and sitting nervously at the table, is trying his hardest to be polite and courteous.

The first course is a particularly heavy soup, after which Dave has a terrible desire to fart. Much as he tries to hold it in, out comes the slightest of bottom burps.

'Rover!' shouts his girlfriend's dad, and to Dave's immense relief he spots a large dog lying under the table.

'Fucking brilliant,' thinks Dave. 'The old boy thinks it was the dog. I'm in the clear.'

The second course is also very heavy with all the trimmings and once again Dave has to fart afterwards. This time though he lets one rip with rather more bravado.

'Rover!' shouts the Dad again. By now Dave is well relaxed and after the pudding throws caution to the wind and lets rip with a real earbuster.

'Rover!' shouts the Dad. 'Get out of there before he shits on you!'

****

They set up the greatest whorehouse in the world. On the ground floor are the French beauties. On the first floor are the Swedish nymphettes. On the second floor are the African Amazons and on the third floor is the whore of whores. The first customer is this big stud. He pays his money and goes in. After half an hour they go to find him. The French beauties are all exhausted and the guy is crawling up the stairs to the Swedish nymphettes.

The next customer is an even bigger stud who pays his money and goes in. After half an hour, they find him halfway up the stairs heading towards the African Amazons, gasping for air.

The third customer is the biggest man-mountain in the world. He slaps his money on the table and struts in. Half an hour later they find him scratching at the door of the whore of whores, on his last legs.

The next bloke to come in is a little geezer with glasses. After they've stopped laughing they take his money and give him five minutes before going to find him. On the ground floor the French beauties are packing their bags and leaving. The Swedish nymphettes on the first floor are aching all over, the African Amazons are hanging out of the windows for air and they find the whore of whores cowering in the corner of her room.

'My God,' they say. 'Where's the little geezer?'

'He's out on the balcony,' whispers the whore of whores, 'having a wank.'

****

Pierre the French fighter pilot was holding his gilrfriend Marie in an amorous embrace. Suddenly, he pulls away from her and pours red wine over her lips.

'Pierre, Pierre, what are you doing?' she demands.

'I am Pierre the French fighter pilot and before I taste red meat, I must taste red wine,' he replies.

As things get saucier, Pierre ripped off Marie's blouse and pours white wine over her breasts.

'Pierre, Pierre, what are you doing?' demands Marie again.

'I am Pierre the French fighter pilot and before I taste white meat, I must taste white wine,' he replies.

As things get even steamier Marie was begging Pierre to go down on her when he ripped off her panties, poured brandy between her legs and lit it.

'Pierre, Pierre, what are you doing?' screamed Marie.

'I am Pierre the French fighter pilot,' said Pierre. 'And when I go down, I go down in flames.'

****

A dumb blonde goes in to the doctor's office for a pregnancy test. A short time later, the doctor returns with the results.

'Yes, madam, you're pregnant!' he announces, beaming.

The dumb blonde is stunned. 'Oh my God,' she says, 'is it mine?'

****

A fantastic-looking woman was walking down the road in the tightest of tight body-hugging jeans one day. It was amazing that she could actually walk in them. Eventually a plucky geezer went up to her and asked, 'Your trousers are incredible. How could anyone get into them?'

'Well,' replied the woman, 'you could start by buying me a drink.'

****

Two mates were chatting down the pub one day. 'You know, no matter what type of girl I bring home, my mother always disapproves and hates her,' complained the one guy.

'I'll tell you what,' said his mate. 'Find a bird who is just like your mum in looks and personality. She can't hate her then.'

A couple of weeks later they meet up again. 'Did you find a bird just like your mum?' asked the one lad.

'Yeah, I did. It was uncanny. She even spoke and dressed like her,' said the other.

'So, what happened?' said the first lad.

'Oh,' replied the second lad, 'when I got her home, my dad hated her.'

****

An irate woman rang up her local vet in the middle of the night and asked him if he could do anything about a dog and a bitch who were making a lot of noise hard at it in her garden.

'Why don't you try telling them they're wanted on the phone?' suggested the vet through slightly clenched teeth.

'Do you think that'll stop them?' asked the woman.

'Well, it worked on me,' replied the vet.

****

An attractive secretary walks into her boss's office and announces that she has some good news and some bad news. Harassed, the boss angrily snaps, 'Look, I haven't got much time today, just tell me the good news.'

'OK then,' says the secretary, 'the good news is that you're not shooting blanks.'

****

Billy goes to the doctor and says, 'Doc, I'm having trouble getting my penis erect. Can you help me?'

After a complete examination the doctor tells Billy that the problem with him is that the muscles around the base of his penis are damaged.

There is nothing he can do for him unless he's willing to try an experimental treatment. Billy asks sadly, 'What is the treatment?'

'Well,' the doctors explains, 'what we would do is take the muscles from the trunk of a baby elephant and implant them in your penis.'

Billy thinks about it for a while then decides that the thought of going through life without ever having sex again is too much, and tells the doctor to go for it.

A few weeks after the operation Billy is given the green light to use his improved equipment. So he plans a romantic evening with this girl that he's been meaning to ask out for a while but didn't dare to until now.

They go to this very nice restaurant in the city. In the middle of dinner Billy feels a stirring between his legs that continues to the point of being uncomfortable. To release the pressure, he unzips his fly under the table thinking nobody is going to see it anyway, but his penis immediately springs from his trousers, grabs a roll from the table and returns to his gaping fly.

His date was completely stunned at first but then says with a sly smile, 'That was incredible! Can you do that again?'

To which Billy replied, 'Well, I guess so, but I don't think I can fit another roll up my arse.'

✳✳✳✳

Running Bear finally woke up one morning to discover that he was a man. As such, he deduced, he would require a woman. So he trekked on over to the Medicine Man's teepee to requisition a woman.

'What you want, Running Bear?' queried the Medicine Man.

'Running Bear want woman!'

'Hmmm,' said the Medicine Man, 'do you know what to do with a woman once you've got her?'

'Uh,' said Running Bear, 'no…'

'Then go into the woods for two months. Find a tree with a hole in it, and practice on the tree. Once you have perfected your technique with the tree, come back to me and I will give you a woman.'

Running Bear agreed, and set off into the woods. Sure enough, he found a tree with the appropriately sized hole, and began his two months of practice.

Two months later, he returned to the Medicine Man with pride in his eyes. 'OK,' he said to the Medicine Man, 'me know what to do. Give me woman.'

The Medicine Man nodded and brought a pretty young squaw from the back of the teepee. 'Little Flower,' he said to her, 'you now belong to Running Bear. Do as he asks.'

Running Bear and Little Flower then retire to a vacant teepee where Running Bear instructs her to bend over. She shrugs and complies. Running Bear then gives her a swift kick in the arse.

'Hey!' cried Little Flower. 'What did you do that for?'

'Me no stupid,' explained Running Bear. 'Me check for bees first.'

✳✳✳✳

A young woman in a REALLY skimpy skirt was at the bus stop. When the bus arrived and the doors opened she tried to climb the steps. However, her skirt was too tight and her legs couldn't move. So, she reached behind her and undid her zip. She tried to step up again, and still couldn't, so she reached behind again and played with the zip. She tried to climb the steps again, but still no luck. So, she reached behind again, but a pair of strong hands picked her up and placed her on the top step.

'What do you think you're doing?' she asked the guy behind her.

'Well, I figured the second time you undid my fly we were at least good friends!'

✳✳✳✳

One evening after attending the theatre, two men were walking down the street when they saw a well-dressed, attractive young woman walking just ahead of them. One turned to the other and said, 'I'd give 50 quid to spend the night with that woman.'

To their surprise, the woman turned and said, 'I'll take you up on that.'

After bidding his friend goodnight the man accompanied the woman to her apartment, where they immediately went to bed. The following morning the man presented her with 25 quid as he prepared to leave.

'If you don't give me the other 25 quid I'll sue you for it,' said the woman.

The man just laughed and said, 'I'd like to see you get it on these grounds.'

The next day he was surprised when he was served with a summons ordering his presence in court as defendant. He hurried to his lawyer and explained the details of the case.

His lawyer said, 'She can't possibly get a judgement against you on such grounds, but it will be interesting to see how her case will be presented.'

After the usual preliminaries, the woman's lawyer addressed the court as follows: 'Your Honour, my client is the owner of a piece of property, a garden spot surrounded by a profuse growth of shrubbery, which property she agreed to rent to the defendant for a specified length of time for the sum of £50. The defendant took possession of the property, used it extensively for the purpose for which it was rented, but upon evacuating the premises tendered only £25. The rent is not excessive since it was restricted property, and we ask judgment to be granted against the defendant to assure payment of the balance.'

The defendant's lawyer was impressed and amused at the way the case had been presented. His defence was therefore somewhat altered from what he had planned.

'Your Honour,' he responded, 'my client agrees the young lady has a fine piece of property, for a degree of pleasure was derived from the transaction. However, my client found a well on the property, around which he placed his own stones, sank a shaft and erected a pump, all labour being personally performed by him. We claim these improvements to the property are sufficient to offset the unpaid balance, and that the plaintiff was adequately compensated for the rental of the said property. We therefore ask that the judgment not be granted.'

The young woman's lawyer's comeback was this: 'Your Honour, my client agrees that the defendant did find a well on the property, and he did make improvements such as described by my opponent; however, had the defendant not known the well existed, he would never have rented the property; also, on evacuating the premises, the defendant moved the stones, pulled out the shaft and took the pump with him. In so doing he not only dragged his equipment through the shrubbery, but left the hole much larger than it was prior to his occupancy, making it easily accessible to little children. We therefore ask that judgment be granted.'

****

There once was a man who had three girlfriends, and he couldn't decide which one to marry. He decided to give £5,000 to each woman to see what she would do with it. The first woman bought new clothes for herself. She got an expensive new hairdo, a massage, a facial, a manicure, and a pedicure. She said, 'I spent the money so that I would look pretty for you because I love you so much.'

The second woman bought a VCR, a CD player, a set of golf clubs and a tennis racket and gave them to the man. 'I used the money to buy you these gifts because I love you,' she told him.

The third woman invested the money in the stock market and within a short time had doubled her investment. She returned the initial £5,000 to the man and reinvested the profit. 'I'm investing in our future because I love you so much,' she said.

The man carefully considered how each woman had spent the money, and then married the woman with the biggest tits.

****

We all know how Cinderella wanted to go to the ball but her wicked stepmother wouldn't let her and then the fairy godmother pops up and gives Cinderella some good news. The fairy godmother tells Cinderella that she'll provide everything she needs to go to the ball, but only on two conditions.

Cinderella asks what she needs to do and the fairy godmother replies, 'First, you must wear a diaphragm.'

Cinderella's mouth drops open and says, 'You must be crazy! I'm on the pill, and I don't need to wear a diaphragm.'

The fairy godmother reminds Cinderella about all the handsome princes that will be attending the ball that night, and Cinderella agrees to wear a diaphragm.

'Well, what's the second condition?' Cinderella asks.

The fairy godmother replies, 'You must be back home by 2am.'

Well, Cinderella explains that if she's gonna party with the princes, she wants to be out all night long. The fairy godmother tells Cinderella that if she's not home by 2am, then her diaphragm will turn into a pumpkin and reminds her that at least she'll be with the princes most of the evening, so Cinderella agrees to be home at 2am.

At 2am, Cinderella doesn't show up. By 3am, there's still no Cinderella. By 4am, still no Cinderella… finally, at 5am, Cinderella shows up at the door with a huge grin on her face.

The fairy godmother stands up and looks at Cinderella and says, 'Where the hell have you been? Your diaphragm was supposed to turn into a pumpkin three hours ago!!!'

Cinderella tells the fairy godmother that she met a prince and he took care of it for her. The fairy godmother wonders about a prince with this type of power and asks Cinderella his name – to which she sheepishly replies, 'Peter, Peter the pumpkin-eater.'

****

Jill was sitting around with her mum, waiting for a bus, on a particularly cold day. When Jill started to complain her mother told her the way to get warm and to be very lady-like is to put your hands between your legs so that they can warm up. Jill tried this, and was amazed at how well it did warm her hands.

A month later Jill and her boyfriend, Paul, were parked up at Lover's Leap when Jill started to feel the cold. Again, very lady-like, she placed her hands together and put them between her legs. Quite bewildered, her boyfriend asked what she was doing, So Jill explained how it warms your hands. Fifteen minutes later Paul starts rubbing his hands together and complaining about the cold... Jill gently takes his hands and very lady-like places them between her legs. Ten minutes later Paul starts rubbing his nose saying how cold it feels. After a short time Paul complains how his penis is so cold it has gone stiff...

The next morning Jill's mother asks how she coped with the cold night. 'Fine, mum,' she replied, 'but penises make a right mess when they thaw out, don't they?'

****

King Arthur was getting ready to go on a quest, but was worried about leaving Queen Guinevere alone with all the horny knights of the Round Table. So he went to Merlin the Magician for advice.

After explaining his problem to Merlin, the wizard thought about the problem for a while and then told the king to come back in a week and he would have a solution to the problem.

The next week the king returned to Merlin to see the new invention. It was a chastity belt, except that it had a rather large hole in the most obvious place.

'This is no good,' said the king . 'Look at this opening. How is this supposed to protect the queen?'

'Ah sire, just observe,' said Merlin as he pulled out an old wand that he was going to throw away. Merlin then inserted the wand into the hole in the chastity belt whereupon a guillotine blade came down and cut the wand neatly in two halves.

'Merlin, you are a genius. Now I can leave knowing that my Queen is fully protected,' said the king.

After putting Guinevere in the device, King Arthur then set out on his quest. Several years later the King returned to Camelot. Immediately, the king assembled all the Knights of the Round Table into the courtyard and had them drop their trousers for inspection. Sure enough every knight was either amputated or damaged in some way, all except for Sir Galahad.

'Sir Galahad, you are the one and only true knight. What is in my power to grant you? Name it and it is yours,' said the King.

Sir Galahad was speechless.

****

A doctor was giving a talk on safe sex and was asking the class who had sex once a week. Most of the hands went up. He then asked who had it once a month. A few hands went up. This went on for a while until the doctor noticed that only one man had not put his hand up.

'And how often do you have sex?' asked the doctor.

'Once every two years,' replied the man happily.

'Once every two years!!' said the doctor. 'You don't seem too unhappy.'

'Well, tonight's the night!' replied the man.

****

A new recruit arrived in a remote fort in the desert for his first day in the French Foreign Legion. He asked the sergeant what the men did for recreation. 'You'll see soon enough,' said the sergeant.

A week later, 300 camels were herded in to a corral and the men went wild trying to fuck the camels.

The new recruit was a bit stunned. 'Why do the men rush?' he asked. 'There are hundreds of camels and only 50 men.'

'That is true,' said the sergeant. 'But do you want to be stuck with the ugly one?'

****

An agent discovered that his leading actress had been selling her body. Having long lusted after her, he asked if he could have a go as well. She said to him, 'OK, but you'll have to pay the same as everyone else.'

He thought this was a bit unfair but agreed and met at her flat later that night. He turned the lights out and they fucked. She fell asleep. Ten minutes later he woke her up and fucked her again. This went on for two hours.

She was amazed at her agent's vitality.

'I never knew agents were so virile,' she said to him.

'I'm not your agent,' came the reply. 'He's at the door selling tickets.'

****

An 84-year-old man went to a famous brothel. 'I want a girl please,' he said.

'I'm sorry?' said the receptionist.

'I want a girl, please,' said the old man.

'How old are you?' said the receptionist.

'Eighty-four,' he replied.

'Eighty-four? You've had it,' she said.

'Oh, have I?' said the old man. 'How much do I owe you?'

****

A blonde gets on an airplane and sits down in the first-class section. The stewardess tells her she must move to economy because she doesn't have a first-class ticket. The blonde replies, 'I'm blonde, I'm smart, I have a good job and I'm staying in first class until we reach Jamaica.'

The stewardess gets the head stewardess who asks the woman to leave and she says, 'I'm blonde, I'm smart, I have a good job and I'm staying in first class until we reach Jamaica.'

The stewardesses don't know what to do because they have to get the rest of the passengers seated to take off, so they get the co-pilot. The co-pilot goes up to the blonde and whispers in her ear. She immediately gets up and goes to her seat in the economy section.

The head stewardess asks the co-pilot what he said to get her to move. The co-pilot replies, 'I told her the front half of the airplane wasn't going to Jamaica.'

****

One day this fellow noticed that a new couple had moved into the house next door. He was also quick to notice that the woman liked to sunbathe in the back garden, usually in a skimpy bikini that showed off her magnificent breasts. He made it a point to water and trim his lawn as much as possible, hoping for yet another look. Finally, he could stand it no more. Walking to the front door of the new neighbour's house, he knocked and waited. The husband, a large, burly man, opened the door.

'Excuse me,' our man stammered, 'but I couldn't help noticing how beautiful your wife is.'

'Yeah? So?' his hulking neighbour replied.

'Well, in particular, I'm really struck by how beautiful her breasts are. I would gladly pay you £10,000 if I could kiss them.'

The burly gorilla is about to deck our poor guy when his wife appears and stops him. She pulls him inside and they discuss the offer for a few moments. Finally, they return and ask our friend to step inside.

'OK,' the husband says gruffly, 'for ten thousand quid you can kiss my wife's tits.'

At this the wife unbuttons her blouse, and the twin objects of desire hang free at last. Our man takes one in each hand, and proceeds to rub his face against them in total ecstasy. This goes on for several minutes, until the husband gets annoyed.

'Well, come on, kiss them!' he growls.

'I can't,' replies our awe-struck hero, still nuzzling away.

'Why not?' demands the husband, getting really angry now.

'I don't have ten thousand quid.'

✳✳✳✳

It was a cold, dark winter night (aren't they all?), and this is woman driving home through the countryside, when suddenly she her tire blows out and she has to stop the car. Since it's late and she doesn't relish the thought of changing the wheel, she walks to a nearby farmhouse to ask if she can stay the night and phone a garage in the morning to fix the car. The farmer agrees to let her stay in his house as long as she doesn't touch the farmers' two sons.

The farmer explains that his wife has died when the boys were young and due to the farm's isolation, the two, who are now young men, have never seen a woman at close quarters before. So the woman goes to bed and halfway through the night, she starts to feel quite randy, and decides to pay one of the lads a visit.

Now, being a careful and sensible woman, she gives him a condom to wear, telling him it will prevent her from getting pregnant. After they make love she goes back to bed. Unfortunately, soon afterwards, she gets the urge again, and goes to see the other son. Once again giving him a condom to wear, they make love.

The next morning she thanks the farmer for his hospitality and phones the garage and goes on her way. Three months later the two sons are working in the fields together, and they discuss their experience with the woman.

The youngest son asks the eldest son, 'Do you really care if that woman gets pregnant?'

'No, not at all,' replies the eldest.

'Well, why don't we take off these damn rubber things, then?'

✳✳✳✳

This bloke took a blind date to a fair. They went for a ride on the Ferris wheel. The ride completed, she seemed rather bored. 'What would you like to do next?' he asked.

'I wanna get weighed,' she said.

So the bloke took her over to the guess-your-weight.

'Eight stone,' said the man at the scale, and he was absolutely right.

Next they rode the roller-coaster. After that, he bought her some popcorn and some candyfloss, then he asked what else she would like to do.

'I wanna get weighed,' she sighed. I really latched on to a saddo tonight, thought the young man, and using the excuse that he had developed a headache, he took the girl home.

The girl's mother was surprised to see her home so early, and asked, 'What's wrong, dear? Didn't you have a nice time tonight?'

'Wousy,' said the girl.

****

Two engineering students meet on campus one day. The first engineer calls out to the other, 'Hey, nice bike! Where did you get it?'

'Well,' replies the other, 'I was walking to a lecture the other day when this pretty young student rides up on this bike. She jumps off, takes off all of her clothes, and says 'You can have ANYTHING you want!!'

'Clever,' says the first, 'her clothes wouldn't have fitted you anyway.'

****

Q: What's the difference between a vitamin and a hormone?
A: You can't hear a vitamin.

****

Q: How do blonde braincells die?
A: Alone.

****

Q: Why is a blonde like a turtle?
A: They both get fucked up when they're on their back.

****

Q: Why are blondes bad with cattle?
A: Because they can't keep two calves together!

****

Q: Why do blondes have orgasms?
A: So they know when to stop having sex!

****

Man: You should learn to iron, then we could do without the ironing lady.
Blonde wife: Well, if you would learn to fuck me properly we could do without the gardener.

****

Q: How can you tell that a blonde's having a bad day.
A: She has a Tampax tucked behind her ear, and she can't find her pencil.

****

Q: Why do men like blonde jokes?
A: Because they can understand them.

****

Q: What kind of clothes are there?
Woman replies: Clean and dirty
Man replies: Clean, almost clean, sort of clean, not bad, dirty, really dirty, pretty shitty, nasty and smelly, really, really shitty. Men will voluntarily wear all but the last of these clothes listed.

****

Q: How was Colonel Sanders a typical male?
A: All he cared about were legs, breasts, and thighs.

****

Q: What would men do if they had breasts?
A: They'd stay at home and play with them all day.

****

Q: Why do men find it difficult to make eye contact?
A: Breasts don't have eyes.

****

Q: Why do men get paid twice as much to complete the same job?
A: The woman can do it right the first time.

****

Q: How can you tell if a man is sexually excited?
A: He's breathing.

****

Q. What did the Leper say to the Hooker?
A. Keep the tip

****

Q: How do you get a blonde pregnant?
A: Come on her shoes and let the flies do the rest.

****

Q: Why did the pervert cross the road?
A: To get to the chicken!

****

Q: What's an Essex girl's favourite wine?
A: 'I wanna go to Spaiiiiiiiiiin.

Chapter 8
On The Wagon

Now, strange as it may seem, there are non-alcoholic drinks available in a pub. And, incredibly, some people do choose to drink them. Now, for most folk the only time they consider getting within a hundred miles of an orange juice is if they're having a bad acid trip or if it's mixed with some other highly alcoholic beverage, but there are those who, because they've overdone it a bit in the past or are only aged nine and are in one of those pubs that allow children in, undergo a more sedate pub experience altogether.

Not for them the deep belly laughs and bits of dribble down the shirt-front of the full, raucous, pissed night out. Their evening is one of gentle banter and amusing jokes, that neither offend nor insult. Incredibly, such jokes do actually exist...

****

'Jimmy, did your mother help you with your homework last night?' the teacher asked.

'No, she did it all,' he replied.

****

Two guys are walking in the jungle. One is carrying a lamp-post, the other one has a telephone box. 'Why are you carrying a telephone box?' the first one asked.

'When the lions come,' says the second, 'I'll put it down, get inside it and I'll be saved'

'Oh,' says the first.

'And why are you carrying a lamp-post?' asks the one carrying the telephone box. 'When the lions come,' he replies, 'I'll throw it away, so I can run faster.'

****

A teacher was working with a group of underprivileged children, trying to broaden their horizons through sensory exploration. With their eyes closed, they would feel objects from pumice stones to pine cones and smell aromatic herbs and exotic fruits. Then one day, the teacher brought in a great variety of boiled sweets, more flavours than you could ever imagine.

'Children, I'd like you to close your eyes and taste these,' announced the teacher. Without difficulty, they managed to identify the taste of cherries, lemons and mint, but when the teacher had them put honey-flavoured sweets in their mouths, every one of the children was stumped.

'I'll give you a hint,' said the teacher. 'It's something your daddy and mummy probably call each other all the time.'

Instantly, one of the children spat the sweet out of his mouth and shouted, 'Ugh... they're arseholes.'

****

While crossing the US-Mexican border on his bicycle, this man was stopped by a guard who pointed to two sacks the man had on his shoulders. 'What's in the bags?' asked the guard.

'Sand,' said the cyclist.

'Get them off – we'll take a look,' said the guard.

The cyclist did as he was told, emptied the bags, and proving they contained nothing but sand, reloaded the bags, put them on his shoulders and continued across the border.

Two weeks later, the same thing happened. Again the guard demanded to see the two bags, which again contained nothing but sand. This went on every week for six months, until one day the cyclist with the sand bags failed to appear.

A few days later, the guard happened to meet the cyclist downtown. 'Say friend, you sure have us beat,' said the guard. 'We know you're smuggling something across the border. I promise I won't say a word, please tell me what it is?'

'Bicycles!' replied the man.

****

Three bulls heard via the grapevine that the farmer was going to bring yet another bull on to the farm, and the prospect raised a discussion amongst them.

'Boys,' said the first bull, 'we all know I've been here five years. Once we settled our differences, we agreed on which 100 of the cows would be mine. Now, I don't know where this newcomer is going to get HIS cows, but I'm not giving him any of mine.'

'That pretty much says it for me, too,' says the second bull. 'I've been here three years and have earned my right to the 50 cows we've agreed are mine. I'll fight him till I run him off or kill him, but I'M KEEPING ALL MY COWS.'

'I've only been here a year,' says the third bull, 'and so far you guys have only let me have 10 cows. I may not be as big as you fellows yet, but I am young and virile, so I simply MUST keep all MY cows.'

They'd just finished their big talk when an 18-wheel lorry pulls up in the middle of the pasture with only ONE ANIMAL IN IT. The biggest bull these guys had ever seen!

'You know,' says the first bull, 'it's actually been some time since I really felt I was doing all my cows justice, anyway. I think I can spare a few for our new friend.'

'I'll have plenty of cows to take care of if I just stay on the opposite end of the pasture from HIM,' says the second bull. 'I'm certainly not looking for an argument.'

They look over at their young friend, the third bull, and find him pawing the dirt, shaking his horns, and snorting the bull's equivalent of 'Stay away from my bird.'

'Son,' says the first bull, 'let me give you some advice. Let him have some of your cows and live to tell about it.'

'Hold on, mate,' says the third bull, 'he can have ALL MY COWS. I'm just making sure he knows I'M a bull!'

****

Waiter, there's a dead fly in my soup!
Yes sir, I expect it's the hot water that kills them.

****

Waiter, there's a fly in my soup!
Keep it down, sir, or they'll all be wanting one.

****

Waiter, what's this fly doing in my soup?
It's fly soup sir!

****

Waiter, what's this fly doing in my soup?
Um, looks to me to be backstroke, sir...

****

Waiter, there's a fly in my soup!
Don't worry sir, the spider on the bread roll will get him.

****

Waiter, there's a fly in my soup!
No sir, that's a cockroach, the fly is on your steak.

****

Waiter, this coffee tastes like dirt!
Yes, sir, that's because it was ground this morning.

****

Waiter, what is this stuff?

That's bean salad sir.

I know what it's been, but what is it now?

****

Waiter: And how did you find your steak sir?

Well, I just rolled a pea over, and there it was!

****

Two hunters got a helicopter pilot to fly them into the highlands for deer hunting. They were quite successful in their venture and bagged six big bucks. The pilot came back, as arranged, to pick them up. They started loading their gear into the chopper, including the deer. But the pilot objected, 'The chopper can only take four of your deer,' he said. 'You'll have to leave two behind.'

They argued with him; the year before they'd shot six and the pilot had allowed them to put all aboard. The helicopter was the same model and capacity. Reluctantly, the pilot finally allowed them to put all six aboard. But when they attempted to take off and leave the valley, the little chopper couldn't make it and they crashed into the wilderness.

Climbing out of the wreckage, one hunter said to the other, 'Do you know where we are?'

I think so,' replied the other hunter. 'Isn't this the same place we crashed last year?'

****

A customer was bothering the waiter in a restaurant. First he asked that the air conditioning be turned up because he was too hot, then he asked it be turned down because he was too cold, and so on for about half an hour.

Surprisingly, the waiter was very patient, he walked back and forth and never once got angry. Finally a second customer asked him why he didn't throw the git out.

'Oh, I don't care,' said the waiter with a smile, 'we don't even have an air conditioner.'

****

When Beethoven passed away, he was buried in a churchyard. A couple of days later, the town drunk was walking through the cemetery and heard some strange noises coming from the area where Beethoven was buried.

Terrified, the drunk ran and got the priest to come and listen to it. The priest bent close to the grave and heard some faint, unrecognisable music coming from the grave.

Frightened, the priest ran and got the town magistrate. When the magistrate arrived, he bent his ear to the grave, listened for a moment, and said, 'Ah, yes, that's Beethoven's Ninth Symphony, being played backwards.' He listened a while longer, and said, 'There's the Eighth Symphony, and it's backwards, too. Most puzzling.' So, the magistrate kept listening; 'There's the Seventh... the Sixth... the Fifth...'

Suddenly, the realisation of what was happening dawned on the magistrate; he stood up and announced to the crowd that had gathered in the cemetery, 'My fellow citizens, there's nothing to worry about. It's just Beethoven decomposing.'

****

Three convicts were going to be executed. As they went out, the first was given one last request. He pointed behind the firing range and shouted, 'Tornado,' and when the firing squad looked round he ran away.

When the second took up his position he was also given one last request. He pointed behind the firing squad and shouted, 'Hurricane,' and he too ran away.

Sadly, the third one didn't get away. When he was given a last request, he pointed behind the squad and shouted, 'Fire!'

A waiter brings the customer the steak he ordered with his thumb over the meat. 'What the hell are you doing holding on to my dinner like that?' screamed the customer.

'What?' answers the waiter, 'You want it to fall on the floor again?'

****

Long ago, when sailing ships ruled the waves, a captain and his crew were in danger of being boarded by a pirate ship. As the crew became frantic, the captain bellowed to his First Mate, 'Bring me my red shirt!'

The First Mate quickly retrieved the captain's red shirt, which the captain put on and led the crew to battle the pirate boarding party.

Although some casualties occurred among the crew, the pirates were repelled.

Later that day, the lookout screamed that there were two pirate vessels sending boarding parties. The crew cowered in fear, but the captain, calm as ever, bellowed, 'Bring me my red shirt!' And once again the Captain and his crew repelled the boarding parties, although this time more casualties occurred.

Weary from the battles, the men sat around on deck that night recounting the day's occurrences when an ensign looked to the captain and asked, 'Sir, why did you call for your red shirt before the battle?'

The Captain, giving the ensign a look that only a captain can give, exhorted, 'If I am wounded in battle, the red shirt does not show the wound, and thus, you men will continue to fight unafraid.'

The men sat in silence marvelling at the courage of such a man. As dawn came the next morning, the lookout screamed that there were pirate ships, ten of them, all with boarding parties on their way. The men became silent and looked to the captain, their leader, for his usual command. The captain, calm as ever, bellowed, 'Bring me my brown trousers!'

****

Two atoms were walking down the street when they bumped into each other. 'Are you OK?' asked the first one.

'No,' replied the second. 'I lost an electron!'

'Are you sure?' asked the first one.

'I'm positive!' replied the second.

****

So there's this magician working on a small cruise ship. He's been doing his routines every night for a year or two now. The audiences appreciate him, and they change over often enough for him not to worry too much about new tricks. However, there's this parrot who sits in the back row and watches him night after night, year after year.

Finally, the parrot figures out how the tricks work and starts giving it away for the audience. For example, when the magician makes a bouquet of flowers disappear, the parrot squawks, 'Behind his back! Behind his back!'

Well, the magician gets really annoyed at this, but he doesn't know what to do. The parrot belongs to the captain, so he can't just kill it. One day, the ship springs a leak and sinks. The magician manages to swim to a plank of wood floating by and grabs on. The parrot is sitting on the other end of the plank. They just stare at each other and drift. They drift for three days and still don't speak. On the morning of the fourth day, the parrot looks over at the magician and says, 'OK, I give up. Where did you hide the ship?'

****

During camouflage training, a private disguised as a tree trunk had made a sudden move that was spotted by a visiting general.

'You simpleton!' the officer barked. 'Don't you know that by jumping and shouting the way you did, you could have endangered the lives of the entire company?'

'Yes sir,' the solder answered apologetically. 'But, if I may say so, I did stand still when a flock of pigeons used me for target practice. And I never

215

moved a muscle when a large dog pissed on my lower branches. But when two squirrels ran up my trouser leg and I heard the bigger say, "Let's eat one now and save the other until winter," that did it.'

****

Two rhinos have been in a cage at the zoo for 10 years when one turns to the other and says, 'Do you know, we've been in this cage for all this time and I don't even know your name.'

'It's Neil,' replies the other.

'Not Rhino Neil?' says the first.

****

Two elephants fell off a cliff. Boom, boom.

****

A guy goes into a pet shop and asks for a wasp. The owner tells him they don't sell wasps, to which the man says, 'Well, you've got one in the window.'

****

Luke Skywalker and Darth Vader are fighting with the light sabres. To put Luke off Darth says, 'Luke, I am your Father.'

'I don't believe you,' says Luke.

'I can prove it,' says Darth.

'OK, prove it then,' says Luke.

'I know what you're getting for Christmas,' says Darth.

'How do you know?' says Luke.

'Because, Luke, I've felt your presents.' says Darth.

****

A sausage walks into pub and asks for a pint. The landlord says, 'Sorry, we don't serve food.'

****

One ghost says to the other, 'How long have you been dead?'
'Six foot two, the same as when I was alive,' says the other.

****

In a restaurant. 'Waiter, why is there a small coffin floating in my wine?'
'Well you did order something with a little body, sir.'

****

Have you heard about the rude ghost?
She goes bum in the night.

****

Man at the restaurant. 'Waiter, there's a dead vampire bat in my meal.'
'Yes, sir, it's the steak that kills them.'

****

Guy goes into a fish shop and says, 'I'd like a piece of cod, please.'
Fishmonger says, 'It won't be long sir.'
'Well, it had better be fat then,' replies the guy.

****

Two peanuts walking down the road. One's assaulted.

****

Two flies were on a lavatory seat. One got pissed off.

****

This guy goes to a camel salesman and says, 'I want to buy a camel, please.'

The salesman hands him two bricks and says, 'This one here is very fast but you'll need these.'

The man asks why. The salesman says, ''Cos when you want the camel to go, you have to take the bricks, place them either side of the camel's balls and smash them together.'

The man asks, 'Doesn't it hurt?'

The salesman says, 'Only if you get your thumbs caught.'

****

There once was a young person named Red Riding Hood who lived with her mother on the edge of a large wood. One day her mother asked her to take a basket of fresh fruit and mineral water to her grandmother's house. Not because this was woman's work, mind you, but because the deed was generous and helped engender a feeling of community. Furthermore, her grandmother was not sick, but rather was in full physical and mental health and was fully capable of taking care of herself as a mature adult.

So, Red Riding Hood set off with her basket through the woods. Many people believed that the forest was a foreboding and dangerous place and never set foot in it. Red Riding Hood, however, was confident enough in her own budding sexuality that such obvious Freudian imagery did not intimidate her. On the way to Grandma's house, Red Riding Hood was accosted by a wolf who asked her what was in her basket. She replied, 'Some healthful snacks for my grandmother, who is certainly capable of taking care of herself as a mature adult.'

The wolf said, 'You know, my dear, it isn't safe for a little girl to walk through these woods alone.'

'I find your sexist remark offensive in the extreme,' said Red Riding Hood, 'but I will ignore it because of your traditional status as an outcast from society, the stress of which has caused you to develop your own, entirely valid, world view. Now, if you'll excuse me, I must be on my way.'

Red Riding Hood walked on along the main path. But, because his status outside society had freed him from slavish adherence to linear, Western-style thought, the wolf knew a quicker route to Grandma's house. He burst into the house and ate Grandma, an entirely valid course of action for a carnivore such as himself. Then, unhampered by rigid, traditionalist notions of what was masculine or feminine, he put on Grandma's night-clothes and crawled into bed.

Red Riding Hood entered the cottage and said, 'Grandma, I have brought you some fat-free, sodium-free snacks to salute you in your role of a wise and nurturing matriarch.'

From the bed, the wolf said softly, 'Come closer, child, so that I might see you.'

'Oh,' said Red Riding Hood, 'I forgot you are so optically challenged. Grandma, what big eyes you have!'

'They have seen much, and forgiven much, my dear,' said the wolf.

'Grandma,' said Red Riding Hood, 'what a big nose you have, only relatively, of course, and certainly attractive in its own way.'

'It has smelled much, and forgiven much, my dear,' said the wolf.

'Grandma, what big teeth you have!' said Red Riding Hood.

'I am happy with who I am and what I am,' said the wolf and leaped out of bed. He grabbed Red Riding Hood in his claws, intent on devouring her.

Red Riding Hood screamed, not out of alarm at the wolf's apparent tendency toward cross-dressing, but because of his wilful invasion of her personal space. Her screams were heard by a passing woodchopperperson (or solid-fuel technician, as he preferred to be called). When he burst into the cottage, he saw the mêlée and tried to intervene. But as he raised his axe, Red Riding Hood and the wolf both stopped.

'And just what do you think you're doing?' asked Red Riding Hood. The woodchopperperson blinked and tried to answer, but no words came to him. 'Bursting in here like a Neanderthal,' continued Red Riding Hood, 'trusting your weapon to do your thinking for you! Sexist! Speciesist! How dare you assume that women and wolves can't solve their own problems without a man's help!'

When she heard Red Riding Hood's impassioned speech, Grandma jumped out of the wolf's mouth, seized the woodchopperperson's axe, and cut his head off. After this ordeal, Red Riding Hood, Grandma, and the wolf felt a certain commonality of purpose. They decided to set up an alternative household based on mutual respect and co-operation, and they lived together in the woods happily ever after.

****

Man: Doctor, I've just swallowed a pillow.
Doctor: How do you feel?
Man: A little down in the mouth.

****

Did you hear about the paranoid with low self-esteem?
He thought that nobody important was out to get him.

****

Man: Doctor, I can't stop singing, 'The Green, Green Grass Of Home.'
Can you help me?'
    Doctor: Ah yes, you appear to be suffering from Tom Jones Syndrome.
    Man: Is it rare?
    Doctor: Well… it's not unusual.

****

A Mother and Father are talking about their son's school progress. 'So how did Peter do in his history exam?' asked the father.

'Not very well,' said his Mother, 'but then he can't really be blamed. A lot of the questions were about things that happened before he was born.'

****

Two women are talking. 'My youngest has trouble with eczema and asthma,' said one.

'Oh, that's nasty,' said the other. 'How did he get them?'

'He hasn't got them,' said the first woman. 'He just can't spell them.'

****

The teacher is handing back the class's homework. 'Johnny,' she says. 'Your homework is very poor. I really don't see how one person can make so many mistakes.'

'It wasn't one person, Miss,' says Johnny. 'My Dad helped me.'

****

A mother is shouting at her cheeky son. 'Stephen, just for once I'd like to go through a whole day without having to tell you off or punish you,' she shouts.

'OK, Mum,' says Stephen. 'You have my consent.'

****

Teacher to pupil: Tell me two pronouns.
Pupil: Who? Me?

****

The young kid went to the sweet shop. 'I want one of those all-day gobstoppers please,' he said. The shop assistant gave him one. 'Here,' said the kid. 'This looks smaller than the one I had before.'

'Well,' said the shop assistant. 'The days are getting shorter.'

****

A Hollywood actor was testifying in a court case. When asked to identify himself he said, 'I am the world's greatest actor.'

The next day his agent was talking to him. 'Don't you think that was a bit much yesterday?' he said.

'Not at all,' replied the actor. 'Don't forget I was under oath.'

****

A doctor is on the phone to a farmer, 'I'm sorry,' says the doc, 'but I can't come out to see you any more.'

'Why not?' asks the farmer.

'Because every time I come to your place your ducks insult me,' says the doctor.

****

Two goldfish are in a tank. One turns to the other and says, 'Do you know how to drive this thing?'

****

A tortoise goes to the police station to report being mugged by three snails. 'What happened?' says the policeman.

'I don't know,' says the tortoise. 'It was all so quick.'

****

A duck goes to a chemist and says, 'Can I have some lipsalve please?'

The chemist goes and gets it and says, 'Will you be paying cash?'

'No thanks,' says the duck, 'put it on my bill.'

****

A tortoise knocks on the door of this big house in winter. A gruff old geezer answers the door. 'What do you want?' he says.

'Please, sir,' says the tortoise, 'I'm so very cold. Can I come in and warm myself by your fire?'

'Certainly not,' says the man, and kicks the tortoise to the end of the garden.

Next Spring there's another knock at the door and the same man answers it. 'Yes?' he says.

'What did you do that for?' says the tortoise.

****

Two Moroccans are introduced to each other at a party. One says to the other, 'I'm sure we've met before. Your fez is very familiar.'

****

This kid walks into a general store one day and asks for a job. The owner tells him that he doesn't need any help. The kid is persistent so the bloke tells him to watch him when the next customer comes in. If he can do what he does, he'll give him a job.

A few minutes later a customer comes in. 'Good afternoon, sir. What can I do for you?'

The bloke says, 'I need some grass seed.' So the owner goes and gets it. When he gets back he says, 'How about a lawnmower to go with this?'

'What do I need a lawnmower for?'

'Well, when the grass grows you're going to need something to cut it with.'

'Yeah, OK, I'll take a lawnmower, too.'

After the customer's gone, the owner turns to the kid and said, 'That's how it's done. Can you do that?'

The kid says, 'Sure.'

So the next customer comes in and says, 'I need some Tampax.'

The kid says, 'Yes sir,' and goes to get them. When he gets back he says, 'Would you like a lawnmower to go with that?'

The bloke says, 'What the hell do I need a lawnmower for?'

The kid replies, 'You might as well cut the grass. Your weekend is shot, that's for sure…'

****

A mother was working in the kitchen and listening to her son playing with his new electric train in the living room. She heard the train stop and her son say, 'All of you fuckers who want to get off, get the fuck off now 'cos this is the last stop. And all of you fuckers who are getting on get your arses in the train 'cos we're leaving.'

The mother went into the living room and told her son, 'We don't use that kind of language in this house. Now I want you to go to your room for two hours. When you come out you may play with your train. But I want you to use nice language.'

Two hours later the son comes out of the bedroom and resumes playing with his train. Soon the train stops and the mother hears her son say, 'All passengers who are disembarking the train please remember to take all of your belongings with you. We thank you for riding with us today and hope your trip was a pleasant one. We hope you will ride with us again soon. For those of you just boarding we ask you to store all your luggage under your seat. Remember there is no smoking on this service. We hope you have a pleasant and relaxing journey with us… And for those of you who are pissed off about the two-hour delay, please see the bitch in the kitchen.'

****

A young lad was playing with his food one dinner time. 'Come on,' said his mum, 'eat up your greens. They'll make you big and strong.'

'Well, why don't you give them to Grandpa, then?' replied the boy.

****

Young Johnny turned up late for Sunday school one morning and the teacher wanted to know why. 'Well, I was going to go fishing, but my dad wouldn't let me,' said Johnny.

'I should think not,' replied the teacher. 'And did your father explain why you should not go fishing on this day?'

'Oh yeah,' said Johnny. 'He said he didn't have enough bait for both of us.'

****

One day, the teacher walks into her classroom and announces to the class that on each Friday, she will ask a question of the class and anyone who answers correctly doesn't have to go to school the following Monday.

On the first Friday, the teacher asks, 'How many grains of sand are on the beach?' Needless to say, no one could answer. The following Friday, the teacher asks the class, 'How many stars are in the sky?' and again no one could answer.

Frustrated, little Johnny decides that the next Friday, he would somehow answer the question and get a three-day weekend. So Thursday night, Johnny takes two ping-pong balls and paints them black. The next day, he brings them to school in a paper bag. At the end of the day, just when the teacher says, 'Here's this week's question,' Johnny empties the bag to the floor sending the ping-pong balls rolling to the front of the room.

Because they are young kids who find any disruption of class amusing, the entire class starts laughing. The teacher says, 'OK, who's the comedian with the black balls?' Immediately, little Johnny stands up and says, 'Lenny Henry, see you on Tuesday!'

****

What do you call a cross between a rooster and an owl?
A cock that stays up all night.

****

A whole family was caught in a small boat during a sudden storm off the coast cf Cornwall, but were towed to safety by the coastguard.

'I always knew God would take care of us,' said the composed five-year old daughter of the boat owner after the family got home.

'I like to hear you say that,' beamed the mother. 'Always remember that God is in His heaven watching over us.'

Oh, I wasn't talking about THAT God,' the five-year-old interrupted. 'I was talking about the COAST God.'

****

A little girl says, 'Grandpa, can I sit on your lap?'

'Why sure you can,' her grandfather replied.

As she's sitting on granddad's lap she says, 'Grandpa, can you make a sound like a frog?'

Perplexed, her granddad says, 'Sweetheart, why do you want me to make a sound like a frog?'

And the little girl says, ''Cause Grandma said that when you croak, we're going to EuroDisney.'

****

A very confused little boy goes to his mother and asks, 'Mummy? Is God male or female?'

'Well, honey,' says his mother. 'He's both.'

'Oh,' says the little boy. 'Mummy? Is God black or white?'

'Well, he's both,' replies his mother.

'Oh...' says the little boy. 'Mummy?'

'Yes, sweetie?'

'Is Michael Jackson God?'

****

A little boy is in school working on his arithmetic. The teacher says,

'Imagine there are five blackbirds sitting on a fence. You pick up your gun and shoot one. How many blackbirds are left?'

The little boy thinks for a moment and says, 'NONE!'

The teacher replies, 'None, how do you figure that?' The little boy says, 'If I shoot one, all the other birds will fly away scared, leaving none on the fence.'

The teacher replies, 'Hmmmm, not exactly, but I do like the way you think!'

The little boy then says, 'Teacher, can I ask you a question? There are three women sitting on a park bench eating ice cream cones. One is licking her cone, another is biting it, and the third one is sucking it. How can you tell which one of the women is married?'

The teacher ponders the question uncomfortably and then finally replies, 'Well, I guess the one sucking her cone.'

To which the little boy replies, 'Actually, it's the one with the wedding ring, but I do like the way YOU think!'

****

A 999 operator gets a call one evening but nobody says anything. Fearing the worst, the operator calls back, and a little boy answers the phone in a whispering voice.

Boy (barely audible): Hello!

Operator: Hello little boy. Did you just call 999?

Boy (barely audible): No!

Operator: O.K., is your mum home?

Boy (barely audible): Yes.

Operator: Can I speak to her, please?

Boy (barely audible): No.

Operator: Why not?

Boy (barely audible): Because she's busy!

Operator: Oh, OK. Is your daddy home then?

Boy (barely audible): Yes.

Operator: Well, can I speak to him?

Boy (barely audible): No!
Operator: Well, my goodness, why not?
Boy (barely audible): Because he's busy too!
Operator: Oh, goodness! What's he busy doing?
Boy (barely audible): Talking to the police.
Operator: Oh, so the police are there?
Boy (barely audible): Yes.
Operator: Can I speak to one of them?
Boy (barely audible): No!
Operator: Why not?
Boy (barely audible): Because they are really busy.
Operator: Well, what's your mum busy doing?
Boy (barely audible): Talking to the firemen.
Operator: Can I speak to one of the firemen then, please?
Boy (barely audible): No.
Operator: Well, goodness, why not?
Boy (barely audible): Because they are really busy, too!
Operator: Well, what are all of these people busy doing?
Boy (barely audible): Looking for me.

✳✳✳✳

A little boy is in a queue with his dad at the supermarket check out. In front of them is a really fat woman. The little boy looks her over and turns to his day and says: 'She is really big and fat, isn't she, daddy?'

The father is embarrassed and tries to get his son to quieten down. In a few minutes the little boy yells out: 'She is the biggest woman I have ever seen!'

The father is embarrassed to tears and bends over and tell his son: 'We do not talk about people looking different from us, especially if they are fat. Don't do it again.'

The little boy got the message and stood for a long time, until the woman's beeper went off. He then shouted: 'Look out, daddy, she's backing up!'

****

A secondary school student asked his teacher if a person should be punished for something he hadn't done. 'No,' said the teacher. 'Of course not,'

'Good,' said the boy. 'I haven't done my homework.'

****

A father and his small son were standing in front of the tiger cage at the zoo. The father was explaining how ferocious and strong tigers are, and the son was taking it all in with a serious expression.

'Dad,' the boy said finally, 'if the tiger got out of his cage and ate you...'

'Yes, son?' the father said expectantly.

'What bus should I take home?' the boy finished.

****

'Are caterpillars good to eat?' asked little Tommy at the dinner table.

'No,' said his father, 'what makes you ask a question like that while we are eating?'

'You had one on your lettuce salad, but it's gone now,' replied Tommy.

****

Mr Baldwin, the biology teacher, asked Mary, 'Tell me the part of the body that, under the right conditions, expands to six times its normal size, and state the conditions.'

Mary gasped and said in a huff, 'Why, Mr Baldwin! That is an inappropriate question and my parents are going to hear of it when I get home!' She sat down, red-faced.

'Susan, can you tell me the answer?' asked Mr Baldwin, 'The pupil of the eye, under dark conditions,' said Susan.

'Correct. Now Mary, I have three things to say to you. First, you have not studied your lesson. Second, you have a dirty mind. And third, boy, are you going to be disappointed some day!'

****

A stern father was taking his little son Johnny for a walk in the park when a bee landed on a rock in front of them. The little boy stepped forward and crushed the bee with his shoe. The father said, 'That was cruel, you'll get no honey for a whole year.'

Later, Johnny deliberately stepped on a butterfly. 'Just for that,' his father said, 'you'll have no butter for a year.'

When they returned home, Johnny's mother was making dinner. As they walked into the kitchen, she spied a cockroach and immediately crushed it. Johnny looked at his father and asked, 'Shall I tell her, Dad, or will you?'

****

A small boy walked into a gents. He saw a sailor in full dress uniform. The little boy got really excited, and asked the sailor, 'Are you a REAL Sailor?'

The sailor replied, 'Why, yes, son, I am. Would you like to wear my hat?'

The little boy said, 'Yes!' and put on the hat.

A Royal Marine entered the bathroom. The little boy, very excitedly asked, 'Mister, are you a REAL Marine?' The Marine answered, 'Yes, son, I am! Why, do you want to suck my dick?'

The little boy exclaimed, 'I'm not a REAL sailor! I'm just wearing the hat!'

****

Little Johnny's teacher asked him, 'Johnny, give me a sentence using the phrase, "bitter end" in it.'

Little Johnny thought for a moment and replied, 'Our dog chased our cat and he bitter end.'

****

One blistering hot day when guests were present for dinner, a mother asked her four-year-old son to say grace.

'But, Mother, I don't know what to say,' he protested.

'Just say what you've heard me say,' she told him. Obediently, he bowed his head and said, 'Oh, Lord, why did I invite those people here on a hot day like this?'

****

This young girl about five years old had a dog which she took for a walk every day after school. Well, one day her dog was on heat, so her father told her that she couldn't walk the dog for a week or so because it wasn't feeling well. His daughter became very upset and cried for most of the night.

The next day the father came up with a plan. He put some petrol on the dog's rear end to conceal the smell from the male dogs. Well, when the girl got home she was happy to find that she could now walk her dog again. About an hour later the girl returned without the dog. The father asked her what on earth had happened to the dog?

The girl replied: 'She ran out of petrol a few streets back and she's being pushed home by another dog.'

****

A couple of young lads were fishing at their special pond off the beaten track when out of the bushes jumped the gamekeeper. Immediately, one of the boys threw his rod down and started running through the woods like a bat out of hell, and hot on his heels came the game keeper. After about half a mile the young lad stopped and stooped over with his hands on his thighs to catch his breath and the gamekeeper finally caught up with him.

'Let's see your fishing licence, lad!' the game keeper gasped.

With that, the young lad pulled out his wallet and gave the gamekeeper a valid fishing licence.

'Well, son,' said the gamekeeper, 'you must be really stupid! You don't have to run from me if you have a valid license.'

'Yes, sir,' replied the young lad, 'but my friend back there, well, he doesn't have one.'

****

Little Johnny sat playing in the garden. When his mother came out to collect him, she saw that he was slowly eating a worm. She turned pale. 'No, Johnny! Stop! That's horrible! You can't eat worms!' Trying to convince him further she said, 'Now the mother worm is looking all over for her nice baby worm.'

'No, she isn't,' said Johnny.

'Why not?' said his mum.

'Because I ate her first!'

****

Eight-year-old Johnny comes into the house for dinner after playing outside all afternoon. His parents ask him what he did today. He says that he played football and then he proposed to seven-year-old Jane, the nextdoor neighbour. They are going to get married. His parents think this is cute, and they don't want to make fun of Johnny so they ask him, 'How are you and Jane going to pay for the expenses of being married?'

Johnny replies, 'Well, with the £1 I get each week from you and the £1 she gets from her mum and dad, we should do OK.'

His father says, 'That's fine, but how will you pay the extra expenses if you and Jane have a baby?'

Johnny answers, 'Well, so far, we've been lucky…'

****

Every day an eight-year-old boy walks home from school past an eight-year-old girl's house. One day he is carrying a football, and he stops to taunt the little girl. He holds up the football and says, 'See this football?

Football is a boy's game and girls can't have one!'

The little girl runs in the house crying and tells her mother about the encounter. She runs out and buys the girl a football. The next day the boy is riding home on his bike, and the girl shows him the football, screaming, 'Nah na nah na nah.'

The little boy gets mad and points to his bike. 'See this bike? This is a boy's bike, and girls can't have them!'

Next day, the boy comes by and the little girl is riding a new boy's bike. Now he's really mad. So he drops his pants, points at his most private of parts, and says, 'You see THIS? Only BOYS have these and your mother can't buy you one!'

The next day as he passes the house he asks the little girl, 'Well, what do you have to say NOW?'

So she pulls up her dress and says, 'My mother told me that as long as I have one of these, I can have as many of THOSE as I want!'

****

'Is your mother home?' the salesman asked a small boy sitting on the frontstep of a house.

'Yeah, she's home,' the boy said, moving over to let him past. The salesman rang the doorbell, got no response, knocked once, then again. Still no one came to the door. Turning to the boy, the salesman said, 'I thought you said your mother was home.'

The kid replied, 'She is, but I don't live here.'

****

One day, a father and his son were walking in the woods on their way home when suddenly they came upon two dogs mating in the bushes.

'What are they doing, Dad?' asked the small child, staring intently at the scene before them.

'They, um, they're making a puppy,' said the boy's father, as he grabbed his coat and moved him along quickly.

A few nights later, the little boy woke up and got up from his bed to go to the bathroom. As he walked by his parents' room, he heard strange noises coming from within. He opened the door and was surprised to see his father on top of his mother, moving in a strange way. His father looked up and saw his son – instantly, both mother and father froze. As the boy's mother grabbed for the sheets to cover herself up, the father got up and hustled his son out of the bedroom.

'What were you doing to Mum, Dad?' asked the little boy, who still wasn't sure what he saw.

'Your mother and I were, well, we were, ah, trying to make a baby – you know, maybe a brother or sister for you,' said the boy's father, now confident that this would satisfy his son's curiosity.

'Oh,' said the little boy, thinking hard for a minute. 'Y'know Dad, when you go back to bed with mum, turn her over, please – I'd rather have a puppy.'

✱✱✱✱

This little boy wakes up three nights in a row when he hears a thumping sound coming from his parents' room. Finally, one morning he goes to his mum and says, 'Mummy, every night I hear you and daddy making noises and when I look in your bedroom you're bouncing up and down on him.'

His mum is taken by surprise and says, 'Oh… well… ah… I'm, er bouncing on his stomach because he's fat and that makes him thin again.'

And the boy says, 'Well, that won't work'

His mum says, 'Why?'

And the boy replies, 'Because the lady next door comes by after you leave each day and blows him back up!'

✱✱✱✱

Mother: Why are you home from school so early?
Son: I was the only one who could answer a question.
Mother: Oh, really? What was the question?

Son: Who threw the rubber at the headmaster?

✳✳✳✳

Little Johnny has a problem. He swears like a trooper. Johnny's teacher is aware of this, so she has got to be extra careful not to let Johnny swear.

'OK, class. We're going to play a game today. I'm going to name a letter of the alphabet and I want you to come up with a word that starts with that letter and put it in a sentence.'

The kids are excited, especially Johnny, who's thinking of every swear word he can.

'OK, class, let's start with the letter A.'

Johnny raises his hand.

'Susie,' the teacher calls.

'A is for apple. Apples grow on trees,' she replies.

'Very good,' the teacher says. 'OK, class, let's do the letter B.'

Johnny raises his hand excitedly.

'Mikey,' the teacher calls.

'B is for brown. Brown is my favourite colour.'

'Very good,' the teacher says. 'OK, class, let's do the letter C.'

Johnny raises both hands! He's going mad! He's got a great word for C!

'Bobby,' the teacher calls.

'C is for cat. A cat lives in my back garden.'

'Very good,' The teacher says. This goes on and on, and the teacher is not going to call on Johnny if there's a swear word that starts with the letter she calls out.

Finally, she gets to the letter R. The teacher can't think of a single swear word that starts with R, and even Johnny looks a little puzzled. So she calls out R and asks Johnny to respond.

Johnny nervously stands up. He looks around the room. Then he says, 'R is for a Rat…' he suddenly gets excited and stretches both arms wide, '…a rat with a dick this big!'

✳✳✳✳

A vampire bat came flapping in from the night covered in fresh blood and parked himself on the roof of the cave to get some sleep. Pretty soon all the other bats smelt the blood and began hassling him about where he got it. He told them to piss off and let him get some sleep but they persisted until finally he gave in.

'OK, follow me,' he said and flew out of the cave with hundreds of bats behind him. Down through a valley they went, across a river and into a forest full of trees. Finally he slowed down and all the other bats excitedly milled around him. 'Now, do you see that tree over there?' he asked.

'Yes, yes, yes!' the bats all screamed in a frenzy.

'Good,' said the first bat, 'Because I didn't!'

****

There was once a Scotsman and an Englishman who lived next door to each other. The Scotsman owned a hen and each morning would look in his garden and pick up one of his hen's eggs for breakfast.

One day he looked into his garden and saw that the hen had laid an egg in the Englishman's garden. He was about to go next door when he saw the Englishman pick up the egg. The Scotsman ran up to the Englishman and told him that the egg belonged to him because he owned the hen. The Englishman disagreed because the egg was laid on his property. They argued for a while until finally the Scotsman said, 'In my family we normally solve disputes by the following actions: I kick you in the balls and time how long it takes you to get back up, then you kick me in the balls and time how long it takes for me to get up; whoever gets up quicker wins the egg.'

The Englishman agreed to this and so the Scotsman found his heaviest pair of boots and put them on. He took a few steps back, then ran toward the Englishman and kicked him as hard as he could in the balls. The Englishman fell to the floor clutching his nuts, howling in agony for 30 minutes.

Eventually the Englishman stood up and said, 'Now it's my turn to kick you.'

The Scotsman said, 'Keep the fucking egg.'

****

A Daughter's Letter Home

Dear Mum and Dad,

It has been three months since I left for college. I have been remiss in writing and I am very sorry for my thoughtlessness. I will bring you up to date now, but before you read on, please sit down. You are not to read any further unless you are sitting down, OK?

Well, I'm getting along pretty well now. The skull fracture and the concussion I got when I jumped out of the window of my halls of residence when it caught fire shortly after my arrival are pretty well healed now. I only spent two weeks in the hospital and I now can see almost as well as before and I only get those nauseating headaches once a week. Fortunately, the fire in the halls of residence and my jump was witnessed by an attendant at the petrol station near the halls and he was the one who called the fire brigade and the ambulance. He also visited me at the hospital and since I had nowhere to live because of the burnt-out halls, he was kind enough to invite me to share his flat with him.

It's really a basement, but it's really quite nice. He is a very good man and we have fallen deeply in love and are planning to get married. We haven't exactly set the date yet, but it will be before my pregnancy begins to show. Yes, Mum and Dad, I am pregnant! I know how you are looking forward to being grandparents and I know you will welcome the baby and give it the same love and devotion and tender care you gave me as a child.

The reason for the delay in our marriage is that my boyfriend has some minor infection which he is waiting to clear up. I carelessly caught it from him. This will soon clear up with the penicillin injections I am taking daily. I know you will welcome him into the family with open arms. He is kind, and, although not well-educated, has ambitions.

Although he is of a different race and religion than ours, I know your oft-expressed tolerance will not permit you to be bothered by the fact that his skin colour is somewhat darker than ours. I am sure you will love him as I do. His family background is good, too, for I hear that his father is an important gun-bearer in the village in Africa from which he comes.

Now that I have brought you up to date, I want to tell you that there was no fire. I do not have a concussion or a skull fracture, I was not in the hospital, I am not pregnant, I am not engaged, I do not have syphilis and there is no African in my life. However, I did fail my exams and I wanted you to see these results in their proper perspective.

Your loving daughter, Gail xxx

****

John Wayne rides in to town, ties up his horse and walks into the saloon.

'Give me a shot of red eye,' says John.

He downs it in one and then walks outside. He notices that his horse is gone so he comes back inside the saloon. 'If my horse isn't returned after I've had another drink,' says John, 'the same thing will happen here that happened in Dodge City. Now, give me another red eye.'

He downs the red eye in one and walks outside to find his horse tied up against the rail. he mounts up and is just about to ride off when this cowboy walks up to him.

'Say, John,' says the cowboy. 'What happened in Dodge City?'

'I had to walk home,' John replies.

****

A three-legged dog walks into a saloon in the Wild West. The piano stops playing, everyone stops talking and a nervous hush descends upon the room.

'What do you want here?' says one brave soul.

'I've come for my paw,' replies the dog.

****

This man went to a casino. Very soon, he'd lost almost all his money. He decided to put the rest on number five on the roulette. The wheel spun and it came up number five. He'd made all his money back and a bit to spare. He was just about to leave the table when the devil appeared on his shoulder.

'Let it ride on number five,' said the devil. The man decided to go for it, the wheel spun and number five came up again. The man was very happy and went to grab his chips when the devil spoke again. 'Let it ride on number five again,' said the devil.

The man wasn't very sure but he decided to have one more go. The wheel spun and number five came up again. The man was now quite rich and was just about to leave the table when the devil piped up once more.

'Let it ride on number five again,' said the devil. The man didn't want to. He'd already planned to start a new life in the Caribbean. But the devil insisted. 'Let it ride on number five again,' said the devil.

The man was extremely doubtful but he left the money where it was. The wheel spun and came up on number five again.

'You jammy git,' said the devil.

****

A posh woman owned a very talented parrot called Charles. Not only could Charles talk but he played the piano as well. Unfortunately, he had one failing. He loved to fuck chickens. Any chance he could get to fuck a chicken, he'd be in there.

This really upset the farmer next door and he complained to the posh lady. She went and told Charles. 'If you mess with those chickens again, you're really going to get it,' she said.

Charles said nothing. He tried to resist, but the next day, he was caught messing around with the chickens. His mistress was very annoyed and punished Charles by shaving his head and nailing him to the piano. That evening, the posh lady had a gala party and all Charles could do was announce the guests.

'Mr and Mrs David Lloyd… Mr and Mrs John Silverman… ' he was saying. Just then two bald-headed men appeared at the door. 'And you two chicken fuckers can come up on the piano with me.' said Charles.

****

'Give me two hot dogs. One with mustard and one without.'
'Which one without?

****

A man was seen walking through town with a desk strapped to his back, a typewriter under one arm, and a wastebasket under the other. A policeman stopped him and asked him what he was doing. He was arrested when he replied, 'Impersonating an office, sir!'

****

What do Saddam Hussein and Little Miss Muffet have in common?
They both have Kurds in their way.

****

This man was walking along a street and met a young boy. The man asked the boy, 'What's your name?'
The boy replied, 'Six and Seven-Eighths.'
The man asked, 'Where did your parents get a name like that?'
The boy said, 'They picked it out of a hat.'

****

A group of chess enthusiasts had checked into a hotel, and were standing in the lobby discussing their recent tournament victories. After about an hour, the manager came out of the office and asked them to disperse. 'But why?'

they asked.

'Because,' he said, 'I can't stand chess nuts boasting in an open foyer.'

****

The first Jewish woman Prime Minister is elected. She calls her Mother: 'Mama, I've won the elections, you've got to come to the swearing-in ceremony.'

'I don't know, what would I wear?'

'Don't worry, I'll send you a dressmaker.'

'But I only eat kosher food!'

'Mama, I am going to be the Prime Minister, I can get you kosher food.'

'But how will I get there?'

'I'll send a limo, just come Mama.'

'OK, OK, if it makes you happy.'

The great day comes and Mama is seated between the Lord Chancellor and the future Cabinet ministers, she nudges the gentleman on her right. 'You see that girl, the one with her hand on the Bible? Her brother's a doctor!'

****

There were three guys on top of this big construction platform. One was a German, the other Italian, and the third one was an Irishman. The German opened his lunchbox and saw sauerkraut for his lunch and said, 'If I haff this stuff vun more time, I'll jump off zis beam.'

The Italian also looked in his lunchbox and saw pasta and said, 'If I 'ave disa pasta one more time I jump offa dis beam.'

Then the Irishman looked in his lunchbox and saw a cheese and tomato sandwich and said, 'If I have this sandwich one more time, I'll jump off this beam.'

So, the next day came and the German opened his lunchbox and saw sauerkraut, and jumped off the beam. Then the Italian looked in his lunchbox and saw pasta, and jumped off the beam. So, the Irishman looks in his lunchbox and sees a cheese and tomato sandwich and jumps.

The three workers' wives showed up at the scene and the workers' boss came over and told them why. He told them he had overheard the conversation saying that the workers would jump if their lunch was the same the next day.

Suddenly the German wife spoke up, 'Dat's veird, he neffer said anyzing to me. If he would haff I wouldn't haff packed it!'

The Italian wife said the same thing. But the Irishman's wife was crying worse now, and was barely able to say, 'That is strange, because he packs his own lunch!'

****

One day a man was walking in the woods when he got lost. For two days he roamed around trying to find a way out. He had not eaten anything during this period and was famished. Over on a rock ledge he spotted a bald eagle, killed it, and started to eat it. Surprisingly a couple of park rangers happen to find him at that moment, and arrested him for killing an endangered species.

At court, he pleaded innocent to the charges against him claiming that if he didn't eat the bald eagle he would have died from starvation. The judge ruled in his favour. In the judge's closing statement he asked the man, 'I would like you to tell me something before I let you go. I have never eaten a bald eagle, nor ever plan on it. What did it taste like?'

The man answered, 'Well, it tasted like a cross between a whooping crane and a lesser spotted owl.'

****

A father decided his son was showing signs of taking him and his mother for granted so he sat him down one day for a chat.

'Right,' said the dad, 'I think it's time you started treating your mother and I with a little more respect, young man. I mean, where would you be if we both died suddenly?'

'Here,' replied the boy. 'The question is, where would you two be?'

****

Q: Why can't women play hockey?
A: They have to change their pads after every period.

****

Q: Do you know how men and floor tiles are alike?
A: If you lay them right the first time you can walk on them the rest of your life.

****

Q: What did the banana say to the vibrator?
A: 'What are you shaking for? She's gonna eat me.'

****

Q: Why do they call seagulls seagulls?
A: Cause if they flew over the bay, they'd be bagels!

****

So these two cannibals were eating this clown and the one cannibal says to the other cannibal, 'Does this taste funny to you?'

****

Q: What is the result of a bomb blast in the middle of a herd of cows?
A: Udder destruction.

****

Q: What did one fly say to another?
A: Time is fun when you're having flies.

****

Q: How do you get down from an elephant?
A: You don't, you get down from a goose.

****

Q: How many mice does it take to screw in a light bulb?
A: Two, the trick is getting them in there.

****

Q: What does a women have two of that a cow has four of?
A: Feet.

****

Q:What's the difference between a porcupine and a Porsche owner?
A:With a porcupine, the prick is on the outside!

****

Q: What happened to the Pope when he went to Mount Olive?
A: Popeye almost killed him!

****

Q: Did you hear about the man who ate his son?
A: He didn't know his wife was pregnant!

****

Q: What's the difference between a pervert and a kinky person?
A: A pervert uses a feather, a kinky person uses the whole chicken!

****

Q: What goes, 'Marc, Marc?'
A: A dog with a hare lip!

****

Q:What's the hardest part about eating a vegetable?
A: Manipulating the wheelchair!

****

Q: What's red and has seven dents?
A: Snow White's cherry!

****

Q: How can you tell a head nurse?
A: She's the one with the dirty knees!

****

Q: What do you have if you have a moth ball in one hand and a moth ball in the other hand?
A: One HELL of a moth!

****

Q: How many Zen masters does it take to screw in a light bulb?

A: None. The Universe spins the bulb, and the Zen master merely stays out of the way.

****

Q: Why did the polygamist cross the aisle?
A: To get to the other bride.

****

Q: Why did the teacher draw a dot on the floor for his students?
A: He wanted to illustrate a point.

****

Q. What do you call a dog with no hind legs and steel balls?
A. Sparky!

****

Q: How do you confuse an idiot?
A: 26

****

Q: How many dope smokers does it take to screw in a light bulb?
A: Two. One to roll it and one to light it up.

****

Q: How many mystery writers does it take to screw in a light bulb?
A: Two. One to screw it almost all the way in and the other to give it a surprising twist at the end.

Chapter 9

Whose Round Is It?

It's a difficult moment, but ultimately unavoidable. At the start of the evening everyone's clear-headed and when John bought the first round, followed by Pete getting the next lot in and then Sandra sharing a round with Ted all was well. Then things became a bit blurred. Firstly, Karl and Janine turned up and got involved in a mini-round of their own with Dave, Ian and Louise. Then Barry, who had been in at the beginning, went to the bog and missed out on Steve's round, and of course with three beers in him John's begun to think that Sandra and Ted sharing a round wasn't really fair and that when it comes round to him again he's only going to buy one of them a drink.

It's complicated, and with money being the root of all evil and alcohol being, well, alcohol, it's surprising that more friendships don't end this way. However, more often than not, the desperation to get more bevvied becomes the overriding drive and that tenner you were saving for the cab home soon becomes two large ones for Sandra and Ted, who have strangely gone to the toilet next time it's their round…

****

A travelling salesman stopped alongside a field on a country road to rest for a few minutes. The man had just closed his eyes when a horse came to the fence and began to boast about his past. 'Yes sir, I'm a fine horse. I've run in 25 races and won over £5 million. I keep my trophies in the barn.'

The salesman computed the value of having a talking horse, found the horse's owner and offered a handsome sum for the animal.

'Aw, you don't want that horse,' said the farmer.

'Yes I do,' said the salesman, 'and I'll give you £10,000 for him.'

Recognising a good deal, the farmer said without hesitation, 'He's yours.'

While he wrote out his check, the salesman asked, 'By the way, why wouldn't I want your horse?'

'Because', said the farmer, 'he's a liar – he hasn't won a race in his life.'

****

The local pub was so sure that its landlord was the strongest man around that they offered a standing £1,000 bet. The landlord would squeeze a lemon until all the juice ran into a glass, and hand the lemon to a customer. Anyone who could squeeze one more drop of juice out would win the money.

Many people had tried over time, but nobody could do it. One day this scrawny little man came into the pub, wearing thick glasses and a polyester suit, and said in a tiny, squeaky voice, 'I'd like to try the bet.'

After the laughter had died down, the landlord said OK, grabbed a lemon, and squeezed away. Then he handed the wrinkled remains of the rind to the little man. But the crowd's laughter turned to total silence as the man clenched his fist around the lemon and six drops fell into the glass.

As the crowd cheered, the landlord paid the £1,000, and asked the little man, 'What do you do for a living? Are you a lumberjack, a weight-lifter, or what?'

The man replied, 'I work for the Inland Revenue.'

****

There's a guy in a pub, it's late, and the guy and the landlord are the only ones left in the pub. The guy pushes his empty pint glass over to the edge of the counter, walks to the other end of the room and says to the landlord, 'If I could spit from here, and get it in the glass without getting any anywhere else, would you give me £50?'

The landlord, not seeing how this bet could be cheated, says, 'OK, you're on. Show me.'

So the guy spits and gets it in the glass without getting any on the counter or the floor. The landlord says, 'That's amazing! You deserve the £50!'

The next day the guy's in the pub again, and asks the landlord, if he could do it again, but with two glasses side by side, would he give him £100.

The landlord agrees and the guys spits from across the pub and makes it in both glasses, without getting any anywhere else.

So the evening rolls on, and the landlord sticks glasses all over the pub and says to the guy, 'If you can spit in all of these glasses at the same time, without getting any anywhere else, I'll give you £200.'

'Sure,' says the guy, 'but I need a little time to get ready.' So after a minute, the guy comes up, and proceeds to spit everywhere at lightning speed. The landlord, seeing that the guy has missed every single glass, jumps up and down for joy, screaming. The guy then pays the landlord and says, 'I don't see what you're so happy about, I just bet the guy in the corner £500 that I could spit all over your pub, and you'd be happy about it.'

****

A man goes into a pub and sees a pile of cash on a table beneath a big sign that reads, '£2,000 Cash Prize! See landlord for details.' Keeping one eye on the stack of money, the man goes over and asks the landlord what he has to do to win the prize. 'You have to do three things and it's all yours,' the landlord says.

'Just three things?' the bloke asks, rubbing his hands now and imagining about walking out of the pub £2,000 richer. 'What are the three things?'

'Well,' the landlord says, 'first you have to go over to that 16-stone bouncer and knock him out. After that, I've got a mean-tempered Pit Bull in the back room who needs a tooth pulled. Then you have to go upstairs and give the 80-year-old lady an orgasm.'

'No problem,' the guy says. He struts over to the bouncer and says, 'Hey pal your shoelace is untied.' When the bouncer looks down at his shoes, the man flattens him with a single, solid uppercut. Next he heads to the back room where the Pit Bull is housed. The landlord can hear a tremendous commotion from the back room and, after a few minutes the man emerges from the back room, quite bloody and cut up and breathing heavily.

'OK,' he says, 'where's the old lady that needs her tooth pulled?'

****

There was a couple who were big over-spenders. They always dreamed of holidaying in Hawaii, but were never able to save any money to do so. One day they had an idea. Each time they had sex, they would put £10 into a piggy bank. So they bought the piggy bank, and followed that procedure for about a year. After that time, they decided that there was enough money for their dream vacation and broke the piggy bank. The husband looked at their savings and said, 'Isn't it strange? Each time we had sex, I put £10 into the piggy bank. But I see here that there are quite a few £20 notes and a few £50 notes.'

'Well,' said his wife. 'Do you think that everybody is as stingy as you are?'

****

After the wedding, the bride's dad took a taxi to the bankruptcy court. As he got out he said to the driver, 'You might as well come, too.'

****

A couple were having a discussion about family finances. Finally the husband exploded, 'If it weren't for my money, the house wouldn't be here!'

'My dear,' the wife replied. 'If it weren't for your money I wouldn't be here.'

****

A man's credit card was stolen but he decided not to report it because the thief was spending less than his wife did.

****

A man walks into a restaurant has a few drinks and then asks what his bill is.

'20 quid,' the waiter says.

'I'll tell you what,' says the man, 'I'll bet you my bill, double or nothing that I can bite my eye.'

The waiter accepts and the man pulls out his glass eye and bites it. He has a few more drinks and asks for his bill again. This time it's £30.

'OK,' says the man. 'I'll bet you my bill, double or quits, that I can bite my other eye.' Knowing that the man can't have two glass eyes the waiter accepts the bet, at which point the guy takes out his false teeth and bites his other eye.

****

A rabbi and a priest were discussing their respective collection boxes and how the money was split.

'We give three-quarters of it to Christian charities,' said the priest, 'and the last quarter we keep for ourselves and for the upkeep of the vicarage.'

'I see,' said the rabbi. 'Well, what we do is this. Each week, my wife and my two children take one corner of a table cloth and put all the money into the middle. We toss the money very high into the air up to God. Whatever he wants, he takes, and the money that falls back to earth we keep!'

****

A priest and a rabbi were talking when the rabbi asked the priest about confession. 'I have an idea,' said the priest. 'Why don't you sit with me on my side of the confession booth and hear it for yourself? No one will ever know.'

A woman came into the booth and said, 'Bless me, Father, for I have sinned.'

'What did you do?' asked the priest.

'I cheated on my husband,' replied the woman.

'How many times?' asked the priest.

'Three times,' says the woman.

'Well,' said the priest, 'say five Hail Marys and put five pounds in the offertory box.'

Another woman came in and said, 'Bless me, Father, for I have sinned.'

'What did you do?' asked the priest. 'I cheated on my husband,' said the woman.

'How many times?' asked the priest.

'Three times,' said the woman.

Again the priest said, 'Say five Hail Marys and put five pounds in the offertory box.'

Then the priest turned to the rabbi and said, 'Would you like to do the next confession?' The rabbi started to object, but the priest said, 'Go ahead. It's easy.'

So another woman came in and said, 'Bless me, Father, for I have sinned.'

'What did you do?' asked the rabbi.

'I cheated on my husband,' said the woman.

'How many times?' asked the rabbi.

'Twice,' said the woman.

'Well, go and do it again,' said the rabbi. 'They're three for five pounds today.'

✳✳✳✳

A young boy goes off to college, but about a third of the way through the term, he has foolishly squandered what money he had. 'Hmmmm,' he wonders, 'how am I gonna get more dosh?' Then he gets an idea. He calls his father. 'Dad,' he says, 'you won't believe the wonders of modern education. Why, they actually have a course here that will teach Fido how to talk!'

'Why that's absolutely amazing!' his father says. 'How do I get him on to this course?'

'Just send him down here with £1,000,' the boy says, 'I'll get him on to the course.'

So his father sends the dog and the money, but very shortly the boy has spent all the money again, so he calls his father.

'So how's Fido doing, son?' his father asks.

'Great dad, he's talking up a storm,' he says, 'but you just won't believe this – now they have a course here that will teach Fido to READ!'

'READ!' says his father, 'That's amazing! What do I have to do to get him on that course?'

'Just send £2,500, I'll get him in the class,' says the boy.

So his father sends the money. At the end of the term, the boy has a problem. When he gets home, his father will find out that the dog can neither talk nor read. So he strangled the dog.

When he gets home, his father is all excited. 'Where's Fido?' he shouts, 'I just can't wait to hear him talk and listen to him read something!'

'Dad,' the boy says, 'I have some grim news. This morning when I got out of the shower, Fido was in the living room sitting on the sofa reading the paper, like he usually does. Then he turned to me and asked, 'So, is your old man still shagging that little redhead that lives down on Oak Street?'

'I hope you wrung the lying bastard's fucking neck!' says his Dad.

****

This geezer just started at his new job, working at a porn shop. His boss comes out and tells him that he has to leave for a while. 'Can you handle it?' he asks the new employee. The new employee is somewhat reluctant, but with the boss' positive comments he finally agrees.

So, the geezer is there by himself for a little while and a white woman comes in. 'How much for the white dildo?' she asks.

'£35,' he answers.

'And how much for the black one?' she asks.

'It's the same price,' he says.

'£35 for the black one, £35 for the white one. I think I'll take the black one,' she says. 'I've never had a black one before.'

She pays him, and off she goes. A little bit later a black woman comes in and asks, 'How much for the black dildo?'

'£35,' says the new employee.

'And how much for the white one?' she asks.

'It's the same price,' he says. '£35 for the black one, £35 for the white one.'

'Hmmm,' says the woman, 'I think I'll take the white one. I've never had a white one before.'

She pays him, and off she goes. About an hour later a young blonde woman comes in and asks, 'How much are your dildos?'

'£35 for the white, £35 for the black,' says the man.

'Hmmmmm....' she muses, 'and how much is that tartan one on the shelf?'

'Well,' he says, 'that's a very special dildo... it'll cost you £165.'

She thinks for a moment and answers, 'I'll take the tartan one, I've never had a tartan one before.'

She pays him, and off she goes. Finally, the guy's boss returns and asks, 'How did you do while I was gone?'

'Really good,' said the new employee. 'I sold one white dildo, one black dildo, and I sold your Thermos flask for £165!'

****

A rather scruffy-looking man went into a bank. Reaching the head of the queue, he said to the bank clerk, 'I wanna open a fucking bank account.'

'Certainly, sir,' answered the bank clerk, 'but there's no need to use that kind of language.'

'Look, lady. I just wanna open a fucking bank account,' growled the would-be customer.

'I'll be glad to be of service, sir,' said the bank clerk, blushing slightly, 'but I would appreciate not being spoken to in that way.'

'Just lemme open a fucking account, OK?' he said.

'I'm afraid I'm going to have to speak to the branch manager,' said the pissed-off bank clerk, slipping off her stool and returning shortly with a dapper middle-aged man who asked how he could be of service.

'I just won 10 million pounds on the lottery,' snarled the man, 'and all I wanna do is open a fucking account.'

'I see,' said the manager sympathetically. 'And this fucking BITCH is giving you trouble?'

****

A man was caught for speeding and went before the judge. 'What will you take, 30 days or £30?' said the judge.

'I think I'll take the money,' the man replied.

****

A biker appeared in court one day to testify on behalf of a friend, when the prosecuting lawyer asked him, 'Isn't it true that you were offered £5,000 to throw this case?' The biker calmly gazed out the window, ignoring the lawyer. Most annoyed, the lawyer again thundered, 'I said, isn't it true that you were offered £5,000 to throw this case?'

The judge, seeing that the biker continued to ignore the question, leaned over and said, 'You will answer the question,' to which the biker replied,

'Oh, sorry, your honour. I thought he was talking to you.'

****

After the student delivered the pizza to old Ken's house Ken asked: 'What is the usual tip?'

'Well,' replied the youth, 'this is my first trip here, but the other blokes say if I get 5p out of you, I'll be doing great.'

'Is that so?' snorted Ken. 'Well, just to show them how wrong they are, here's five quid.'

'Thanks,' replied the youth, 'I'll put this towards my studies.'

'What are you studying?' asked Ken. The lad smiled and said:

'Applied psychology.'

****

A shoplifter was caught red-handed trying to steal a watch from an exclusive jewellery store. 'Listen,' said the shoplifter, 'I know you don't want any trouble either. What say I just buy the watch and we forget about this?'

The manager agreed and wrote up the sales slip. The crook looked at the slip and said, 'This is a little more than I intended to spend. Can you show me something less expensive?'

****

A man walks into a bank and says he wants to borrow £200 for six months. The manager asks him what kind of collateral he has. The man says, 'I've got a Rolls-Royce. Keep it until the loan is paid off. Here are the keys.'

Six months later the man comes into the bank, pays back the £200 loan, plus £10 interest, and regains possession of the Rolls-Royce. 'Sir,' says the manager, 'if I may ask, why would a man who drives a Rolls-Royce need to borrow £200?'

'I had to go to abroad for six months, and where else could I store a Rolls-Royce for that long for only £10?'

****

There were two evil brothers. They were rich, and used their money to keep their ways from the public eye. They even attended church, and looked to be perfect Christians. Then their vicar retired, and a new one took over. Not only could he see right through the brothers' deception, but he also spoke well and true and the church started to swell in numbers.

A fund-raising campaign was started to repair the roof. All of a sudden, one of the brothers died. The remaining brother sought out the new vicar the day before the funeral and handed him a cheque for the amount needed to finish paying for the roof.

'I have only one condition,' he said. 'At his funeral, you must say my brother was a saint.' The vicar gave his word, and deposited the cheque. The next day, at the funeral, the vicar did not hold back.

'He was an evil man,' he said. 'He cheated on his wife and abused his family.' After going on in this vein for some time, he concluded with, 'But compared to his brother, he was a saint.'

****

A man tried to sell his neighbour a new dog. 'This is a talking dog,' he said. 'And you can have him for £5.'

'Who do you think you're kidding with this talking-dog stuff?' said the neighbour. ' There's no such animal.'

Suddenly the dog looked up with tears in his eyes. 'Please buy me, sir,' he pleaded. 'This man is cruel. He never buys me a meal, never bathes me, never takes me for a walk. I used to be the richest trick dog in Asia. I performed before kings. I was in the army and was decorated 10 times.'

'Hey!' said the neighbour. 'He can talk. Why sell him for just £5?'

'Because,' said the seller, 'I'm getting tired of all his damn lies.'

****

A new man is brought into prison cell 102. Already there is a long-time resident who looks 100 years old. The new man looks at the old-timer inquiringly. 'Look at me,' says the old timer. 'I'm old and worn out. You'd never believe that I used to live the life of Riley. I wintered on the Riviera, had a boat, four fine cars, the most beautiful women, and I ate in all the best restaurants in France.'

'What happened?' asked the new man.

'One day Riley reported his credit cards missing!' said the old-timer.

****

A group from Chicago spent a weekend gambling in Las Vegas. One of the men on that trip won $100,000. He didn't want anyone to know about it, so he decided not to return with the others, but took a later plane home, arriving back at 3am.

He immediately went out to the back garden of his house, dug a hole and planted the money in it.

The following morning he walked outside and found only an empty hole. He noticed footsteps leading from the hole to the house next door, which was owned by a deaf mute. On the same street lived a professor who understood sign language and was a friend of the deaf man. Grabbing his pistol, the enraged man went to awaken the professor and dragged him to the deaf man's house.

'You tell this guy that if he doesn't give me back my $100,000 I'm going to kill him!' he screamed at the professor. The professor conveyed the message to his friend, and his friend replied in sign language, 'I hid it in my backyard, underneath the cherry tree.'

The professor turned to the man with the gun and said, 'He's not going to tell you. He says he'd rather die first.'

****

The neatly-dressed salesman stopped a man in the street and asked, 'Sir, would you like to buy a toothbrush for 10 quid?'

Aghast, the man said, 'I should say not, that's robbery!'

The salesman seemed hurt. 'Well, then, how about a piece of homemade chocolate cake for 5p?'

This seemed fair, and the man handed a five-pence piece to the salesman. Unwrapping the cake, he took a bite.

'Urgh,' he snarled, 'this chocolate cake tastes like shit!'

'It is,' replied the salesman. 'Want to buy a toothbrush?'

****

A little old lady walked into the main branch the Bank of England holding a large paper bag in her hand. She told the young man at the window that she wished to take the £3 million that she had in the bag and open an account with the bank. But first, she said that she wished to meet the manager of the bank due to the large amount involved.

After looking into the bag and seeing an awful lot of money the bank clerk called the manager's office and told him the old lady wanted to see him.

The lady was escorted upstairs and ushered into the manager's office. Introductions were made and she explained that she liked to know the people that she did business with on a more personal level.

The manager then wondered her how she came into such a large amount of money. 'Was it an inheritance?' he asked.

'No,' she replied.

'Was it the lottery?' he asked.

'No,' she replied.

He was quiet for a minute trying to think where she could have come into £3 million.

'I bet,' she stated.

'You bet!' repeated the manager. 'As in horses?'

'No,' she replied. 'I bet on people.' Seeing his confusion, she explained that she just bet different things with people. All of a sudden she said, 'I'll bet you £25,000 that by 10am tomorrow morning your balls will be square.'

The bank manager figured that she must be off her rocker and decided to take her up on the bet. He didn't see how he could lose. For the rest of the day he was very careful. He decided to stay home that evening and take no chances – after all there was £25,000 at stake.

When he got up the next morning and took his shower, he checked to make sure that everything was OK. There was no difference, he looked the same as he always had. He went to work and waited for the little old lady to come in at 10am, humming as he went about his business. He knew that this would be a good day. How often do you get handed £25,000 for doing nothing?

At 10 sharp, the little old lady was escorted into his office. With her was a younger man. When the manager inquired as to the purpose of his being there, she informed him that he was her lawyer, and that she always took him along when there was a large amount of money involved.

'Well,' she asked. 'What about our bet?'

'I don't know how to tell you this,' he replied, 'but I'm the same as I have always been, only £25,000 richer!'

The lady seemed to accept this, but requested that she be able to see for herself. The manager thought that this was reasonable and dropped his trousers. She instructed him to bend over, then she grabbed hold of him. Sure enough, everything was fine. The manager then looked up and saw her lawyer banging his head against the wall.

'What's wrong with him?' the manager asked.

'Oh, him,' she replied. 'I bet him £100,000 that by 10am this morning, I would have the manager of the Bank of England by the balls.'

✳✳✳✳

A man calls his lawyer and asks: 'How much would you charge me to answer three questions?'

'£400,' the lawyer replies.'

' Jesus,' says the man, 'that's a lot of money, isn't it?'

'I guess so,' replies the lawyer. 'What's your third question?'

✳✳✳✳

One day little Johnny went to his father, and asked him if he could buy him a £200 bicycle for his birthday. Johnny's father said, 'Johnny, we have a £80,000 mortgage on the house, and you want me to buy you a bicycle? Wait until Christmas.'

Christmas came around, and Johnny asked again. The father said, 'Well, the mortgage is still extremely high, sorry about that. Ask me again some other time.'

Well, about two days later, the boy was seen walking out of the house with all his belongings in a suitcase. The father asked him why he was leaving. The boy said, 'Yesterday I was walking past your room, and I heard you say that you were pulling out, and mummy said that you should wait because she was coming too, and I'll be damned if I'm going to get stuck with an £80,000 mortgage!'

✳✳✳✳

A newly-wed couple had recently opened a joint bank account. 'Darling,' said the man. 'The bank has returned that cheque you wrote last week.'

'Great,' said the woman. ' What shall I spend it on next?'

****

John's wife was not so good with money and, determined to economise, he'd decided to have a chat with her about it. The following day he met up with his mate.

'So,' asked his mate, 'do you think your little chat worked?'

'Yes, I think so,' said John. 'I'm going to give up beer and fags.'

****

Three engineers and three accountants are travelling by train to a conference. At the station, the three accountants each buy tickets and watch as the three engineers buy only a single ticket.

'How are three people going to travel on only one ticket?' asks an accountant.

'Watch and you'll see,' answers an engineer.

They all board the train. The accountants take their respective seats but all three engineers cram into a toilet and close the door behind them. Shortly after the train has departed, the conductor comes around collecting tickets. He knocks on the toilet door and says, 'Ticket, please.' The door opens just a crack and a single arm emerges with a ticket in hand. The conductor takes it, clips it and moves on.

The accountants see this and agree it's quite a clever idea. So after the conference, the accountants decide to copy the engineers on the return trip and save some money (being clever with money and all that). When they get to the station, they buy a single ticket for the return trip. To their astonishment, the engineers don't buy a ticket at all.

'How are you going to travel without a ticket?' says one perplexed accountant.

'Watch and you'll see,' answers an engineer.

When they board the train the three accountants cram into a toilet and the three engineers cram into another one nearby. The train departs. Shortly afterward, one of the engineers leaves his toilet and walks over to the toilet where the accountants are hiding. He knocks on the door and says, 'Ticket, please.'

****

A butcher is in his shop and he's busy working when he notices a dog in the shop. He shoos him away, but later, he notices the dog is back again. So he goes over to the dog, and notices he has a note in his mouth. He takes the note and it reads, 'Can I have 12 sausages and a leg of lamb, please? The dog has money in his mouth.' The butcher looks inside the dog's mouth and, lo and behold, there is a £10 note in there. So he takes the money, and puts the sausages and lamb in a bag and places it in the dog's mouth. The butcher is well impressed, and since it's close to closing time, he decides to shut up shop and follow the dog.

So off he goes. The dog is walking down the street, when he comes to a level crossing. The dog puts down the bag, jumps up and presses the button and waits for the lights to change. They do, and he walks across the road, with the butcher following him all the way. The dog then comes to a bus stop, and starts looking at the timetable. The butcher is in awe by this stage. The dog checks out the times, and then sits on one of the seats provided. Along comes a bus. The dog walks around the front, looks at the number, and goes back to his seat. Another bus comes. Again the dog goes and looks at the number, sees it's the right bus, and climbs on.

The butcher, by now open-mouthed, follows him onto the bus. The bus travels through the town and out into the suburbs with the dog looking at the scenery. Eventually he gets up, and moves to the front of the bus. He stands on his hind legs and pushes the bell to stop the bus. Then he gets off, his groceries still in his mouth.

Well, dog and butcher are walking along the road, and then the dog turns into a house. He walks up the path, and drops the bag on the step.

Then he walks back down the path, takes a big run, and throws himself – whap!– against the door. He goes back down the path, runs up to the door and – whap!– throws himself against it again.

There's no answer at the house, so the dog goes back down the path, jumps up on a narrow wall, and walks along the perimeter of the garden. He gets to the window, and beats his head against it several times, walks back, jumps off, and waits at the door. The butcher watches as a big guy opens the door, and starts laying into the dog, kicking him and punching him and swearing at him. The butcher runs up, and stops the guy.

'What the hell are you doing ? The dog is a genius. He could be on TV, for God's sake !'

The big guy responds, 'Clever, my arse. This is the second time this week that he's forgotten his key.'

****

Two weevils grew up in London. One went to Hollywood and became a world-famous actor. The other stayed behind in the cotton fields and never amounted to much. The second is now known as the lesser of two weevils.

****

An engineer, a manager and a computer programmer driving down a steep mountain road. The brakes failed and the car careered down the road out of control. Halfway down the driver managed to stop the car by running it against the embankment, narrowly avoiding going over a cliff. They all got out, shaken by their narrow escape from death, but otherwise unharmed.

The manager says, 'To fix this problem we need to organise a committee, have meetings, and develop a solution.'

The engineer says, 'No, that would take too long, and besides that method never worked before. I have my trusty pen-knife here and will take apart the brake system, isolate the problem and correct it.'

The computer programmer says, 'I think you're both wrong! We should all push the car back up the hill and see if it happens again.'

Chapter 10
Quiz Night

265

It is now a legal requirement for each and every pub in the land to have a night where some local loudmouth is given a microphone so that they can become even louder, as they blast out an astonishing array of questions supposed to be general knowledge, but in fact requiring a Phd or 10 hours a day surfing the Internet to answer.

They do this to various groups of people huddled round tables masquerading under some highly comical team name such as 'The Studs,' or 'The Cranial Crusaders,' who then scribble answers down whilst simultaneously operating a NATO-style defence manoeuvre so that other comically-named teams can't see their answers. At the end of it all the winners get a bottle of whisky, containing about the amount they would have drunk if they hadn't been spending so much time trying to answer the questions. Now that's entertainment…

****

Q: What's the last thing to go through a bug's mind as it hits the windscreen?
A: His arse!

****

Q: How do most men define marriage?
A: A very expensive way to get your laundry done free.

****

Q: Why do policemen have bigger balls than firemen?
A: They sell more tickets.

****

Q: How do you make a bunch of little old ladies say 'fuck'?.
A: Shout 'Bingo!'

****

Q: What do you call a man with a shovel in his head?
A: Doug.

****

Q: What do you call a man without a shovel in his head?
A: Douglas.

****

Q: What do you call a lady with a toothpick in her head?
A: Olive.

****

Q: What do you call a lady with one leg longer than the other?
A: Eileen.

****

Q: What do you call a Chinese lady with one leg longer than the other?
A: Irene.

****

Q: What do you call a lady with both legs the same length?
A: Nolene.

****

Q: What do you call an epileptic in a pile of leaves?
A: Russell.

****

Q: What do you call a man with a wooden head?
A: Edward.

****

Q:What do you call a man with three wooden heads?
A: Edward Woodward.

****

Q: What do you call a man with four wooden heads?
A: I don't know, but Edward Woodward would.

****

Q: What do you call a man with a rabbit up his bum?
A: Warren.

****

Q: What do you call a man with his legs chopped off at the knees?
A: Neil.

****

Q: What do you call a man who is being electrocuted?
A: Buzz.

****

Q: What do you call a man who sits at your front door?
A: Matt.

****

Q: What do you call a man who has his head stuck under your car?
A: Jack.

****

Q: What do you call a man who has no arms and legs who is nailed to the wall?
A: Art.

****

Q: What do you call the arms and legs of the above-mentioned man?
A: Pieces of Art.

****

Q: What do you call a man with no arms and legs floating in the ocean?
A: Bob.

****

Q: What do you call a lady who is the stand-in for Polly in *Fawlty Towers*?
A: Polly-filler.

****

Q: What do you call a whole bunch of dead, bald, smokers floating in the ocean at Christmas?
A: Yul-tide.

****

Q: What do you call a man with toilet paper in his mouth?
A: John.

****

Q: What do you call a man who has been buried for 2,000 years?
A: Pete.

****

Q: What do you call a dog with no legs?
A: It doesn't matter what you call him – he still won't come.

****

Q: What do you call a deer with no eyes?
A: No idea.

****

Q: What do you call a deer with no eyes and no legs?
A: Still no idea.

****

Q: What do you call a deer with no eyes and no legs who is chewing a razor?
A: Still no bloody idea.

****

Q: What do you call a man who hangs off the back of a car?
A: Reg.

****

Q: What do you call the man who hangs off the back of a car's brother?
A: Our Reg.

****

Q: What do you get when you cross a penis and a potato?
A: A dictator!

****

Q: What's the difference between a terrorist and a women with PMS?
A: You can negotiate with a terrorist!

****

Q: Why was the mushroom invited to all the parties?
A: Because he was a fungi.

****

Q: Why does a prostitute earn more money than a drug dealer?
A: 'Cos she can wash her crack and use it again.

****

Q: How do you turn a duck into a soul singer?
A: Put it in a microwave till its bill withers.

****

Q: What do you call a man with no arms and no legs swimming the Channel?

A: Clever Dick.

****

Q: What do you call a man with no arms, no legs and no dick, swimming the Channel?
A: Smart Arse.

****

Q: What's red and invisible?
A: No tomatoes.

****

Q: What do you call a sheep with no legs?
A: A cloud.

****

Q: What do you call a greenfly without legs?
A: A bogey.

****

Q: What's green and spongey?
A: A green sponge.

****

Q: How do you reunite The Beatles?
A: Three more bullets.

****

Q: What's 10 foot long and stinks of piss?
A: Old people doing the conga.

****

Q: What do ghosts do if they want to have a party?
A: See if they can dig up a few old friends.

****

Q: What do you call two ghosts in an aeroplane?
A: High spirits.

****

Q: Why did King Kong buy 15 pairs of shoes?
A: Because he was a 30-foot monster.

****

Q: Why did the ghost spend so long in the bathroom?
A: Because the spirit was willing but the flush was weak.

****

Q: What's got a big stomach and lives in the Himalayas?
A: The Abdominal Snowman.

****

Q: How could the vampire's mum tell he'd been smoking?
A: Because of his coffin.

****

Q: What lies in a garden and trembles?
A: A nervous rake.

****

Q: What sits on the beach and cackles?
A: A sand witch.

****

Q: What sits in the desert and cackles?
A: A toasted sand witch.

****

Q: Where does Quasimodo keep his pet rabbit?
A: In a hutch, back of Notre Dame.

****

Q: What's brown and sticky?
A: A stick.

****

Q: What do you call a boomerang that doesn't come back?
A: A stick.

****

Q: What does a ghost take for constipation?
A: Spirit of figs.

****

Q: What's hot, meaty and chases Ebeneezer Scrooge?
A: The ghost of Christmas Pasties.

****

Q: Why do hippos make love in water?
A: Do you have any idea how difficult it is to keep a seven-pound clitoris moist.

****

Q: What's the difference between cheese and men?
A: Cheese matures.

****

Q: Why is a cucumber and a beer better than a man?
A: Because the beer comes in a can, not your mouth, and the cucumber stays hard for a week.

****

Q: Why did God create men?
A: Because vibrators can't mow the lawn.

****

Q: How many men does it take to open a beer?
A: None: it should be open by the time she brings it to the couch.

****

Q: What's the smelliest thing in the world?
A: An anchovy's bottom.

****

Q: What's the difference between ignorance and apathy?
A: I don't know and I don't care!

****

Q: How are a haemophiliac and a virgin alike?
A: One prick… and it's all over!

****

Q: What's green and red and faster than an airplane?
A: A frog in a blender!

****

Q: Why is a man like a Rubik cube?
A: The longer you play with one, the harder it gets.

****

Q: How many Zen Masters does it take to change a lightbulb?
A: Two, one to change it and one not to change it.

****

Q: What's blue and screws old ladies?
A: Hypothermia.

****

Q: Why do farts smell?
A: So that deaf people can enjoy them, too!

****

Q: What do you call a truck full of vibrators?
A: Toys for twats.

****

Q: How many Vietnam vets does it take to change a light bulb?
A: I don't know. That's right, you don't know because you weren't there.

****

Q: Why do blondes wear panties?
A: To keep their ankles warm.

****

Q: What do you call two lesbians in a boat?
A: Fur traders!

****

Q: What should you do with your arsehole before you have sex?
A: Drop him off at the golf club.

****

Q: How do you make six pounds of fat look attractive?
A: Put a nipple on it.

****

Q: What do you get when you mix a Jehovah's Witness with a Hell's Angel?
A: Someone who knocks on your front door at 7.30 on a Sunday morning, and tells you to fuck off.

****

Q: What do men and parking spaces have in common?
A: The good ones are always gone first and the ones that are left are disabled.

****

Q: How do you kill a circus?
A: Go for the juggler.

****

Q: What do you call the useless bit of skin at the end of a penis?
A: A man.

****

Q: What do elephants use as a vibrator?
A: A python with Parkinson's disease.

****

Q: What's the difference between a pub and a clitoris?
A: Most men can find a pub.

****

Q: What does tofu have in common with a vibrator?
A: They're both meat substitutes.

****

Q: What's the best way to get in touch with your long-lost relatives?
A: Win the lottery.

****

Q: Did you hear about the devil-worshipping dyslexic?
A: He sold his soul to Santa.

****

Q: How do you stop a dog from barking in the back garden?
A: Put it in the front garden.

****

Q: Why do cows have bells?
A: Because their horns don't work.

****

Q: How do you get two whales in a Mini?
A: One in the back, one in the front.

****

Q: How do you get two ants in the same Mini?
A: You can't, it's full of whales.

****

Q: Why was Cinderella chucked out of Disneyland?

A: Because she was caught sitting on Pinnochio's face saying, 'Lie, lie, lie.'

****

A man goes into a fish and chip shop and orders fish and chips twice. The shop owner says, 'I heard you the first time.'

****

Two crisps were walking down the road when a passing motorist offers them a lift. 'No thanks,' say the crisps, 'we're Walkers.'

****

Two lepers were walking down the street. 'How are you?' says one. 'Mustn't crumble,' replies the other.

****

Q: What do you call a Spice Girl with two brain cells?
A: Pregnant.

****

Q: What do you call a Spice Girl sitting behind a steering-wheel?
A: An airbag.

****

Q: What do you call a polar bear in the jungle?
A: Lost.

****

Q: What do you get if you cross a hyena with an Oxo cube?
A: An animal that makes itself a laughing stock.

****

Q: What do you get if you cross a grass field with a cow?
A: A lawn-mooer.

****

Q: What do you get if you cross a herd of cows with an emergency?
A: Udder chaos.

****

Q: What do you get if you cross a cow with a major American city?
A: Moo York.

****

Q: What do you get if you cross a whale with a nun?
A: Blubber and sister.

****

Q: What do you get if you cross a cow with a sheep and a baby goat?
A: The milky baa kid.

****

Q: What do you get if you cross a thief with an orchestra?
A: Robbery with violins.

****

Q: What do you get if you cross a successful book with perfume?
A: A best smeller.

****

Q: What do you get if you cross a pool of water with a spy?
A: James Pond.

****

Q: What do you get if you cross a lost property office with two vicars?
A: The missing parsons bureau

****

Q: What do you get if you cross a famous composer with an Indian?
A: Haydn Sikh.

****

Q: What did Snow White say when the chemist lost her film?
A: Some day my prints will come.

****

Q: Why couldn't the viper viper nose?
A: Because the adder adder handkerchief.

****

Q: What do you get if you cross an ancient English king with a chiropodist?
A: William the Corn-curer.

****

Q: How do you know when elephants have been making love in your garden?
A: The grass is rolled flat and all the bin-liners are missing.

****

Q: Why do elephants paint the soles of the feet yellow?
A: So they can hide upside-down in the custard.

****

Q: How do you know when an elephant has been in your fridge?
A: There are footprints in the butter.

****

Q: Why are elephants large, grey and wrinkled?
A: If they were small, round and white they'd be aspirins.

****

Q: Have you ever seen an elephant swimming in the custard?
A: No, but that just proves the efficiency of their camouflage.

****

Q: What's grey, has four legs, and a trunk?
A: A mouse going on holiday.

****

Q: What's brown, has four legs, and a trunk?
A: The same mouse coming back from holiday.

****

Q: How can you tell when there's an elephant in bed with you?
A: Because they have a big 'E' on their pyjamas.

****

Q: How can you tell when there's an elephant under the bed?
A: Your nose is touching the ceiling.

****

Q: What should you do if you come across an elephant in the jungle?
A: Wipe it off and say you're sorry.

****

Q: How do elephants get up trees?
A: They sit on an acorn and fall asleep.

****

Q: How do elephants get down from trees?
A: They sit on a leaf and wait for Autumn.

****

Q: Why are crocodiles long, thin and flat?
A: They walk under trees in Autumn.

****

Q: How do you get four elephants into a Mini?

A: Two in the front, two in the back.

****

Q: How do you know when an elephant is visiting your house?
A: There's a Mini outside with three elephants in it.

****

Q: What do elephants use as tampons?
A: Sheep.

****

Q: Why do elephants have long trunks?
A: Sheep don't have strings.

****

Q: How do you get an elephant into a matchbox?
A: Take out all the matches first.

****

Q: Why are elephants large, grey and wrinkled?
A: Have you ever tried ironing one?

****

Q: What's the similarity between an elephant and a blue plum?
A: They are both grey. Well, except the plum.

****

Q: What did Tarzan say, when he saw the elephants coming down the hill?
A: 'Look, the elephants are coming down the hill.'

****

Q: What did Julius Caesar say, when he saw the elephants coming down the hill?
A: 'Look, the plums are coming down the hill' – he was colour-blind.

****

Q: How many hippies does it take to screw in a light bulb?
A: Oh wow, is it like dark, man?

****

Q: How many Paras does it take to screw in a light bulb?
A: 50. One to screw in the light bulb and the remaining 49 to guard him.

****

Q: How many members of the U.S.S. Enterprise does it take to change a light bulb?
A: Seven. Scotty will report to Captain Kirk that the light bulb in the Engineering Section is burnt out, to which Kirk will send Bones to pronounce the bulb dead. Scotty, after checking around, notices that they have no more new light bulbs, and complains that he can't see in the dark to tend to his engines. Kirk must make an emergency stop at the next uncharted planet, Alpha Regula IV, to procure a light bulb from the natives. Kirk, Spock, Bones, Sulu, and three red shirt security officers beam down. The three security officers are promptly killed by the natives and the rest of the landing party is captured.

Meanwhile, back in orbit, Scotty notices a Klingon ship approaching and must warp out of orbit to escape detection. Bones cures the native king who is suffering from the flu, and as a reward the landing party is set free and given all of the light bulbs they can carry. Scotty cripples the Klingon ship and warps back to the planet just in time to beam up Kirk et al. The new bulb is inserted, and the Enterprise continues with its five-year mission.

****

Q: How many pygmies does it take to screw in a light bulb?
A: At least three.

****

Q: How many actors does it take to change a light bulb?
A: Only one. They don't like to share the spotlight.

****

Q: How many Dadaists does it take to screw in a light bulb?
A: To get to the other side.

****

Q: How many consultants does it take to change a light bulb?
A: We don't know. They never get past the feasibility study.

****

Q: How many Ukrainians does it take to screw in a light bulb?
A: They don't need to, they glow in the dark.

****

Q: How many stockbrokers does it take to change a light bulb?
A: Two. One to take out the bulb and drop it, and the other to try to sell it

before it crashes (knowing that it's already burned out).

****

Q: How many magicians does it take to change a light bulb?
A: Depends on what you want to change it into.

****

Q: How many missionaries does it take to change a light bulb?
A: 101. One to change it and 100 to convince everyone else to change light bulbs, too.

****

Q: How many Californians does it take to change a light bulb?
A: Six. One to turn the bulb, one for support, and four to relate to the experience.

****

Q: How many psychiatrists does it take to change a light bulb?
A: Only one, but the bulb has got to really WANT to change.

****

Q: How many graduate students does it take to screw in a light bulb?
A: Only one, but it may take upwards of five years for him to get it done.

****

Q: How many 'Real Men' does it take to change a light bulb?
A: None: 'Real Men' aren't afraid of the dark.

****

Q: How many folk singers does it take to screw in a light bulb?
A: Two. One to change the bulb, and one to write a song about how good the old light bulb was.

****

Q: How many surrealists does it take to change a light bulb?
A: Two. One to hold the giraffe, and the other to fill the bathtub with brightly coloured machine tools.

****

Q: How many Hassidic Jews does it take to change a light bulb?
A: None. They will never change anything.

****

Q: How many accountants does it take to screw in a light bulb?
A: What kind of answer did you have in mind?

****

Q: How many civil servants does it take to change a light bulb?
A: 45. One to change the bulb, and 44 to do the paperwork.

****

Q: How many nuclear engineers does it take to change a light bulb?
A: Seven. One to install the new bulb and six to figure out what to do with the old one for the next 10,000 years.

****

Q: What do you get if you cross a Cuban with an Icelandic person?
A: An ice cube.

****

Q: What do you get if you cross a piece of paper with two composers?
A: A Chopin Listz.

****

Q: What do you get if you cross a joker with a pile of knickers?
A: A jester drawers.

****

Q: What do you get if you cross a fruit with a Welshman?
A: A taffy apple.

****

Q: What do you get if you cross a Greek singer with a yellow fruit?
A: Banana Mouskouri.

****

Q: What do you get if you cross a highwayman with a pickle?
A: Dick Gherkin.

****

Q: What do you get if you cross a chicken with a parrot?
A: Fowl language.

****

Q: What do you get if you cross a mass murderer with a fish?
A: Jack the Kipper.

****

A down and out approached a well-dressed bloke. 'Ten pence for a cup of tea, Guv?' he asked.
The bloke gave him the money and after waiting for five minutes said, 'So where's my cup of tea, then?'

****

Q: How many ears did Davy Crockett have?
A: Three. A left ear, a right ear and a wild frontier.

****

Q: What's a Hindu?
A: Lay eggs.

****

Q: Who rides around on a camel carrying a lamp?
A: Florence of Arabia.

****

Q: What do zebras have that no other animals have?
A: Baby zebras.

****

Q: What's the difference between a dead skunk on the road and a

dead lawyer?
A: There are skid marks in front of the skunk.

****

Q: Why did the chicken cross the road
A: Because is was stuck to the chicken-fucker's knob.

****

Q: Why was the skeleton afraid to cross the road?
A: He had no guts!

****

Q: Why have elephants got big ears?
A: Because Noddy won't pay the ransom

****

Q: What do vampires become after they reach the age of 200?
A: 201

****

Q. Why is 6 afraid of 7?
A. Because 7 ate 9

****

Q: Why was the legless dog called Woodbine
A: Because it's owner took it out for a drag in the garden twice a day

****

Q: What do you call two elephants on a bicycle ?
A: Optimistic!

****

Q: What do you get if you take an elephant into the city?
A: Free Parking.

****

Q: What do you get if you take an elephant into work ?
A: Sole use of the lift.

****

Q: How do you know if there is an elephant in the pub?
A: It's bike is outside.

****

Q: How do you know if there are two elephants in the pub?
A: There is a dent in the cross-bar of the bike outside.

****

Q: How do you know if there are three elephants in the pub?
A: Stand on the bike and have a look in the window.

****

Q: What do you call a small box with a sattelite dish on the side?
A: A council house.

****

Q: Why did the chicken cross the road?
A: To get to the otherside.

****

Q: How can keep an Irishman busy?
A: Give him two shovels and tell hims to take his pick.

****

Q: Did you hear about the Irish woodworm?
A: It was found dead in a brick.

****

Q: How can you spot an Irish aeroplane?
A: It's got an outside lav.

****

Q: What happened at the Irish Water Polo championships?
A: All the horses drowned.

****

Q: What do you call a scouser in a suit?
A: The accused.

****

Q: What do you call a cockney in a detatched house?
A: A burglar.

Chapter 11
Pissed As A Fart

Reality, eh? Maybe as the philosophers would have us believe we're all living in some ludicrous dream where nothing is real, yet everything is real, and we could all fly if we really wanted to in craft made out of eggshells and those bits of black stuff you get between your toes. Then again maybe philosophers are the biggest bunch of pissheads around, who spend their lives in that state somewhere just past 'lively' and just before, 'pass out' where the most ludicrous of suggestions seems like a very sensible idea, and the worst puns and crappiest jokes get massive laughs. At least we hope they do...

****

Two bits of vomit were walking down the street when one of them began to cry.

'What's the matter?' asked the first.

'I'm sorry,' said the other, 'but I always get a bit sentimental when I pass the place I was brought up.'

****

'Hello, and welcome to the Psychiatric Hotline. If you are obsessive-compulsive, please press 1 repeatedly. If you are co-dependent, please ask someone to press 2. If you have multiple personalities, please press 3, 4, 5 and 6. If you are paranoid-delusional 36.

****

Three cons escape from prison. They make it to a nearby town, but are confronted by a policeman. 'Hey, aren't you those three escaped cons?' asked the policeman.

Thinking on his feet the first con looked around him and said 'no, I'm Mark... Mark Spencer.'

The second followed his lead and said, 'My name is William, W H Smith.'

The third said, 'My name is Ken... Tucky Fried Chicken.'

****

A man sits down at a restaurant and looks at the menu. He tells the waiter, 'I think I will have the turtle soup.' The waiter leaves, but the man changes his mind to pea soup. He yells to the waiter, 'Hold the turtle, make it pea!'

****

A drunk decides to go ice fishing, so he gathers his gear and goes walking around until he finds a big patch of ice. He heads into the centre of the ice and begins to saw a hole. All of a sudden, a loud booming voice comes out of the sky and says, 'You will find no fish under that ice.'

The drunk looks around, but sees no one so he starts sawing again. Once more, the voice speaks. 'As I said before, there are no fish under the ice.'

The drunk looks all around, high and low, but can't see a single soul, so he picks up the saw and tries one more time to finish. Before he can even start cutting, the huge voice interrupts. 'I have warned you three times, now. There are no fish!'

'The drunk is now flustered and somewhat scared, so he asks the voice, 'How do you know there are no fish? Are you God trying to warn me?''

'No,' the voice replies. 'I am the manager of this ice rink.'

****

A man walks into a pub with his monkey. He orders a pint and sits down to drink it. While he's sitting at the bar, his monkey is out of control. It jumps up on the pool table and eats the cue ball. The landlord runs up to the man and says, 'Did you see what your stupid monkey just did?'

'No, what did that stupid fucker do this time?' says the man.

'He just ate the cue ball!' shouts the landlord.

'I hope it kills the stupid bastard,' says the man.

About two weeks later, the man comes back to the pub with his monkey.

While he's drinking at the bar, his monkey is again out of control. The monkey finds a grape at the bar, picks it up, sticks it up his arse, and eats it. The landlord, having seen this, asks the man: 'Did you see what your sick monkey just did?'

'No,' says the man.

'He just stuck a grape up his arse and ate it,' the landlord tells him.

'Well, what do you expect?' asks the man. 'Since that pool ball he measures everything first.'

****

A thirsty-looking big, bad, brown bear comes walking into a pub and shouts, 'Oi, landlord, give me a pint!'

The landlord walks over to the bear and confidently says, 'Sorry but we don't serve beers to big, bad, brown bears in this pub.'

This pisses the bear off as he's growing thirstier by the second. So, the bear leans on the bar and says, 'Just give me a beer.'

The landlord replies again, 'Sorry, but we don't serve beers to big, bad, brown bears in this pub.' The bear, who is really pissed off now, leans over the bar, looks the landlord square in the eyes and says, 'If you don't give me a beer, I'm going to go bite that girls head off!' pointing to the women at the end of the bar.

The landlord repeats himself, 'Sorry but we don't serve beers to big, bad, brown bears in this pub.'

So the bear walks down to the girl... GGGRRRRRRRR... CHOMP... GULP. He bites her head off and swallows it whole. The bear walks back over to the bartender, slams his bloody paws on the table and says, 'Give me a fucking beer!'

The landlord looks the bear straight in the eyes and says, 'Sorry but we don't serve beers to big, bad, brown bears WHO DO DRUGS in this pub.'

The bear, who's a bit confused, shouts, 'WHAT?'

The landlord points to the half-eaten girl and says, 'that was a Bar-Bitch-U-ate.'

****

A panda sauntered into the pub, sat down at the bar and said to the landlord, 'Give me a sandwich and a pint.'

The landlord had seen many strange characters in his time, and knew it was important to keep his cool, so he replied, 'Sure, mate,' and slapped a ham sandwich and a lager in front of the panda. The panda chomped on the sandwich and gulped down the beer. He then deftly pulled out a pistol, aimed at a whisky bottle behind the counter, and pulled the trigger. The bottle exploded into pieces and shattered onto the floor. The landlord was dumbfounded as he watched the panda return his gun to his holster and walk out the front door.

'Hey, what the hell is going on?' shouted the landlord as he ran after the beast.

The panda stopped and said, 'What do you want?'

'Well, I didn't expect you to come into my pub and start shooting the place up. Besides, you still owe me for lunch.'

'I'm a PANDA. Look it up,' replied the panda and went on his way.

The landlord was too upset and nervous to rile such an unpredictable sort, so he picked up his unabridged dictionary from the shelf, and found the entry for 'panda'. 'Shit!' he muttered. He realised that there was nothing he could do about it. There it was, in black and white, written by an authority no less than Oxford University itself: 'panda n. A large bear-like member of the raccoon family native to the mountains of China and Tibet, with distinctive white and black markings. Eats shoots and leaves.'

****

An Indian tribe had a chief named Shortcake. He was highly regarded by all the members of the tribe and when he died, all the braves took him out and prepared to bury him. Just then his wife came running up and shouted, 'Wait! Wait! Squaw bury Shortcake.'

****

Charles was working for many years as the elephant trainer in a local circus. Then, after a few rough years, the circus went bust and he was let go with a 'thank you', one of the elephants and a few bales of hay.

Feeling rather depressed, Charles got to wondering how he was going to survive with only an elephant and no career. Then he remembered his days in the circus and realised he was on to a good thing. In all his years in the circus, he had trained elephants to lift one leg off the ground, lift two legs off the ground and even lift three legs off the ground, but NEVER had he seen four legs off the ground at once. Near and far he advertised, '£1 a go, win £1,000 if you can make the elephant lift four legs off the ground at once.'

People came from near and far to try and Charles was raking in the money. He had made about £700 when one day a fellow arrived in a red convertible. He asked about the rules of the contest and paid his money. He walked back to the car, took out a baseball bat, walked to the front of the elephant, looked him in the eye long and hard. Then he walked around the back of the elephant, took a mighty swing and struck the animal in the testicles. At once the elephant leapt into the air and Charles was down £1,000 and feeling very sorry for himself. Then he remembered his days at the circus and in all his days he had never seen an elephant move his head from side to side. Up and down he had seen, round and round he had seen but NEVER from side to side.

Near and far he advertised, '£1 a go, win £1,000 if you can make the elephant move his head from side to side.People came from near and far to try and Charles was raking the money in when one day the same fellow arrived in his red convertible. Again he asked the rules and walked to his car. He returned with a baseball bat, walked to the front of the elephant, looked the animal in the eye long and hard and said, 'You remember me, don't you?'

The elephant nodded.

'You remember what I did to you?'

The elephant nodded.

'You remember the PAIN?'

The elephant nodded.

'Do you want me to do it again?'

****

So, this guy, Bill is sitting at the bar and pulls out this tiny little piano and a little guy about a foot tall. The little guy sits down and starts playing the piano quite beautifully. The fellow on the next bar stool, Joe, says, 'That's amazing. Where did you get him?'

Bill says, 'Well, I got this magic lamp with a genie.'

'That's great,' says Joe. 'Could I use it?'

Bill says, 'Sure,' and hands him the lamp.

Joe rubs the lamp and out comes the genie. He says,' I want a million quid.' Suddenly the room is entirely filled with octopuses! Joe exclaims, 'Hey! I asked for a million QUID! not SQUID!'

'Yeah, sorry about that, the genie is a bit deaf,' says Bill. 'You don't think I really asked for a 12-inch-pianist, do you?'

****

Then there's the drunk who went out on a long bender. Somewhere in the course of his wanderings the right pocket was ripped out of his trousers. The drunk, sobering up somewhat after several days, begins to take stock of himself and his condition. He reaches into his coat pocket, pulls out the contents and checks them. All is well. He reaches into his left trouser pocket, pulls out the contents – again all is well. Then he reaches into his right trouser pocket. He feels around a bit then, with a quizzical look on his face says to himself, 'Prunes, prunes... now why in the hell did I buy prunes?'

****

A neutron walks into a pub. 'I'd like a beer,' he says. The landlord promptly serves him a beer. 'How much will that be?' asks the neutron.

'For you?' replies the landlord, 'no charge.'

****

Three bits of string walked by a pub and noticed a sign outside it that said, 'NO STRING ALLOWED'. Indignant at the discrimination the first piece of string decided to go in and order a drink.

'Can't you read?' said the landlord, and when the string refused to leave he picked it up and tossed it out the door. The second piece of string tried the same thing and when it also refused to leave, the landlord punched it and threw it out the door as well. The third piece of string thought for a few seconds, then scraped itself along the pavement harshly until it was ragged all over. Then it twisted itself inside out and around and around until its middle was all in a bunch, then it entered the pub, got upon a stool and ordered a pint.

'Hey,' asked the landlord suspiciously, 'aren't you the string I just threw out of here?'

'No,' replied the string, 'I'm a frayed knot.'

****

A duck goes into a pub and asks the landlord, 'You got any fish?'

The landlord says, 'No. This is a pub, we don't sell fish.' So the duck leaves. The next day, the duck goes back to the pub and asks, 'You got any fish?'

The landlord says, 'I told you yesterday. This is a pub and we don't sell fish.'

The following day, the duck returns and asks, 'You got any fish?'

The landlord loses it, grabs the duck by the neck, and screams, 'I TOLD YOU TWICE. THIS IS A PUB! WE DON'T SELL FISH! IF YOU ASK AGAIN, I'M GONNA NAIL YOUR FUCKING WEBBED FEET TO THE FLOOR!'

The next day, the duck goes in the pub and asks, 'Got any nails?'

The landlord sighs and says, 'No, we don't have any nails.'

'Good,' says the duck. 'Got any fish?'

****

The landlord got tired of hearing these five drunks arguing about who had the biggest dick. So he shouts out, 'I'm tired of this shit. Pull them out and put them up on the bar and I'll tell you who has the biggest.'

They were drunk enough that all five of them responded and placed their dicks up on the bar. Just then a gay guy walks in, and the landlord asks, 'May I help you?'

To which he responds: 'Well, I came in for a pint and a sandwich but I think I'll have the smorgasbord.'

****

The first little pig walked into the pub and said, 'Can I have a rum and Coke?'

'OK,' said the landlord. Then the little pig said, 'Can I use your toilet?' and similarly the landlord agreed.

Then a second little pig walked into the pub and said, 'Can I have a rum and Coke?' and once again the landlord poured him one.

Then the little pig said, 'Can I use your toilet?' to which the landlord similarly agreed. Then a third little pig walked into the pub and said, 'Can I have a rum and Coke?'

'OK,' said the landlord, 'and I suppose you want to use the toilet, too'.

But the third little pig said, 'No, I'm the lttle pig that goes wee, wee, wee all the way home'

****

One night, after closing time, a landlord is sitting at his bar minding his own business, when a spectral hound floats in through the door. The landlord, being an exceptionally cool kind of geezer, asks, 'Yeah, what do you want?'

The phantom hound explains, in a haunting voice, 'I've lost my tail and cannot rest until a kindly landlord stitches it back on.' At this request the landlord stands back astonished and says to the phantom dog.

'Sorry, but we don't re-tail spirits at this time of night.'

****

A doctor made it his regular habit to stop off at a bar for a hazelnut daiquiri on his way home. The bartender knew of his habit, and would always have the drink waiting at precisely 5:03pm. One afternoon, as the end of the working day approached, the bartender was dismayed to find that he was out of hazelnut extract. Thinking quickly, he threw together a daiquiri made with hickory nuts and set it on the bar.

The doctor came in at his regular time, took one sip of the drink and exclaimed, 'This isn't a hazelnut daiquiri!'

'No, I'm sorry,' replied the bartender, 'it's a hickory daiquiri, doc.'

****

A bloke goes to the doctor with a heavily-infected arm, all yellow and pussy. After examining it the doc asks, 'What is it that you do?'

'I work in the circus,' replies the man.

'I see,' says the doc. 'And what do you do in the circus?'

'I work with the elephants,' replies the man.

'I see,' says the doc. 'And what do you do with the elephants?'

'Well,' says the man. 'It's my job to give them enemas. I put my arm right up their backsides and get on with it.'

'I think,' says the doc, 'that therein lies your problem. You're going to have to stop doing that and find another job.'

'What and give up showbiz?' replies the man.

****

There was a woman who was pregnant with twins, and shortly before they were due, she had an accident and went into a coma. Her husband was away on business, and couldn't to be reached. While in the coma, she gave birth to her twins, and the only person around to name her children was her brother.

When the mother came out of her coma to find she had given birth and that her brother had named the twins, she became very worried, because he wasn't a very bright guy. She was sure he'd named them something absurd or stupid. When she saw her brother she asked him about the twins.

He said, 'The first one was a girl.'

'What did you name her?' asked the woman.

'Denise!' said her brother.

'Oh, that's not bad,' she said. 'What about the second one?'

'The second one was a boy,' said her brother.

'Oh, and what did you name him?' she asked.

'Denephew,' said the brother.

✱✱✱✱

One afternoon this young woman called on her neighbour for a chat. She walked in and said, 'You look depressed.'

'You bet I am,' replied the neighbour. 'Look what my bloody husband sent me – six dozen roses. Now I'm going to have to spend the entire weekend flat on my back with my legs open.'

'Don't be silly,' said the first woman, 'why don't you just use a vase?'

✱✱✱✱

It seems a man got turned in by his neighbour who saw him having sex with a goat. He was arrested and told to get a lawyer. He had a choice of two. It was a small town. One lawyer was very expensive. He usually won his case by having costly out-of-town experts testify. The other was cheap. His forte was jury selection, he could usually get a juror or two that would be sympathetic to his client. The defendant chose the less expensive lawyer.

The first day of the trial the witness was told to tell the jury exactly what he saw on the morning of March 15th. He stated that he happened to look out his kitchen window about 8am and he saw farmer Brown drop his pants and have sex with a tan-coloured goat. And when he finished the goat turned around and licked his penis. At this time a front-row juror was heard to say to another juror, 'You know, a good goat will do that.'

****

Woman goes to the doctor and says, 'Doctor, my husband limps because his left leg is an inch shorter than his right leg. What would you do in his case?'

'Probably limp, too,' says the doc.

****

A 60-year-old woman came home one day and heard strange noises in her bedroom. She opened the door and discovered her 40-year-old daughter playing with her vibrator. 'What are you doing?' asked the Mum.

'Mum, I am 40 years old and look at me,' said the daughter. 'I am ugly. I will never get married, so this is pretty much my husband.' The mother walked out of the room, shaking her head.

The next day the father came home and heard noises in the bedroom and upon entering the room found his daughter using the vibrator. 'What the hell are you doing?' he asked.

His daughter replied, 'I already told Mum. I am 40 years old now and ugly. I will never get married so this is as close as I'll ever get to a husband.' The father walked out of the room shaking his head too.

The next day the mother came home to find her husband with a beer in one hand and the vibrator sitting next to him, watching the football.

'For Christ's sake, what are you doing?' she cried.

'What does it look like I'm doing?' replied her husband. 'I'm having a beer and watching the game with my new son-in-law!'

****

Two guys wandered into a pub. One of the men shouted to the landlord, 'Hiya, Mike. Set 'em up for me and my mate here.' Then he turned to his slightly dim partner and boasted, 'This is a great pub. For every two drinks you buy, the house gives you one and the fruit machines are free!'

'"That's not so great,' responded the friend. 'There's a pub across town that'll match you drink for drink, and you can get laid for free.'

'Where is this place?' the first guy exclaimed.

'Oh, I don't know,' the dim fellow replied, 'but my wife goes there all the time.'

****

A man walked in to a pub after work. As he began to drink his beer, he heard a voice say seductively, 'You've got great hair!' The man looked around but couldn't see where the voice was coming from, so he went back to his beer.

A minute later, he heard the same voice say, 'You're a handsome man!' The man looked around, but still couldn't see where the voice was coming from. When he went back to his beer, the voice said again, 'What a stud you are!' The man was so baffled by this that he asked the landlord what was going on. The landlord said, 'Oh, it's the nuts – they're complimentary.'

****

An 80-year-old couple decide they want kids again. They visit the doctor who suggests, since they are a little older than usual, some tests might be in order. He hands the couple a small jar and asks them to go next door and for the gentleman to fill it so they can test his sperm count.

A few minutes later the couple returns and hands back the jar. 'But it's still empty!' exclaims the doctor.

'I know,' replies the man. 'I tried with my right hand, I tried with my left hand, then I tried with both hands, and I still couldn't do it. Then my wife tried with her right hand, then her left hand, and with both hands. She tried with her teeth in and her teeth out, and we still couldn't get the lid off that jar!'

****

Two old ladies were waiting for a bus and one of them was smoking a cigarette. It started to rain, so the old lady reached into her handbag, took out a condom, cut off the tip and slipped it over her cigarette and continued to smoke. Her friend saw this and said, 'Hey that's a good idea! What is it that you put over your cigarette?'

The other old lady said, 'It's a condom.'

'A condom?' said her friend. 'Where do you get those?'

The lady with the cigarette told her friend that you could purchase condoms at the chemist.

When the two old ladies arrived in town, the second old lady went into a chemist shop and asked the pharmacist if he sold condoms. The pharmacist said yes, but looked a little surprised that this old lady was interested in condoms. 'What size do you want?' he asked her.

The old lady thought for a minute and said, 'I'd like one that will fit a Camel.'

****

Two missionaries in Africa were apprehended by a tribe of very hostile cannibals who put them in a large pot of water, built a huge fire under it, and left them there. A few minutes later, one of the missionaries started to laugh uncontrollably. The other missionary couldn't believe it!

'What's wrong with you?' he shouted. 'We're being boiled alive! They're gonna eat us! What could possibly be funny at a time like this?'

' Well,' said the other missionary. 'I just pissed in the soup!'

****

It's been a hard year in the jungle, so when these two cannibals finally catch this one missionary they have a discussion about how they are each going to get a fair share. They finally reach the conclusion that they will start at opposite ends and meet in the middle.

After starting the meal one cannibal asks the other, 'How you doing down there?'

'Oh I'm having a ball!' replies the other cannibal.

'No, no!' screamed the first cannibal, 'you're eating too fast!'

****

The devil told the Pope, 'No one in the world has a better memory than I do.'

'Oh!' replied the Pope. 'Well, I know this American Indian who has the best memory in the world and I'll even prove it.'

'OK,' said the devil, 'I'll take up your offer and if I have a better memory I get your soul.'

'It's a deal,' said the Pope.

So off they went to a remote village. There they met Roaming Bull, who was the Indian the Pope had been talking about. The devil asked Roaming Bull what meal he had eaten 20 years ago to the day.

'Eggs,' replied Roaming Bull.

'Thank you,' said the devil and left. Although a short while after leaving town he realised that this could quite easily have been a trick answer and vowed to clear this up the next time he was free.

The devil can be a busy chap, what with all the idle hands in the world and 50 years passed before he returned to the village. This time he greeted the now wizened Roaming Bull in the traditional Indian way. 'How,' said the devil.

'Scrambled,' replied the Indian.

****

A vicar stepping up into the pulpit spots a woman he thinks he knows wearing a mini-skirt seated on the front pew. He leans over to his organist and asks, 'Isn't that Fanny Blue?'

'No,' says the organist, 'I think it's just the way the light's coming through the stain-glass window.'

****

A woman telephoned a vet and asked him to come and examine her cat.

'I don't know what's wrong with her,' the woman told him. 'She looks as if she's going to have kittens, but that's impossible. She's never been out of the house except for when I had her on a leash.'

The vet examined the cat and said there was no question about her pregnancy.

'But she can't be,' protested the woman. 'It's impossible.'

At that point a large tom-cat emerged from under the sofa.

'How about him?' asked the vet.

'Don't be silly,' answered the woman. 'That's her brother.'

****

Three monks are meditating far from the madding crowd, in the Himalayas. One year passes in silence, and one of them says to the others, 'Pretty cold here.'

Another year passes and the second monk says, 'You know, you are quite right.'

Another year passes and the third monk says, 'Hey, I'm going to leave unless you two stop jabbering!'

****

One day two nuns were sitting in their convent talking and drinking tea when a priest arrived. The nuns invited him to sit and have tea with them. He accepted and sat down to discuss upcoming events at their parish.

Suddenly the priest stopped talking in mid-sentence because his eyes had wandered to the piano in the room. Sitting on top of it was an opened unrolled latex condom. He was appalled. 'Sisters,' he said pointing to the piano, 'what do you call that?'

The nuns were oblivious to his shock and simply explained to the priest why the condom was sitting on the piano, 'Well,' said the first nun, 'we saw them advertised on the TV…'

'…And,' finished the second nun, 'the people in the ad said they were really good for you and that everybody should use them every time.'

'So,' said the first nun, 'we went to the shop and bought some. When we got back to the convent, we read the instructions on the back of the box. It said , "Carefully place it on your organ." So we did.'

****

A man saw a priest walking down the street. Noticing his collar, he stopped him and said, 'Excuse me, but why are you wearing your shirt backwards?'

The priest laughed, 'Because, my son,' he said, 'I am a Father!'

The man scratched his head. 'But I am a father too,' he said, 'and don't wear my shirt backwards!'

Again the priest laughed. 'But I am a Father of thousands!'

To which the man replied, 'Well then you should wear your underwear backwards!'

****

Ian is sitting on a bench in front of the Pearly Gates waiting for St Peter to show up when his best friend Tim comes and sits down next to him. They talk for a while until St Peter shows up at the gate.

'I'm sorry, lads,' says the winged one, 'but we only have room for one more person right now.' So the two friends started arguing about who should go in.

'You go Tim,' says Ian.

'No, no,' says Tim. 'You go Ian.'

'No, Tim, I couldn't,' says Ian. 'You go.'

This continues for some time until St Peter stops them and says, 'Right, each one of you will write me a poem about my favourite place, Timbuctoo, and whoever's is best will go to heaven.'

So they both wrote a poem and Ian, wanting his friend Tim to go to heaven rather than him, decides to write a really bad one. When they're both done they go back to St Peter who asks Tim to read his poem first. He does so and it's pretty good. Next St Peter asks the Ian to read his poem. He clears his throat and reads, 'Me and Tim a-hunting went, spied three maidens in a tent, since they were three and we were two, I bucked one and Tim bucked two.'

****

Three old ladies are sitting in a cafe chatting about various things. 'You know,' says one lady, 'I'm getting really forgetful. This morning, I was standing at the top of the stairs, and I couldn't remember whether I had just come up or was about to go down.'

'You think that's bad?' says the second lady. 'The other day, I was sitting on the edge of my bed, and I couldn't remember whether I was going to bed or had just woken up!'

The third lady smiles smugly. 'Well, my memory's just as good as it's always been,' she says, 'touch wood,' and she knocks the table. Then with a startled look on her face, she says, 'Who's there?'

****

An elderly husband and wife noticed that they were beginning to forget many little things around the house. They were afraid that this could be dangerous, as one of them might accidentally forget to turn off the stove and thus cause a fire.

So, they decided to go to see their doctor to get some help. Their doctor told them that many people their age found it useful to write themselves little notes as reminders. The elderly couple thought this sounded wonderful, and left the doctor's office very pleased with the advice. When they got home, the wife said, 'Dear, will you please go to the kitchen and get me a dish of ice cream? And why don't you write that down so you won't forget?'

'Nonsense,' said the husband, 'I can remember a dish of ice cream!'

'Well,' said the wife, 'I'd also like some strawberries on it. You'd better write that down, because I know you'll forget.'

'Don't be silly,' replied the husband. 'A dish of ice cream and some strawberries. I can remember that!'

'OK, dear, but I'd like you to put some whipped cream on top. Now you'd really better write it down now. You'll forget,' said the wife.

'Come now, my memory's not all that bad,' said the husband. 'No problem, a dish of ice cream with strawberries and whipped cream.' With that, the husband shut the kitchen door behind him. The wife could hear him getting out pots and pans, and making some noise inconsistent with his preparing a dish of ice cream, strawberries, and whipped cream.

He emerged from the kitchen about 15 minutes later. Walking over to his wife, he presented her with a plate of bacon and eggs. The wife took one look at the plate, glanced up at her husband and said, 'Hey, where's the toast?'

****

There is this guy who really takes care of his body. He lifts weights and jogs five miles every day. One morning he is looking into the mirror and admiring his body when he notices that he is really sun-tanned all over, except for his penis. So he decides to do something about it.

The next day he goes to the beach, strips completely and buries himself in the sand, except for his penis which he leaves sticking out. Two little old ladies are strolling along the beach and one looks down and says 'There is no justice in this world.'

'What do you mean?' says her friend.

'Look at that,' she says. 'When I was 10 years old I was afraid of it. When I was 20, I was curious about it. When I was 30, I enjoyed it. When I was 40, I asked for it. When I was 50, I paid for it. When I was 60, I prayed for it. When I was 70, I forgot about it. And now that I'm 80, the damn things are growing wild!'

****

Two teenage boys are talking, and the first boy asks the second boy, 'How many wings does a bird have?'

'Two wings,' the second boy replies.

'How many stingers does a bee have?' the first boy asks next.

'One stinger,' responds the second boy.

'And how many ribs does a cat have?' asks the first boy.

'I don't know,' replies the second boy.

'Well,' says the first boy. 'You may know about the birds and the bees, but you don't know much about pussy.'

****

A murderer, sitting in the electric chair, was about to be executed. 'Have you any last requests?' asked the chaplain.'

'Yes,' replied the murderer. 'Will you hold my hand?'

****

Once upon a time there were two deaf mutes standing on a street corner talking to each other with sign language.

Mute One: 'What would you like to do?'

Mute Two: 'I don't know, what about you?'

Mute One: 'Let's get my car, find some girls, drive to a dark space and have some fun.'

Mute Two: 'Good idea.'

So they get his car, find some girls, drive to a dark spot and are having a ball when the guy in the back seat taps the guy in the front seat on the shoulder.

Front Seat Mute: 'What?'

Back Seat Mute: 'Have you got any protection?'

Front Seat Mute: 'No. Have you?'

Back Seat Mute: 'No. We'd better go to a chemist and get some.'

They drive to a chemist and the man in the back seat gets out and goes inside. In two minutes he is back outside and taps on the car window.

Inside Mute: 'What?'

Outside Mute: 'I can't make the chemist understand what I want.'

Inside Mute: 'I know what to do.'

Outside Mute: 'What?'

Inside Mute: 'Go back inside. Put £5 on the counter and put your pecker on the counter. He'll know what you want.'

Outside Mute: 'Good idea.'

The man goes back into the chemist and two minutes later he's back at the car window.

Inside Mute: 'Well?'

Outside Mute: 'It didn't work.'

Inside Mute: 'What do you mean?'

Outside Mute: 'I did what you told me to do. I went inside. I put £5 on the counter and I put my pecker on the counter. Then he put his on the counter. It was bigger than mine so he took my £5.'

****

A blind man was standing on the corner with his dog when the dog raised his leg and pissed on the man's trouser leg. The man reached in his pocket and took out a doggie biscuit. A busybody who had been watching ran up to him and said, 'You shouldn't do that. He'll never learn anything if you reward him when he does something like that!'

'I'm not rewarding him,' the blind man retorted, 'I'm just trying to find his mouth so that I can kick him up the arse.'

****

There were these two guys out hiking when they came upon an old abandoned mine-shaft. Curious about its depth they threw in a pebble and waited for the sound of it striking the bottom, but they heard nothing. They went and got a bigger rock, threw it in and waited. Still nothing. They searched the area for something larger and came upon a large metal fence.

With great difficulty, the two men carried it to the opening and threw it in. While waiting for it to hit bottom, a goat suddenly darted between them and leapt into the hole! The guys were still standing there with astonished looks upon their faces from the actions of the goat when a man walked up to them. He asked them if they had seen a goat anywhere in the area and they said that one had just jumped into the mine shaft in front of them.

'Oh no,' replied the man, 'that couldn't be my goat, mine was tied to a fence.'

****

There were these two statues and they were both a couple of hundred years old. One day, a fairy flew over them and tapped their heads with her wand.

'You have 24 hours to do WHATEVER YOU WANT,' she said to the statues.

Twenty-three hours and 57 minutes later the male statue says to the female statue, 'Why don't we do it again?'

'We don't have enough time!' says the female statue.

'Sure we do!' says the male statue.

'Just ONE MORE TIME, please?'

'Oh, all right!' says the female statue, 'but this time YOU hold the pigeon and I'LL crap on it!'

****

One sunny afternoon Superman was out flying around. Crime was slow that day, so he decided to go over to Spiderman's house. 'Hey, Spidey,' said Superman, 'let's go get a burger and a beer'

'No can do, Supe,' said Spiderman, 'I've got a problem with my Web-shooter. Can't fight crime tomorrow without it.'

So Superman went over to the Bat Cave to see what was up there.

'Hey, Batman!' said Superman, 'Let's go get a burger and a beer!'

'Not today, my friend,' said Batman, 'my Batmobile is down and it must be fixed today. Can't fight crime tomorrow without it.'

Disgruntled, Superman takes to the air, cruising around the skies when he flies over a penthouse apartment. Thanks to his supervision he is able to see Wonderwoman, lying on the balcony, spread eagle and stark naked! So he zooms down and thanks to his superspeed shags her in a flash and is gone before anyone can notice. All of a sudden Wonderwoman sits up and says, 'What was that!?'

'I don't know,' says the Invisible Man, 'but it hurt like hell!'

****

The curator of an art gallery asked an artist for a painting depicting General Custer's last thoughts. Two weeks later, the artist unveiled a painting of an enormous canvas with a lovely blue lake painted in the centre, with a fish leaping from the water with a shining halo around its head.

On the shores of the lake were the most detailed pictures of American Indians fornicating. After gaping at the painting for some time, the enraged curator demanded to know what the theme was supposed to be.

'You asked for a painting of Custer's last thoughts,' he explained. 'That's it… Custer was thinking: 'Holy Mackerel, look at all those fucking Indians?'

****

Two men are approaching each other on a pavement in America. Both are dragging their right foot as they walk. As they meet, one man looks at the other knowingly, points at his foot and says, 'Vietnam, 1969.' The other hooks his thumb behind him and says, 'Dog shit, 20 feet back.'

****

Two British Gas servicemen, a senior training supervisor and a young trainee, were out checking meters in a suburban neighbourhood. They parked their van at the end of the street and worked their way to the other end.

At the last house a woman looking out her kitchen window watched as the senior supervisor challenged his young colleague to a race down the street back to the van to prove that an older guy could outrun a younger one. As they came tearing up to the van, they realised the lady from that end house was huffing and puffing right behind them.

They stopped immediately and asked her what was wrong. 'When I saw two gasmen running as fast as you were,' gasped the woman, 'I figured I'd better run too!'

****

Unable to attend the funeral after his father died, a son who lived far away called his brother and told him, 'Do something nice for Dad and send me the bill.'

Later, he got a bill for £200, which he paid. The next month, he got another bill for £200, which he also paid, figuring it was some incidental expense. Bills for £200 kept arriving every month, and finally the man called his brother again to find out what was going on.

'Well,' said the other brother, 'you said to do something nice for Dad. So I rented him a dinner jacket.'

****

A tourist is travelling through the thickest jungles in South Africa when he comes across an temple. The tourist is entranced by the temple, and asks a local guide for details. The guide says that archaeologists are excavating, and still finding great treasures. The tourist then asks how old the temple is.

'This temple is 1,503 years old,' replies the guide. Impressed at this accurate dating, he inquires as to how he gave this precise figure. 'Easy,' replies the guide, 'the archaeologists said the temple was 1,500 years old, and that was three years ago.'

****

Three men are abducted by cannibals and thrown into a hut to await their fate. The chief tells them that they will be dealt with on a one per day basis. The first day, one man is dragged out and presented with a choice.

'Death or JoJo,' says the chief. The man has no idea what JoJo is, but at least it can't be worse than death, so he accepts JoJo. Immediately, he is strapped naked to a tree face first and one by one the cannibals all fuck him. Torn and bleeding, he is thrown into the hut after that, where he pleads to his companions, 'Don't accept JoJo, accept death.'

The second man is dragged out the second day and presented with the same choice. With his partner's condition still fresh in his mind, he is very afraid, but thinks that at least the guy survived. Hence he also opts for JoJo. He gets fucked again and again and is thrown back into the hut looking twice as bad as his first partner.

The third person is scared out of his wits. When asked the third day, he immediately selects death. The chief nods and passes the sentence, 'Death by JoJo.'

****

Upon entering a fashionable restaurant a couple saw a sign proclaiming it to be 'The World's Most Sanitary Restaurant.' Their waiter came to their table and used a pair of tongs to hand them the menus. All of the silverware and place settings were also placed on their table using tongs. When they questioned the waiter about this, he indicated tongs were used to perform all service functions and was the primary reason the restaurant claimed to be so sanitary.

During the meal, they noticed their waiter had a string hanging out of his fly. The husband called the waiter over and asked about it. The waiter explained the string was tied to his penis and when he had to urinate, he used it to pull it out of his pants without having to touch it which made things even more sanitary. The couple was impressed with all these sanitary procedures.

However, after a few minutes the husband got a puzzled look on his face, again called the waiter over and asked, 'I'm curious about something. How do you manage to get your penis BACK in your trousers?'

'With the tongs, sir,' the waiter replied.

****

A local policeman had just finished his shift one cold November evening and was at home with his wife.

'You just won't believe what happened this evening,' he said to his wife. 'In all my years on the force I've never seen anything like it.'

'Oh yes dear,' she said, 'what happened ?'

'I came across two guys down by the canal,' he told her. 'One of them was drinking battery acid and the other was eating fireworks.'

'Drinking battery acid and eating fireworks?' exclaimed his wife. 'What did you do with them?'

'Oh, that was easy,' said the copper. 'I charged one and let the other off.'

****

An Avon lady was alone in an elevator when suddenly she had to fart. She promptly reached into her bag and sprayed the air with her deodoriser. Two floors later, a gentleman got on the elevator. He began to sniff, and the Avon lady asked, 'Do you smell something?'

'Well, yes I do,' he replied.

'What does it smell like?'

The bemused gentleman answered, 'I'm not sure, but it kind of smells like someone crapped in a pine tree.'

****

Mickey Mouse is in the divorce court and the judge is explaining to him that he can't grant him a divorce on the grounds that Minnie has buck teeth.

'You don't understand,' cries Mickey, 'that's not what I meant when I said she was fucking Goofy.'

****

A fellow was going on a tour of a factory that produces various latex products. At the first stop, he's shown the machine that manufactures baby-bottle teat. The machine made a loud 'hiss pop!' noise.

'The hiss is the rubber being injected into the mould,' explained the guide. 'The popping sound is a needle poking a hole in the end of the teat.'

Later, the tour reached the part of the factory where condoms were manufactured. The machine made a 'hiss, hiss, pop' noise

'Wait a minute!' said the man. 'I understand what the "hiss, hiss" is, but what's that "pop" every so often?'

'Oh, it's rather like the baby-bottle teat machine,' said the guide, 'but here the needle pokes a hole in every fourth condom.'

'Well, that can't be good for the condoms!' said the man.

'No,' the guide said, 'but it's great for the baby-bottle teat business!'

****

A guy goes to work in a zoo. The first job he's given is to clean out the finches' cage, but he's told to be careful because finches are expensive and it'll cost him a tenner for each one he kills. So he's cleaning away when he reaches for a bucket and treads on two finches. 'Shit,' he thinks, 'I know, I'll throw them into the lions' cage and they'll get eaten.'

The next job he's given is to clean the chimps' cage and this time he's told it will cost him £400 if he accidentally kills one. Unfortunately he's a clumsy fellow and in reaching for the polish treads on two chimps. As with the finches, though, he bungs them in the lions' cage and no one is any the wiser.

His final job that day is to clean out the apiary where the bees are kept. Each dead bee will cost him a pound, he's told, and this time he slips over and squashes a large number which of course find their way into the lions' cage, too.

The following day a new lion comes along. Eager to find out about his new home he asks one of the other lions what the food's like.

'It's terrible,' says the other lion, 'all we get are finch, chimps and mushy bees.'

****

A bell ringer is happily ringing the bells one day when he tugs a bit too hard and the rope comes down. Undeterred, he goes up into the bell tower and pushes the bell with his hands. Unfortunately, after a while he loses concentration and the bell smashes into his face. He goes flying out of the window and is killed instantly as he lands on the ground outside.

Two passers by are the first to the scene of the accident. One turns to the other and says, 'Do you know him?'

And the other say, 'No, but his face rings a bell.'

****

During a particularly harsh winter a farmer discovers that all his cows are frozen solid in the meadows. Whilst he's contemplating what to do a little old lady drives up to him in her car and asks for directions. She can see he's a bit down so asks him what's wrong. After finding out the lady goes round every meadow and miraculously, as she goes past each cow, it defrosts and comes back to life.

Amazed and very grateful the farmer says, 'That's incredible Miss, Miss… I'm sorry, I don't even know your name.'

'Oh, it's Thora Hird,' says the little old lady.

****

A man goes into a pub and order a pint of bitter. Halfway through drinking it he has to go for a piss and while he's gone a large black woman, who'd been sitting in the pub, positions herself over his pint and farts into it. She then goes and sits back down again.

When the man comes back from the toilet he's just about to finish his drink when the barman stops him and tells him what happened. Somewhat annoyed the man storms over to the woman and says, 'Oi, you fart in my Whitbread?'

'No,' says the woman, 'I'm Tessa Sanderson.'

✱✱✱✱

A missionary goes to Africa. As soon as he gets off the plane he is amazed at how authentic everything looks. It's all exactly as he expected. Even the sounds are what he had come to associate with Africa, an incessant beating of drums. As he leaving the airport he turns to the baggage handler and asks him, 'Do the drums continue all the time?'

'Oh yes,' he replies, 'if the drums stop, it's very bad news'

'So he gets into a taxi and, still hearing the beating drums, asks again, 'Do the drums ever stop?'

'Oh no,' replies the taxi driver, 'if the drums stop, it's very bad news.'

Eventually he arrives at his hotel and still the drums are beating. 'Tell me,' he says to the hotel receptionist, 'do the drums continue all the time?'

'Oh yes,' he replies, 'if the drums stop, it's very bad news.'

That evening he comes down from his room and still the drums are beating. He goes for a drink in the hotel bar and, of course, has to have a word about the drums to the barman. 'Tell me,' he says to the barman, 'do the drums ever stop?'

'Oh no,' replies the barman, 'if the drums stop, it's very bad news.'

'But why,' asks the missionary, 'is it such bad news when the drums stop?'

'Because,' explains the barman, 'when the drums stop it's the bass solo.'

✱✱✱✱

It's a son's birthday and he asks his father for a ride in a helicopter for a present. The father phones up a mate of his who works as a helicopter stuntman and asks him if that will be OK. The pilot says, 'OK, I'll do it but I can only fly in complete silence. If you make a noise, I'll have to charge you double.' The father thinks about this for a while and says OK.

The next week, father and son strap themselves in and the father says, 'Now listen to me son. The pilot can only fly in complete silence so you mustn't make a sound.'

'OK, dad,' says the son as they take off. Pretty soon, they're soaring through the sky and the pilot thinks to himself, 'I don't want to pay for this flight. I'll do some really scary stunts and the boy will make a noise.' So he starts doing loop-the-loops and flying upside-down. Not a sound comes from behind him. He lands 40 minutes later and shakes the father's hand. 'That was amazing. I tried everything to make you to make a noise but you were completely quiet.' The father says 'Yes, it was hard. I really had to keep my lip buttoned when the lad fell out.'

****

A director is talking to an actor. 'Now, in the next scene,' he says. 'Make love to her like an animal. Imagine you're a gorilla or a lion or a bear or something.'

'OK,' says the actor. 'I'll do the beast I can.'

****

An MP was in bed with his wife when there was a massive thunderstorm. A huge bolt of lightning landed nearby and lit up the whole area at which point the MP sat up and shouted, 'I'll buy the negatives, I'll buy the negatives.'

****

Two office workers were chatting during the lunch break one day. 'It really pisses me off,' said one. 'The boss keeps taking an hour-and-a-half for his lunch break, whilst you and I only get half an hour. That's not fair. I mean if I had an extra fifteen minutes I could pop home for lunch.'

' Well, why don't you?' said the other one. 'The boss is away so long he'd never know.'

So the very next day the first guy decides to do just that. On arriving at home he can't find his wife anywhere downstairs so he goes up to the bedroom. As he's opening the bedroom door he catches a glimpse of his missus in bed with the boss. Before they see him, he shuts the door and rushes back to work.

When he gets back his mate says, 'So, are you going to do that again tomorrow?'

'No way,' he says. 'I nearly got caught today.'

✴✴✴✴

A highly excited man rang up for an ambulance. 'Quickly, come quickly,' he shouted, 'my wife's about to have a baby.'

'Is this her first baby?' asked the operator.'

'No, you fool,' came the reply, 'it's her husband.'

✴✴✴✴

After having been woken up in the middle of the night by his wife pouring petrol over him, the husband was recounting the incident to the police. 'What do you think she was going to do to you?' asked the officer.

'I'm not sure,' said the man, 'but I think she was trying to make a fuel of me.'

✴✴✴✴

'I don't think we should have any more kids,' said the wife to her husband.

'But why not, dear?' said the husband. 'I thought you always wanted four.'

'Not any more,' said the woman. 'I've just heard on the radio that every fourth child born in the world today is Chinese.'

****

Did you here about the dyslexic pimp?
He bought a warehouse.

****

A bear and a rabbit are chatting in the woods.

'Tell me, rabbit,' says the bear, 'when you shit, does it stick to your fur?'

'Why, no,' says the rabbit, 'it doesn't.'

'That's great,' says the bear, picking up the rabbit and wiping his arse with it.

****

Brian is walking by the canal when he sees a guy drowning. He dives in and saves him. When they get back on to dry land the guy says to him, 'I am the grand wizard of Pittiland. For saving me I grant you three wishes.'

'Right,' says Brian. 'First up I want a million quid.'

'OK,' says the wizard. 'It's in your bank account.'

'Now I want a massive mansion in the country with a swimming pool and tennis courts,' says Brian.

'Consider it done,' says the wizard.

'And I want 500 women at my beck and call,' says Brian for his third wish.

'They will be waiting for you at the mansion,' says the wizard, 'as long as I can fuck you first.'

Still reeling from all this, Brian agrees to the wizard's request. After they've had sex, the wizard turns to Brian and says, 'Tell me Brian, how old are you?'

'Thirty,' replies Brian.

'And you still believe in wizards, eh?' says the wizard.

****

A carpet layer had just finished installing a carpet for a lady. He stepped out for a smoke, only to realise he'd lost his cigarettes. In the middle of the room, under the carpet, was a bump.

'No sense pulling up the entire floor for one pack of smokes,' he said to himself and proceeded to get out his hammer and flatten the hump. As he was cleaning up, the lady came in. 'Here,' she said, handing him his pack of cigarettes. 'I found them in the hallway. Now if only I could find my parakeet.'

****

Late one night, a burglar broke into a house he thought was empty. He tiptoed through the living room, but suddenly froze in his tracks when he heard a loud voice say, 'Jesus is watching you!' Silence returned to the house, so the burglar crept forward again. 'Jesus is watching you,' the voice boomed again. The burglar stopped dead again. He was frightened. Frantically, he looked all around. In a dark corner, he spotted a bird cage and in the cage was a parrot. He asked the parrot, 'Was that you who said Jesus is watching me?'

'Yes,' said the parrot. The burglar breathed a sigh of relief, and asked the parrot: 'What's your name?'

'Clarence,' said the bird. 'That's a stupid name for a parrot,' sneered the burglar. 'What idiot named you Clarence?'

'The same idiot who named the Rottweiler Jesus,' said the parrot.

****

In a busy hotel lobby, a receptionist shouts out, 'Telephone call for Mr Grobenstatermeisterhimbergmansturnumbagrat!'

At which an old geezer comes to the desk and asks, 'What's the initial?'

****

Everybody who has a dog calls him, 'Rover' or 'Fido'. I call my dog 'Sex'. Now, Sex has been very embarrassing to me. When I went to get his licence, I told the official I would like to have a licence for Sex. He said, 'I'd like to have one, too.'

Then I said, 'But this is a dog.' He said I didn't care what she looked like. Then I said, 'You don't understand, I've had Sex since I was nine years old.' He said I must have been quite a kid.

When I got married and went on my honeymoon, I took the dog with me. I told the hotel receptionist that I wanted a room for my wife and me and a special room for Sex. She said that every room in the place was for sex. I said, 'You don't understand, Sex keeps me awake at night.'

She said, 'Me too.'

One day I entered Sex in a contest but before the competition began, the dog ran away. Another contestant asked me why I was just standing there looking around. I told him I had planned to have Sex entered in the contest. He told me that I should have sold tickets. 'But you don't understand,' I said, 'I had hoped to have Sex on television.' He called me a show-off.

When my wife and I separated, we went to court to file for custody of the dog. I said, 'Your Honour, I had Sex before I got married.'

The judge said, 'Me too.' Then I told him that after I was married, Sex had left me. He said, 'Me too.'

Last night Sex ran off again. I spent hours looking around town for him. A copper came over to me and asked, 'What are you doing in this alley at four in the morning?'

I said, 'I'm looking for Sex…' My case comes up on Friday.

****

Q: Why don't blind people go skydiving?
A: It scares the shit out of their dogs.

****

Chapter 12
The Pub Team

It's a mystery how they came about, but at some point in time someone must have spoiled a perfectly good drink by suggesting to the gathered throng that they do something active. Presumably this person was drummed out of town time and time again, but at some point someone must have agreed to play a game with them.

This was a defining moment because from then on the human competitive element kicked in and spread like wildfire. Before you knew where you were people were spending valuable drinking time at the dart board and pool table, and then actually organising teams to play football or cricket, games which don't even take place in the pub.

Today, of course, there isn't a pub in the land that doesn't boast a crack team of super-fit athletes ready to represent their gaff at whatever contest they've been challenged to. People who put in hours of speech training every day so that they can come back to the pub after the match and talk the best game of their lives…

****

A golfer, encountering a genie, was granted one wish. The man thought a while and said, 'Well, I've always been embarrassed by being rather small, if you know what I mean; could you make me larger?'

'Done,' said the genie and disappeared. Continuing his game, the man noticed an immediate change in his 'size'. Within several holes, it was down to his knee, and by the 18th, it had crept into his sock. After holing his final putt, the man hurriedly returned to where he'd met the genie.

'Problem?' inquired the genie.

'Yes,' the man responded, 'Do you think I could trouble you for one more wish?'

'And what might that be?' asked the genie.

'Could you make my legs longer?'

****

While playing golf, the man finds a corked bottle on the green. Upon opening it, a genie appears and grants the fellow one wish. After thinking about it for a while, the man says, 'I'd like to shoot par golf regularly.'

'No problem,' says the genie, 'But understand that your sex life will be greatly reduced as a side effect.'

'I can handle that,' the man says, and POUF! the deed is done. Several months later, the genie reappears on the same golf hole and asks the man how his golf is going.

'Fantastic!' says the man, 'I'm now carrying a scratch handicap.'

'And what effect has it had on your sex life?' the genie inquires.

'I still manage to have relations a couple of times a month,' the fellow answers calmly.

'A couple of times a month,' the genie says, 'That's not much of a sex life.'

'Well,' the fellow responds, 'It's not bad for a middle-aged priest with a very small parish.'

****

Fay Lewis was a busy housewife with a demanding husband, six children and a large house. The only relief she got from her chores was the weekly bridge game she shared with a dozen other women. The only flaw in the bridge club relationship was that Fay loved to tell off-colour stories and the girls didn't want to hear them.

To teach Fay a lesson, the other women decided that the next time she told such a story, they'd just get up, walk out and meet at another home, but without Fay. Sure enough, at the next meeting, Fay started, 'You know, girls, there's a rumour going around that a plane-load of prostitutes will be leaving Heathrow in the morning for that big gold find in Alaska, and they say…'

Just then, the women all stood up and started for the door. Fay was disconcerted, but only for a moment. 'Hey! Girls!' she shouted. 'Hold on, hold on! There's plenty of time. The plane doesn't leave till morning!'

✱✱✱✱

A man phones home from his office and tells his wife, 'Something has just come up. I have a chance to go fishing for a week. It's the opportunity of a lifetime. We leave right away. So pack my clothes, my fishing equipment, and especially my blue silk pyjamas. I'll be home in an hour to pick them up.'

He goes home in a hurry and grabs everything and rushes off. A week later he returns.

'Did you have a good trip, dear?' asks the wife.

'Oh yes, great,' he says, 'but you forgot to pack my blue silk pyjamas.'

'Oh no I didn't,' replies the wife. 'I put them in your tackle box!'

✱✱✱✱

A vicar wanted to raise money for his church, and being told that there was a fortune in horse racing, decided to buy a horse and enter him in the races. However, at the local auction, the going price for a horse was so high that he bought a donkey instead. He figured that since he had it he might as well go ahead and enter it in the races, and to his surprise the donkey came in third.

The next day, the racing papers carried this headline:" 'VICAR'S ASS SHOWS'. The vicar was so pleased with the donkey that he entered it in the races again, and this time it won! The paper read: 'VICAR'S ASS OUT IN FRONT.'

The bishop was so upset with this publicity that he ordered the vicar not to enter his donkey in another race. The headlines read: 'BISHOP SCRATCHES VICAR'S ASS.'

This was too much for the bishop and he ordered the vicar to get rid of the animal. The vicar decided to give it to a nun in the nearby convent. The headlines read: 'NUN HAS BEST ASS IN TOWN.'

The bishop fainted! He informed the nun that she would have to dispose of the donkey. She finally found a farmer willing to buy him for £10. The paper read: 'NUN PEDDLES ASS FOR TEN POUNDS.' They buried the bishop the next day. The headline?: 'NUN'S ASS KILLS BISHOP.'

****

One day a nun was fishing and caught a huge, strange-looking fish. A man was walking by and said, 'WOW!! What a nice Gauddam Fish!'

'Sir,' said the sister, 'you shouldn't take God's name in vain.'

'But that's the SPECIES of the fish,' said the man. 'It's a Gauddam Fish.'

So the Sister took the fish back home and said, 'Mother Superior, look at the Gauddam Fish I caught.'

Shocked, the Mother Superior said, 'Sister, you should know better than that.'

'No, Mother Superior,' said the sister, 'you don't understand. That's the name of the species of fish. It's a Gauddam Fish.'

'Well, give me the Gauddam Fish and I'll clean it,' said the Mother Superior. While she was cleaning the fish, the Monsignor walked in.

'Monsignor,' said the Mother Superior, 'look at the Gauddam Fish that the sister caught.'

'Mother Superior!' said the Monsignor rather taken aback, 'you shouldn't talk like that!'

'But that's the species of fish Monsignor,' explained the Mother Superior. 'It's a Gauddam Fish.'

'Well,' said the Monsignor, 'give me the Gauddam Fish and I'll cook it.'

That evening at supper there was a new priest at the table, and he said, 'Wow, what a nice fish.'

'Thank you,' said the sister. 'I caught the Gauddam Fish.'

'And I cleaned the Gauddam Fish,' said the Mother Superior.

'And I cooked the Gauddam Fish,' said the Monsignor.

The priest looked around in disbelief, quite shocked, and said, 'Well let's eat the fucking thing.'

****

A man went to confession and said to the priest, 'Forgive me, Father. I used the F-word this week.'

'Ah, my son,' said the priest. 'Tell me the circumstances which caused you to use the F-word. After all, I can understand a person being provoked into using it.'

'Well, I was golfing,' said the man, 'and I had just hit a beautiful tee-shot that sailed straight as an arrow for 280 yards, but then suddenly sliced into the woods.'

'That is when you used the F-word?' said the priest. 'I can appreciate your frustration my son, as I am a golfer myself.'

'No, I stayed cool at that point, Father,' said the man. 'I then hit a perfect shot out of the woods, but suddenly it landed in the sand trap.'

'Now, I can understand you saying the F-word at that point,' said the priest.

'No, Father, I was calm even then,' said the man. 'I got out my sand wedge and hit a perfect shot out of the trap right at the pin, but suddenly the ball stopped an inch from the cup.'

'Ah, that is when you used the F-word. How frustrating,' said the priest.

'No, Father, I was still cool at this point,' said the man.

'Don't tell me you missed the fucking putt?' said the priest.

****

It was a cold winter day when an old man walked out on to a frozen lake, cut a hole in the ice, dropped in his fishing line and began waiting for a fish to bite.

He was there for almost an hour without even a nibble when a young boy walked out onto the ice, cut a hole not to far from the old man and dropped in his fishing line. It only took about a minute and WHAM!, a Largemouth Bass hit his hook and the boy pulled in the fish.

The old man couldn't believe it, but figured it was just luck. But the next time the boy dropped in his line, within just a few minutes he had pulled in another one. This went on and on until finally the old man couldn't take it any more, since he hadn't caught a thing all this time.

He went to the boy and said, 'Son, I've been here for over an hour without even a nibble. You have been here only a few minutes and have caught about half-a-dozen fish! How do you do it?'

To which the boy responded, 'Roo raf roo reep ra rums rrarm.'

'What was that?' the old man asked.

Again the boy responded, 'Roo raf roo reep ra rums rrarm.'

'Look,' said the old man, 'I can't understand a word you're saying.'

So the boy spat into his hand and said, 'You have to keep the worms warm!'

****

One night, at the lodge of a hunting club, two new members were being introduced to other members and shown around. The man leading them around said, 'See that old man asleep in the chair by the fireplace? He is our oldest member and can tell you some hunting stories you'll never forget.'

They awakened the old man and asked him to tell them a hunting story. 'Well,' he began, 'I remember back in 1944, we went on a lion-hunting expedition in Africa. We were on foot and hunted for three days without seeing a thing. On the fourth day, I was so tired I had to rest my feet. I found a fallen tree, so I laid my gun down, propped my head on the tree, and fell asleep. I don't know how long I was asleep when I was awakened by a noise in the bushes. I was reaching for my gun when the biggest lion I've ever seen jumped out of the bushes at me like this, ROOOAAAARRRRRRRRRR! I tell you, I just shit myself.'

The young men looked astonished and one of them said, 'I don't blame you, mate. I would have shit myself too if a lion jumped out at me.'

The old man shook his head and said, 'No, no, not then, just now when I said ROOOAAAAARRRRRRRRRRR!'

****

A blackjack dealer and a player with a 13 count in his hand were arguing about whether or not it was appropriate to tip the dealer. The player said, 'When I get bad cards, it's not the dealer's fault. By the same token, when I get good cards, the dealer obviously had nothing to do with it so why should I tip him?'

The dealer said, 'When you eat out do you tip the waiter?'

'Yes,' said the player. 'Well then,' said the dealer, 'he serves you food, I'm serving you cards, so you should tip me.'

'OK,' said the player, 'but the waiter gives me what I ask for… I'll take an eight.'

****

While sport-fishing off the Florida coast, a tourist capsized his boat. He could swim, but his fear of alligators kept him clinging to the overturned craft. Spotting an old beachcomber standing on the shore, the tourist shouted, 'Are there any 'gators around here?'

'Naw,' the man hollered back, 'they ain't been around for years!'

Feeling safe, the tourist started swimming leisurely toward the shore. About halfway there he asked the guy, 'How'd you get rid of the 'gators?'

'We didn't do nothin',' the beachcomber said. 'The sharks got 'em.'

****

There was a Liverpool fan with a really crappy seat at Anfield. Looking with some binoculars, he spotted an empty seat on the halfway line. Thinking to himself, 'What a waste' he made his way down to the empty seat. When he arrived at the seat, he asked the man sitting next to it, 'Is this seat taken?'

'This was my wife's seat,' said the man. 'She passed away recently… She was a big Liverpool fan.'

'I'm so sorry to hear of your loss,' said the first man.

'May I ask why you didn't give her ticket to a friend or a relative?'

'Because they're all at her funeral,' replied the man.

****

A group of blind people are playing a round of golf. Naturally enough they are going round quite slowly. Behind them are a priest, an imam and a rabbi. The priest says, 'What a marvellous achievement to see them overcoming their disability.'

The imam says, 'Much as I'm humbled to see these people doing what they're doing I do wish they could go a bit faster,' and the rabbi says 'What, they can't play at night?'

****

After a particularly poor game of golf, a popular club member skipped the clubhouse and started to go home. As he was walking to the car park to get his car, a policeman stopped him and asked, 'Did you tee off on the 16th hole about 20 minutes ago'

'Yes,' replied the golfer.

'Did you happen to hook your ball so that it went over the trees and off the course?' asked the policeman.

'Yes, I did. How did you know?' he asked.

'Well,' said the policeman very seriously, 'your ball flew out on to the highway and crashed through a driver's windscreen. The car went out of control, crashing into five other cars and a fire engine. The fire engine couldn't make it to the fire and the building burned down. So, what are you going to do about it?'

The golfer thought it over carefully and responded, 'I think I'll close my stance a little bit, tighten my grip and lower my right thumb.'

****

Matt and his secretary are having an affair. They decide to leave the office early one day and go to the secretary's flat for an afternoon of lovemaking. They fall asleep after and don't wake up until 8pm. They quickly get dressed and the man asks his secretary to take his shoes and go and rub them in the grass.

The secretary thinks this is pretty weird, but she does it anyway. The man finally gets home and his wife meets him at the door. The wife is very upset and asks him where he has been.

The husband replies, 'I can not tell a lie. My secretary and I are having an affair. We left work early today, went to her place, made love all afternoon, and then we fell asleep. That's why I'm late!'

The wife looks at him, notices the grass stains on his shoes and says, 'You lying bastard. You've been playing golf again, haven't you?'

****

A bishop was an active golfoholic. But he always put his clubs away on saturday night and would not pick them up again till Monday morning. One Sunday, after a particularly ugly week of rain, the bishop got up very early and sneaked on to a public golf course to play one quick round before mass.

At that moment, St Peter looked down from heaven and saw what the Bishop was up to. 'God,' St Peter cried, 'God... Get over here and take a look at this. He is BLASPHEMOUS.'

'Don't worry, Pete,' said the Lord. 'I saw this coming. I'll take care of it.'

At that very moment, the Bishop teed off at the first hole, a 515-yard, dog-leg right, par five. The ball leapt from the pin, soared through the air, executed a text book right curve, struck the ground 298 yards from the tee with incredible velocity, jumped forward and, miracle of miracles, after three bounces dropped into the hole without even striking the flag stick.

The bishop is astonished, as is St Peter. 'Did You see that? He dropped it straight into the hole. That was a miracle. I thought You were punishing him.'

'With time, you will understand,' said God as he walked away. St Peter watched with astonishment as the bishop, hole after hole, dropped the tee shot into the cup. As the bishop puts his ball down on the tee at 18, St Peter summoned God once again. 'He's about to set a record, sir, and You are doing nothing about it.'

God said nothing and they watched as the bishop's shot flew threw the air and dropped effortlessly into the hole.

'I am most confused,' said St Peter to his boss.

'Pete,' explained the Lord, 'think about it. He is a man of God, a vicar of the holy word. He has just shot the perfect game… on a Sunday…. without paying the green fees. Who can he tell?'

****

Harry sliced his tee shot way off into a field beside the golf course. Finally, he found the ball nestled in some buttercups. On his back swing he heard a voice say, 'Please don't hurt my buttercups.' He stopped his swing, looked around, sees no one, and prepares to hit again. 'Please don't hurt my buttercups,' comes the voice again. He stopped again, looked up and sees a beautiful woman approaching. 'I am mother nature,' she said. 'If you promise not to harm my buttercups, I can guarantee you an abundant supply of butter for the rest of your life.'

Harry thought about this and said, 'Where were you last week when I hit my ball into the pussywillows?'

****

At the Olympic wrestling event it is narrowed down to the Russian or the American for the gold medal. Before the final match, the American wrestler's trainer comes to him and says, 'Now don't forget all the research we've done on this Russian. He's never lost a match because of this "pretzel" hold he has. Whatever you do, don't let him get you in this hold! If he does, you're finished!' The wrestler nods in agreement.

As the match begins the American and the Russian circle each other several times looking for an opening. All of a sudden the Russian lunges forward, grabbing the American and wrapping him up in the dreaded "pretzel" hold. A sigh of disappointment goes up from the crowd, and the trainer buries his face in his hands for he knows all is lost. He can't watch the ending.

Suddenly, though, there's a scream, a cheer from the crowd, and the trainer raises his eye just in time to see the Russian flying up in the air. The Russian's back hits the mat with a thud, and the American weakly collapses on top of him, getting the pin and winning the match.

The trainer is astounded! When he finally gets the American wrestler alone, he asks, 'How did you ever get out of that hold? No one has ever done it before!'

The wrestler answers, 'Well, I was ready to give up when he got me in that hold, but at the last moment, I opened my eyes and saw this pair of balls right in front of my face. I thought I had nothing to lose, so with my last ounce of strength I stretched out my neck and bit those babies just as hard as I could. You'd be amazed how strong you get when you bite your own balls!'

****

Two old boys were playing golf. After one particularly long and arduous hole one turned to the other and said, 'So how many did you take?'

'Nine,' came the reply.

'Well, I took eight,' said the first. 'So I guess that's my hole then.'

The next hole was equally long, after which the same old boy turned to his pal and asked the question again.

'No, no,' said his pal. 'It's my turn to ask first.'

****

A passer-by spots a fisherman by a river. 'Is this a good river for fish?' he asks.

'Yes,' replies the fisherman, 'it must be. I can't get any of them to come out.'

****

Two women were talking. 'Listen, I don't want to bring you down,' said one, 'but surely you don't believe that story about your husband being out all night fishing? I mean, he hasn't even brought any fish back.'

'That's why I believe him,' said the other.

****

One day at the golf club Jim spots the most beautiful woman he's ever seen in the clubhouse. Even more incredibly, she comes over and suggests that they play a round together.

She turns out to be a very fine player and gives Jim a good game, after which they go back to his place for some oral sex.

The following day they meet up for another game, followed by another bout of oral sex. This goes on for a week, at the end of which Jim says, 'I'm sorry, but I don't think I can keep this up much longer.'

'That's OK,' says the woman. ' There's something I have to tell you as well. I'm a transvestite.'

'Shit,' says Jim. 'All week you've been playing off the ladies' tees.'

****

A cricket player's wife rang the club during a game to be told that her husband had just gone in to bat. 'That's fine,' she said. 'I'll hold.'

****

A husband and wife were celebrating their anniversary with a romantic dinner. 'Do you remember proposing to me?' said the wife.

'Yes of course,' said the husband. 'It was just next to the pavilion when we were playing Little Sedgewick.'

'Oh, you were bold,' recalled the wife.

'No, as far as I remember it was LBW,' said the husband.

****

A fielder who had dropped eight easy balls in one particularly awful match was blaming his poor display on ill health.

'I'm not well,' he said. ' I think I must have caught a cold.'

'Thank God you're able to catch something,' came the retort.

****

The top scorer of a Premier League team was tragically killed in a car accident one season. Seeing an opportunity for glory, the reserve striker went in to see the boss. 'How about the possibility of me taking his place?' he asked.

'I'm not sure about that,' said the guv'nor, 'I'll have to speak to the undertaker first.'

****

At a football match one day a man tried to get into the game with a gorilla. 'Look,' said a copper, 'I saw you with him yesterday and told you to take him to the zoo.'

'Yes I did that, and then we went to the cinema and had a meal. So today I thought he might like to see a football match.'

****

On Cup Final day a massive crowd is approaching Wembley when a funeral procession goes past. Seeing this, one bloke takes his hat off and stands motionless for a moment before walking on. 'That was a nice thing to do,' said his mate.

'Well,' said the bloke, 'she was a good wife to me.'

****

At a Celtic/Rangers match one season, things got a bit hairy in the crowd and bottles began flying from one set of supporters to the others. A young spectator stuck in the middle of this was naturally somewhat concerned, so an old boy went to reassure him. 'Don't worry son,' he said. 'It's like bombs in the war. One of those won't hit you unless it's got your name on it.'

'That's what I'm worried about,' said the young fellow. 'My name's Johnny Walker.'

****

After a string of ten defeats on the trot the manager of a local football team was at the end of his tether. 'Look,' suggested a friend. 'Why don't you take the whole squad out for a ten mile run every day?'

'What good will that do?' moaned the manager. 'Well, today's Sunday,' said his pal. 'By next Saturday they'll be 60 miles away and you won't have to worry about them.'

****

A fan arrives at a football match midway through the second half. 'What's the score?' he asks his mate as he arrives.

'Nil-nil,' is the reply.

'And what was the half-time score?' he asks.

****

Stuck in the centre of a defensive wall at a free kick, the centre forward took a ball full in the cods and was knocked out cold. When he woke up he found himself in hospital. Still in some pain he asked the doctor, 'Doc, is it bad? Will I be able to play again?'

'Yes, you should be able to,' confirmed the doc.

'Oh, great. So I can play for my club again?' said the relieved forward.

'Well, just as long as they've got a women's team,' said the doctor.

****

After a considerable win on the footie pools, Mr Smith was asked if it would change him. 'No, not at all. My life won't change a bit,' he insisted.

'But what about the begging letters?' asked a reporter.

'Oh, I'll still send them,' he replied.

****

A group of Catholic priests were due to play a group of rabbis in a big inter-faith game. A couple of days before the match, disaster struck the Catholic team when their star player broke his ankle.

'What are we going to do?' moaned Father Bradley.

'Well,' said Father Turner. 'I just happen to be a good friend of Teddy Sheringham's. We could ask him to play for us.'

'But that wouldn't be ethical, now would it?' said Father Bradley.

'No, but if we called him Father Sheringham, no one need know,' replied the other priest.

Having agreed to this devious plan, Father Bradley was then called away and was unable to watch the match. However, as soon as he could he phoned Father Turner for the result.

'I'm afraid they beat us,' said Father Turner, 'Six-two.'

'But how come?' exclaimed Father Bradley, 'we had Father Sheringham on our side.'

'Yes,' said Father Turner, 'but they had Rabbi Seaman and Rabbi Shearer playing for them.'

****

A great footballer was tragically killed and arriving at heaven met the angel on duty at the gates. 'Is there any reason,' asked the angel, 'why you should not be allowed to enter the kingdom of heaven?'

'Well,' said the footballer, 'there was this one time when I cheated in a big international football match.'

'I see,' said the angel, 'tell me about it.'

'Well,' said the player, 'I was playing for Wales against England and I used my hand to push the ball past an English defender. The ref never saw it and I went on to score.'

'And what was the final score?' asked the angel.

'That was the only goal,' said the player, 'we won one-nil.'

'Well, that's not too bad. I think we can let you in,' said the angel.

'Oh great!' exclaimed the footballer, 'that's been on my mind for years. Thanks a lot, St Peter.'

'That's OK,' said the angel as he ushered the player in, 'and by the way, it's St Peter's day off today, I'm St David.'

****

A wee lad was crying his eyes out at a football match one day. 'What's the matter?' asked a policeman.

'I've lost my Dad,' cried the boy.

'What's he like?' asked the copper.

'Beer, women and fags,' said the boy.

****

Two boys were playing with a new football in the street outside their house. 'Hey,' shouted their mother, 'where did you get that football?'

'We found it,' replied one of the boys.

'Are you sure it was lost?' asked the mum.

'Yes,' replied the other boy, 'we saw people looking for it.'

****

Midway through what was turning into a disastrous season, the coach of a third-division side decided to get the team together and really go back to basics. Picking up a football he went, 'Right now, lads, what I have in my hands is called a football, and the object of the game is…'

'Hang on a minute,' came a shout, 'you're going too fast.'

****

A so-called football widow was having a go at her husband. 'Your whole life is football,' she moaned. 'You never take me out, you never buy me presents. You're either at a match or watching one on the telly. I bet you can't even remember when our wedding anniversary is'

'Yes, I can,' retorted the husband, 'it's the same date that Slovan Bratislava beat Barcelona in the Cup-Winners' Cup.'

****

In a nasty challenge a football player dislocated his shoulder. He was still screaming in agony when they got him to hospital.

'For God's sake,' shouted the doctor, 'you're supposed to be a big, tough defender. There's a woman having a baby next door and she's not making anything like the noise that you are.'

'That's as may be,' wailed the player, 'but in her case, nobody's trying to push anything back in.'

****

A team of mammals were playing a team of insects. The first half very much belonged to the mammals, and at half-time they were leading 46-nil. However, at half-time the insects made a substitution and brought on a centipede, which turned out to be a top move.

The centipede scored 300 goals as the insects went on to win 401-290. After the game the captain of the mammals was chatting to the insect captain. 'That centipede of yours isn't half bad, is he? Why don't you play him from the start?' he asked.

'We'd like to,' replied the insect captain, 'but it takes him 45 minutes to get, his boots on.'

****

A Sunday League team were in the dressing-room, one player short. 'Where's Jeff?' said the full back to the captain. 'Oh, apparently he was getting married at 2.30,' said the captain.

'Shit,' said the full back, 'that means he won't get here till the second half'.

****

Another Sunday League team were in the pub having a constitutional before a match. 'Why are you looking so glum, Pete?' asked the landlord.

'My wife ran off with my best mate last night,' replied Pete.

'Oh no,' said the landlord, 'that's bad news.'

'You're not wrong,' said Pete, 'he was meant to be playing in goal today.'

****

A defender with a reputation for being well hard was sent off during a football match. Returning to the changing room, he had a terrible leg on him. It was covered in cuts and bruises and had a massive gash from the top of the thigh to the knee. He had no idea whose it was.

****

Two guys were watching a live Premiership footie game between Manchester United and Arsenal in their local. 'You see the Arsenal,' said one of them, 'their manager's been after me for months.'

'Really?' said his mate.

'Yeah,' he said, 'I'm shagging his wife.'

****

Amazingly, Torquay found themselves at the top of the third division one season mainly due to the goal-scoring talents of their striker. Eager to keep him at the club the manager called him into his office one day about halfway through the season.

'Well done, son,' said the boss. 'Here's a token of our appreciation.' And with that he handed the player a cheque for £5,000.

'Cheers boss,' said the player. 'This really means a lot to me.'

'Pleased to hear it, lad,' said the manager, 'and if you keep this up all season the chairman might even sign it for you.'

****

An old boy turned up at the offices of a large company one afternoon. 'Hello, I'm Tommy Wheeler's Uncle. I've come to ask if he can have the afternoon off so I can take him to the match.'

'I'm afraid he's not here,' came the reply, 'we already gave him the afternoon off so he could attend your funeral.'

****

A young autograph hunter was chuffed to bits when he got Julian Dicks' autograph after a game. The following week he accosted Mr Dicks again and got his autograph, and after the very next game he tried to get it again.

'Look,' said Julian, 'this is the third time you've asked me for my autograph. What's going on?'

'Well,' said the youngster, 'if I can get eight more of yours I can swap them for one of Gazza's.'

****

After going to the doctor a man popped into his local for a stiff one. 'What's up pal?' asked his mate, 'you look perturbed.'

'Yeah, I am,' he said. 'I've just been to the doctor's and he told me I can't play football.'

'Oh, really?' said his mate. 'He's seen you play, then.'

****

A woman goes to the doctor. 'Doctor, doctor. I'm really worried about my son. All he does is play football all day, then come in covered in mud and walk all over my clean carpet,' she said.

'I think you're over-reacting,' said the doctor. 'Sons do those kind of things.'

'Yes,' said the woman, 'but it's not just me that's worried. His wife is also very concerned.'

****

Two men are discussing a golf game. 'Well, I was playing golf with my wife. I'd been having a great game but unfortunately she wasn't. On the 15th tee I hit a beautiful shot, 270 yards straight down the fairway. My wife steps up and hits a tremendous slice that leaves the course and lands in the pasture out of bounds. We both went looking for the ball and just as we were about to give up I spotted a glint of white coming from a cow's behind, just under its tail. I lifted the tail to make sure and then called to my wife saying, "Here, honey, this looks like yours." That's the last thing I remember.'

****

Fred got home from his Sunday round of golf later than normal and very tired. 'Bad day at the course?' his wife asked.

'Everything was going fine,' he said. 'Then Harry had a heart attack and died on the 10th tee.'

'Oh, that's awful!'

'You're not kidding. For the whole back nine it was hit the ball, drag Harry, hit the ball, drag Harry…'

****

A couple of women, Janice and Sherrill, were playing golf one sunny Saturday morning. Sherrill, the first of the twosome teed off and watched in horror as the ball headed directly toward a foursome of men playing the next hole. Indeed, the ball hit one of the men, and he immediately clasped his hands together at his crotch, fell to the ground and proceeded to roll around in agony.

Sherrill rushed down to the man and immediately began to apologise. She then explained that she was a physical therapist and offered to help ease his pain. 'Please allow me to help. I'm a physical therapist and I know I could relieve your pain if you'd just allow me!' she told him earnestly.

'Ummph, oooh, nnooo, I'll be alright... I'll be fine in a few minutes,' he replied as he remained in the fetal position still clasping his hands together at his crotch. But she persisted; and he finally allowed her to help him.

She gently took his hands away and laid them to the side, loosened his trousers and put her hands inside, beginning to massage him. 'Does that feel better?' she asked.

'It feels great,' he replied. 'But my thumb still hurts like hell.'

✳✳✳✳

Barely 20 minutes after teeing off, a woman came into the clubhouse, grimacing in pain. 'What happened?' the club pro asked.

'I got stung by a bee,' she replied.

'Where?'

'Between the first and second holes.'

'Hmmm,' the pro murmured. 'Sounds like your stance was a little too wide.'

✳✳✳✳

There was an engineer, a manager and a computer programmer driving down a steep mountain road. The brakes failed and the car careered down the road out of control. Halfway down the driver managed to stop the car by running it against the embankment, narrowly avoiding going over a cliff.

They all got out, shaken by their narrow escape from death, but otherwise unharmed.

The manager said, 'To fix this problem we need to organise a committee, have meetings, and, through a process of continuous improvement, develop a solution.'

The engineer said, 'No, that would take too long, and besides that method never worked before. I have my trusty pen-knife here and will take apart the brake system, isolate the problem and correct it.'

The computer programmer said, 'I think you're both wrong! I think we should all push the car back up the hill and see if it happens again.'

****

Once the club duffer challenged the local golf pro to a match, with a £100 bet on the side. 'But,' said the duffer, 'since you're obviously much better than me, to even it a bit you have to let me have two "gotchas".'

The golf pro didn't know what a 'gotcha' was, but he went along with it. And off they went. Coming back to the 19th hole, the rest of the club members were amazed to see the golf pro paying the duffer £100.

'What happened?' asked one of the members.

'Well,' said the pro, 'I was teeing up for the first hole, and as I brought the club down, the lunatic stuck his hand between my legs, and grabbed my balls and yelled "Gotcha!" Have you ever tried to play 18 holes of golf, waiting for the second "Gotcha"?'

****

An international sportsstar is on a long-haul flight and he desperately needs to go to the bog, but there's a long queue of people in front of him. He isn't averse to taking advantage of his status as an instantly recognisable brat and so he starts having a temper tantrum.

The stewardess, having little option, and wanting to spare the other passengers' patience tells him to go into the Ladies, but warns him not to play with any of the buttons.

The man agrees. While he's sitting on the toilet in the Ladies, however, he sees four buttons in front of him – one marked WW, one marked WA, another marked PP, and one marked ATR. Despite his promises his curiosity gets the better of him, and, he decides what the fuck does it matter if he presses them or not – so he presses the button marked WW. Suddenly, a jet of warm water sprays gently on his arse. Then he presses the button marked WA and warm air dries his arse.

'Wow,' says the man, 'the girls really have it easy!'

Next he presses the button marked PP and a power puff pats his arse with a scented powder.

'This is great!' he thinks. 'I wonder what the last button does?'

On pressing it he's suddenly knocked unconscious. When he wakes up he finds he's in the hospital. Totally confused he calls out for a nurse to find out what the fuck happened.

'The flight attendant told you not to touch any of the buttons,' explains the nurse. 'And you pressed the one marked ATR.'

'What does ATR stand for?' asks the man, completely bewildered.

'Automatic tampon remover,' replies the nurse. 'You'll find your penis under your pillow.'

****